Delhi Sultanate

Urbanization and Social Change

Delhi Sultanate

Urbanization and Social Change

Iqtidar Husain Siddiqui

Viva Books

New Delhi | Mumbai | Chennai | Kolkata | Bangalore | Hyderabad | Kochi | Guwahati

First Published 2009
Reprinted 2012

Viva Books Private Limited

4737/23, Ansari Road, Daryaganj, New Delhi 110 002
Tel. 42242200, 23258325, 23283121, Email: vivadelhi@vivagroupindia.net

76, Service Industries, Shirvane, Sector 1, Nerul, Navi Mumbai 400 706
Tel. 27721273, 27721274, Email: vivamumbai@vivagroupindia.net

Jamals Fazal Chambers, 26 Greams Road, Chennai 600 006
Tel. 28294241, 28290304, Email: vivachennai@vivagroupindia.net

B-103, Jindal Towers, 21/1A/3 Darga Road, Kolkata 700 017
Tel. 22816713, Email: vivakolkata@vivagroupindia.net

7, GF, Sovereign Park Aptts., 56-58, K. R. Road, Basavanagudi, Bangalore 560 004
Tel. 26607409, Email: vivabangalore@vivagroupindia.net

101-102, Moghal Marc Apartments, 3-4-637 to 641, Narayanguda, Hyderabad 500 029
Tel. 27564481, Email: vivahyderabad@vivagroupindia.net

First Floor, Beevi Towers, SRM Road, Kaloor, Kochi - 682 018, Kerala,
Tel. 0484-2403055, 2403056, Email: vivakochi@vivagroupindia.net

232, GNB Road, Beside UCO Bank, Silpukhuri, Guwahati 781 003
Tel. 0361-2666386, Email: vivaguwahati@vivagroupindia.net

www.vivagroupindia.com

ISBN : 978-81-309-1014-7

Published by Vinod Vasishtha for Viva Books Private Limited
4737/23 Ansari Road, Daryaganj, New Delhi 110 002

Printed & bound by Raj Press, R-3, Inderpuri, New Delhi - 110 012.

For my grandsons
Atif Asad Siddiqui and
Daud Asad Siddiqui

Contents

Contents

Preface

This book has grown out of a paper titled, 'Money and Social Change in India during the Delhi Sultanate Period' for a symposium sponsored by Indian History Congress at its 56th session held in Rabindra Bharti University, Kolkata, 29 December 1995. The paper was appreciated and I was persuaded by my friends and students to investigate further the points raised therein and publish a monograph outlining the different factors responsible for social change and economic development in the Sultanate. While pioneering efforts have been made by eminent scholars, the paucity of relevant evidence in conventional sources was a handicap preventing an indepth analysis of complex socio-economic phenomena. Fresh evidence discovered in contemporary literary works of miscellaneous nature as well as foreign sources enables our study to now have a scientific basis. It is worth pointing out that many important aspects of cultural life during the Delhi Sultanate period remain unexplored and their study makes the history of the Mughal period more intelligible.

The foundation of an independent Sultanate in the beginning of the thirteenth century exposed India to foreign influence. With it, processes of social and economic changes were let loose. The introduction of new institutions, political as well as cultural, played an important role in shaping the culture and life of people. Foreign trade carried on by merchants who had acquired a dominant position in world trade linked the countries of the Mediterranean and the Indian ocean. The merchants came not only with choice foreign merchandise that led to the introduction of new crafts and modification of indigenous ones but also information about different cultural traditions, scientific ideas, instruments and literature. Besides, port towns and urban centres situated along routes of merchant caravans prospered, owing to mercantile expansion.

Equally important is the study of the role performed by the royal court. Progress of intellectual culture resulted from royal patronage to the men of learning and talent. The Indo-Persian literature produced under the patronage of the sultans and members of ruling elite does not serve as a source of information alone but provides us with images of the past embedded in language which are no less important. My study examines this literature critically, in order to study different aspects of life and culture in medieval India during the Delhi Sultanate period. This culture continued to exercise its influence on the society during the Mughal period as well. Besides the royal court, the metropolitan city of Delhi being an integrative nucleus influenced art, architecture, literature and aesthetics in provincial cities.

Lastly I should express my indebtedness to my predecessors for the gaps found in their works that made me search for materials in unconventional sources helping me in the preparation of the work. I hope this work will encourage the scholars interested in the study of Indian history and culture to undertake further investigation.

I. H. Siddiqui

Introduction

The imposition of political domination by the Arabs following their conquest of Sind and the Punjab in AD 712-13, led to important changes in India's traditional socio-political system. In fact, Arab conquest marks the beginning of the medieval age that exposed Sind and Punjab to foreign influence. The introduction of new political and cultural institutions by the new rulers played an important role in shaping the culture as well as the destinies of the peoples. Equally important was the establishment of a symbiotic relationship between Brahmanism and Islam. Doubtless, if the effect of interaction between the followers of the two religions (Brahmanism and Islam) first under the Arabs and then under Sultan Mahmud of Ghazna and his successors remained confined to Sind and the Punjab from the eighth to the close of the twelfth century AD, the Ghurian conquest of north India led to far-reaching socio-economic changes in the subcontinent. It paved the way for the emergence of an independent Sultanate that brought in due course of time almost the whole of the subcontinent under its sway. The relevant evidence contained in contemporary sources of information about patterns of political behaviour of the individual sultans, suggests that it often made a great impact on the social and economic life under the Delhi Sultanate. Many important social changes resulted from the policies followed by certain sultans. The present work attempts to develop an argument on important factors responsible for social change in India during the Delhi Sultanate period.

The process of change began from Makran, the Western region bordering Iran. This was the first region to be conquered by the Arabs after Iran during the early period of the rise of Islam (seventh century AD). It was largely inhabited by the nomadic tribes, mainly the Balochs, in its southern part, and the Turks, Scythians, and Afghans, in its north. The Turks living in the territory, known as Kaikan, were a sedentary people and had developed horse-breeding centres and the Kaikanian horse enjoyed great popularity in Arabia.[1] The region was mostly a barren desert with little water available from streams and rivulets. It, however, attracted Arab traders for its geographical location on the trade route along India, Iran and Central Asian Khurasan, i.e. Sistan and the region of Ghazna and Kabul. These merchants settled in different parts of the region subject to availability of water. In time these merchants began to form an important link in the overseas and overland trade controlled by the Arabs and the region became a high road for international trade between the Islamic world and the countries of Europe, Africa and South-East Asia. These traders not only brought foreign merchandise to Europe, Africa and Asia, but also information about different cultural traditions and scientific ideas.[2] Evidence available in the Arab classics about the merchants in Makran shows how the cultural background of the new settlers played an important role in the process of acculturation there. Makran's postoral economy was gradually changed into a monetized economy following the progress of overland trade and urbanization.[3]

Amongst the famous Arab trading centres in Makran by the turn of the tenth century, Qandabil in its northern part had emerged as a famous market town.[4] The urban centres were soon linked to the inter regional and inter continental trade routes. Moreover in all the towns, the Arabs mingled with the local people after the latter had become Islamized. In due course of time the Turks, who had maintained their ethnic identity from ancient times upto the Arab invasion, weakened and became a part of the Muslim population. The region of Kaikan however continued to be designated by later Arab writers as Turan. Another important development was the introduction by the Arabs of a uniform administrative system under a bureaucracy, the members of which were transferred territorially.

Makran became independent like other provinces of the Abbasid Empire during the period of its disintegration. It was ruled over by Sultan Tajuddin Abul Makarim towards the close of the twelfth century. It is worth mentioning that the local Sultan patronized scholars and poets in the tradition of the Muslim rulers of the lands of higher culture. He also maintained an army with which he could defeat the Ghuzz Turks and save his territories from their tyranny.[5] Later on, Sultan Tajuddin Abul Makarim is reported to have acknowledged the suzerainty of Sultan Ghiyas u'ddin Muhammad bin Sam after the latter Sultan had emerged as the ruler of a powerful Empire (called in history as the Ghurid empire)[6]. The Ghurid dynasty does not seem to have survived the Mongol occupation of Iran and Khurasan, including Ghazna and Peshawar regions.

Other than Makran, Sind and the territory of Multan were the other regions that underwent social and demographic changes following their conquest by the Arabs in AD 712-13. Here, as elsewhere, Islamic proselytization brought about social change among the people of the region. The reference in *Chachnama* to *Maula-i-Islam,*[7] a term used for a convert of high status to Islam, reveals that not only did the downtrodden adopt the new faith for freedom from caste restrictions but so did some local chiefs. Sind also had a sizeable Buddhist population oppressed by the members of a Brahman ruling elite. The religious tension in Sind led Buddhist chiefs to come to co-operate with the Arabs.[8] It may also be recalled that the Arab conqueror Muhammad bin Qasim al-Thaqafi did not interfere with the social system of the conquered people. He is said to have sanctioned the privileges of the Brahmans as well as the degradation of the low-caste Jats. The Jats were kept as degraded as they were under Dahar, the overthrown Brahman ruler of Sind. Muhammad bin Qasim al-Thaqafi was informed by his Brahman and other advisers that 'the Jats were forced (by Dahar) to wear coarse clothing and to move out bare footed and bare-headed', and that while going out of doors, 'they had to take their dogs with them so that they might by this means be recognized. None of them was allowed to ride on horseback; if he had to, he rode without saddle or reins. Having heard all this, Muhammad bin Qasim al-Thaqafi became convinced that they were depraved people and decided to perpetuate their lowly status'.[9]

Yet, it may be recalled that the introduction of Arab polity was accompanied by important changes; the foundation of new cities, such as al-Mausura and al-Mahfuza increased demographic mobility and also paved the way for an advanced monetized economy. Daibul, the principal sea port of Sind also expanded on account of the planting of Arab colonies with Arab merchants and consequently became an important port of call. The cash-nexus became widespread, owing to the expansion of agriculture and horticulture and the diffusion of new crops with new farming methods. All this seems to have influenced the caste mentality of people in the conquered regions. Certain tribes or low-castes, such as the Sumeras, Sammas and Jats began to move up the social ladder and after the *shari'a* law had been enforced, all were treated equal irrespective of birth. Ultimately they became politically assertive in due course of time. The Jat revolt against Sultan Mahmud of Ghazna in AD 1025 is indicative of the fact that by this time they had gained prominence. They were the supporters of the Ismaili local ruler of Sind. It is probable that they had already entered the fold of Islam under the influence of Shi'a Ismaili *da'is* (preachers). The latter infiltrated the lands under the Arab Sunni Muslims, preached their religious doctrines among the Hindus secretly, in the guise of non-Muslims, and when the number of their followers became quite large they subverted Sunni rule. They captured power around the year AD 985.[10]

It is also noteworthy that the members of the tribal castes who converted to Ismaili Shi'ism did not undergo complete social transformation immediately. They lived in the countryside and were generally cultivators. For example, Ibn Battuta found the Sumeras endogamous and adhering to their old customs even in the fourteenth century. He states, 'The people called Somira never eat with anyone … nor do they marry anyone outside their class, nor do they allow anyone to marry into it'.[11]

Unlike the tribes, the converts to Islam in urban centres not only changed their customs and mingled with the Arab settlers but also had their children educated in the Islamic tradition. Some of the Sindis, belonging to the second and third generation of converts to Islam, distinguished themselves as leading scholars of the Quran and *hadith* (Prophetic tradition). 'Muhammad bin Abd ur Rahman of Bailman whose father and uncle had embraced Islam earlier, grew up as a distinguished scholar of *hadith.* Bukhari in *al-Tarikh al-Saghir* includes his name among those traditionalists who had died between AH 140-50. Yaqut also mentions (under Najran) another eminent Bailmani traditionalist Muhammad bin Ibrahim al-Bailmani, from whom 'Ubaidullah bin al-Abbas bin al-Rabi al-Najrani had heard hadith'.[12] These Sindi scholars also introduced Indian sciences to the Islamic World and carried with them Sanskrit treatises on mathematics, astrology, medicine, etc., which they helped the Arabs to render into Arabic.[13]

Likewise, the territorial unit of Multan also underwent demographic and socio-economic changes. Nowhere was the existing demographic pattern changed or touched in the urban centres. The addition of the colonies of Muslim settlers however provided a catalyst for change through interaction between the followers of two different cultural traditions. The Muslim settlers included officers, soldiers, scholars and merchants who were engaged in overland and oversea trade with different foreign countries. As a result, Multan was also included into the complex trading network dominated by the Arab and Irani merchants who carried on trade with China in the east and Europe in the west. The artisans and craftsmen not only benefited from their commercial activities but also appear to have become aware of the tastes of the Arabs and adapted their conventional styles accordingly. For instance, pieces of Indian block-printed textiles found in Egypt and available in the Ashmolean Museum, Oxford, shed light on the brisk trade between India and the Arab world extending as far as Egypt.[14] Since fine quality cotton was grown in the territories of Sind and Multan, the community of weavers appears to have benefited greatly from foreign trade. Mention may be made of the fragment of a cotton sheet, carbon dated AD, 1010 + (55 years), which was produced for export. Its texture had borders of the Arabic Kufic script with the Arabic phrase '*Li Sahibi hi*' (to its owner) added to the main decoration of traditional vine patterns. This block-printed resist-dyed fragment point to the adaptability of the Sindi and Multani craftsmen to local needs.[15]

As for the introduction of new crafts, the making of so-called Islamic glazed tiles, faience and faience-mosaics are worth mentioning as they later formed one of the outstanding characteristics of Multan architecture.[16] The introduction by the emigrants from Arabia, Iran and Khurasan (i.e. present-day Afghanistan) of the Arabic and Persian languages also went a long way to enrich literary culture. Al-Masudi, who visited Multan in AD 916, found the Multanis speaking Arabic, Persian and the local dialects.[17]

The north-western frontier region underwent cultural change after its annexation by Sultan Mahmud to his Empire of Ghazna at the beginning of the eleventh century. Though Sultan Mahmud is regarded as a plunderer, and his invasions of different territories in India caused large-scale suffering, the territories annexed to his Empire benefited greatly from the socio-economic development of the region. The entire region from the north-western frontier to Daibul in Sind was integrated with the Sultanate of Ghazna that had trade relations with the outside world. Moreover, this region was divided into manageable territorial units and garrisons were established at strategic points for the maintenance of law and order along the highways linking different provincial units to the Centre (Ghazna). The construction of *ribat*[18] (resthouses) for providing facilities to the travellers helped the process of urbanization. The description by Gardezi of the *ribat* of Margala (near Islamabad) casts light on its spaciousness and function. He writes that after the defeat of Sultan Masud by the Saljuq Turks in the battle of Dandaniqan (in AD 1041), he decided to leave Ghazna for Hindustan, to make war preparations and then return to retrieve his prestige. The Sultan started with treasures and reached Margala. At Margala the army mutinied and the Sultan was forced to take shelter inside the *ribat* of Margala along with his body guards and war elephants. The mutineers laid siege to the *ribat* and ultimately arrested the Sultan and put him to death.[19] Soon after the construction of such *ribats*, shopkeepers came and settled down around them to sell essential commodities to travellers and these places gradually developed into townships.

The scanty authentic evidence available in the sources reveals that Peshawar, Nandana and Lahore emerged as centres of learning and culture on account of the posting of officers, scholars along with deployment of army contingents.[20] The origin and development of the dialect spoken in Peshawar and the area around, called Hindko, can be traced back to this period, as the Peshawar valley is surrounded by the land of Pushto speaking people. Similarly, Lahore began to develop into an important city and ultimately emerged as a centre of learning and culture. A number of villages were founded around Lahore where leading scholars and poets were settled with landgrants. All this led to important changes in demographic and cultural patterns in the Punjab. Nandana town (in modern Jhelum district of Pakistan Punjab) was also garrisoned and adorned with mosques and madrasas.[21]

It is also worth recalling that the Sultanate polity under the Ghaznavid Sultans was a centralized one in which people could rise from below in the official hierarchy on account of their merit.

Baihaqi, the contemporary historian states the interesting case of Tilak. Tilak was the handsome son of a Hindu barber. He could write the Hindwi and Persian languages fluently and was also known for his eloquence. In Kashmir, he learnt magic, dissimulation and witchcraft. First, he joined the service of Abul Hasan, known as Qazi Shiraz, and was then employed by Wazir Ahmad-i-Hasan Maimandi as an interpreter. Later, impressed by his intelligence and competence, Sultan Mahmud took him in his personal service. He was now in a position to make the most for himself and attained a high status in the state service. In, 1030, a civil war was fought between the Princes for the throne. The Victor Sultan Masud appointed Tilak the commander of the Hindu troops stationed in Ghazna, on the fall of General Sohand Rai. He was honoured with the grant of drums and banners, the privilege that was enjoyed by the leading nobles of the Sultanate. Baihaqi makes the following comment on his rise, 'Wisemen do not wonder at such facts because nobody is born great, men become such. This Tilak had excellent qualities and all the time he lived he sustained no injury on account of being the son of a barber'[22]. All this indicates that an aristocratic background was irrelevant to status, the only thing that mattered was talent and skill.

The relevant evidence contained in the contemporary source *Jawami 'ul-Hikayat* provides us with interesting information about visits by merchant caravans that were a source of enrichment for local traders and craftsman. The compiler Sadid u'ddin 'Awfi mentions that in Punjab, goldsmiths minted silver coins in the name of the Sultan. Some of the Indians took advantage by minting dirham of full standard that gained circulation even outside the frontiers of the Sultanate. Merchants coming from *Darul Islam* (the Muslim world) purchased these for circulation in Khurasan and elsewhere. Over time the goldsmiths began to debase the standard dirham by degrees but the foreign merchants continued to trade in them without knowing of their depreciated value. They brought gold and silver to India from different parts of the Muslim world, in order to have the coins minted for use in other countries. When Sultan Masud III (d.1114) was informed about the matter, he decided to check the corruption and compensate the traders. The Sultan ordered the debased silver coins to be exchanged by the royal treasury with the standard legitimate ones.[23]

It may also be added that Firdausi Tusi indirectly gives hints in his celebrated work, *Shahnama* about the flourishing overland trade between India, Iran and the Central Asian lands. He sheds light on the cultural and commercial ethos when he mentions in his work the large number of merchants moving in caravan across the Indus. As regards the export of Indian commodities, amber, aloe-wood and camphor seem to have been special items in demand in neighbouring countries, while Chinese silk, called *deba-i-chin* was supplied to India. In fact, Firdausi projects what was a reality in his own time. In the *Shahnama* we also find the earliest reference to the *Luliyan-i-Hind* (nats, the dancers) who travelled to the foreign countries through Iran.[24] Sadi Shirazi also mentions a rich Irani merchant who carried on trade with Turkestan, India, Alexandria and China. He is also said to have had a rich stock of choice products from these countries, besides forty slaves. Of the Indian products, the articles of Indian steel appear to have been much valued in the middle eastern lands.[25]

Some words are in order about Lahore that was made the centre of governance of all the provincial units of the Ghaznavid Sultanate in India. Thereafter, it rapidly developed into a city. Further the flight of Khusrau Shah, one of the last descendants of Sultan Mahmud, from Ghazna to Lahore in 1159, paved the way for its rise as a trade emporium of international importance. As Ghazna was seized by the Ghuzz Turks and its residents were subjected to tyranny, the elite also fled to Lahore. They included scholars of distinction, poets, artists and rich merchants, with the result that Lahore emerged as a centre of high culture in place of Ghazna. The merchants from Lahore carried on trade with foreign countries as far as China. Upon the conquest of Central Asia and China by the Mongols, these merchants are reported to have obtained travel permits from the Mongol rulers for travelling in their lands safely. They were rich people, supremely self-confident, and at times even indifferent to the governor.[26] Hasan Nizami was not exaggerating when he called Lahore a city of enrichment, containing beautiful mansions and palaces.[27] In fact, it was Lahore's importance and grandeur that led Sultan Muiz u'ddin Muhammad bin Sam to make it his winter capital, after he had seized it from Khusran Malik, the last Sultan of the Ghaznavid house in 1186.[28] On the assassination of the Sultan, his lieutenant in India, Malik Qutb uddin Aibak also moved from Delhi to Lahore to ascend the throne.[29] He made Lahore the capital of his Sultanate. Delhi was still a *pargana* headquarters of little importance.[30]

Brief mention should be made of the contribution made by the poets of Lahore during the Ghaznavid period because their *diwans* (collections of Persian verses) are included among the classics of Persian literature. The tradition set by them inspired the future poets in India and abroad as well. Abul Faraj Runi and Masud S'ad Salman are recognized as the outstanding poets of Persian language. They composed verses in chaste Persian; 'Their style is plain and simple and in all their verses they have shown to their best advantage, their power, their resources, their fertility and their fine artistic instincts.'[31]

Born and brought up in Lahore, these poets had an attachment to the land and they composed beautiful poems in praise of its climate, fauna and flora, and the seasons, particularly the rainy season. Welcoming the monsoon, Masud S'ad Salman, calls it the spring of India that provides relief from the extreme heat of the summer and brings fresh life to vegetation and imparts sweetness to mankind.[32] He welcomes the rainy season:

> Bar shikal ai Bahar –i- Hindustan,
> Ai nijat az bala-i-tabistan.
> (O, the rainy season, thou art the spring of India,
> Thou provideth protection from the heat of summer).

Significantly, we find the beginning of the use of local Punjabi words in Masud S'ad Salman's Persian verses. In a *qasida,* for example depicting the scene of the siege of Agra fort by the governor of Lahore, the poet uses the Indian phrase *mara mar* in the second line.

As the sound came forth *Chu r'âd az abr begharid Kus-i-Mahmudi, Baramad as Pas-i-divar-i-hisn mara mar* from the Mahmudi drum, sound followed from behind the fortification, 'strike, strike'.[33]

To conclude, it may be stated that the Sultanate polity and culture that developed under the patronage of the Ghaznavid Sultans continued to provide a reference point in India through out the Delhi Sultanate period. The Ghaznavid rule created an atmosphere in which interaction between the followers of two different cultural traditions took place and then their fusion became possible. Thus the Punjab, with Lahore as its centre had become the nucleus of composite culture even before the foundation of the Delhi Sultanate. The foundation of the Delhi Sultanate paved the way for its spread in the entire subcontinent. An effort is made in the following chapters to focus on the social and economic changes that took place during the Sultanate period along with the cultural orientation of its polity.

Endnotes

1. Ahmad bin Yahiya Baladhuri, *Futuh al-Buldan*, Leiden, 1866, p. 433, cited by N.B. Baloch in his commentary on *Fathnama,* known as *Chachnama,* Persian translation of an Arabic work by Ali bin Hamid bin Abu Bakr al-Kufi, Islamabad, 1983, p. 42.
2. Ibid., pp. 20 & 51; idem, *Advent of Islam in Indonesia,* National Institute of Historical and Cultural Research, Islamabad, 1968, pp. 7-9.
3. Cf. Iqtidar Husain Siddiqui, 'The Process of Acculturation in Regional Historiography: The Case of Delhi Sultanate,' in *Art and Culture, Endeavours in Interpretation,* ed. A.J. Qaisar and S.P. Verma, New Delhi: Abhinav Publications 1996, pp. 1-8; also fn. 13.
4. Ibn Hauqal, *Kitab al-Masalik,* Leiden: E.J. Brill, 1983, p. 231.
5. Siraji Khurasani, *Diwan-i-Siraji Khurasani,* ed. Nazir Ahmad, Aligarh, 1975, pp. 226 & 245. Siraji who was associated with the court of Makran, composed a number of *qasidas* (panegyrics) in praise of the Sultan and the princes of Makran.
6. Minhaj-i-Siraj Juzjani, *Tabaqat-i-Nasiri,* 2 vols, ed. Abdul Ha'i Habibi, vol. 1, Kabul: Historical Society of Afganistan, 1963, p. 368.

7. Generally, people in the countries conquered by the Arabs were called *Maula* (client), in case they converted to Islam. They often associated with an Arab family for getting acquaintance with Islam and were then called the *Maula* of that family. Unlike them, those who did not get attached to a family, owing to their aristocratic background were known as *Maula-i-Islam*. *Fathnama-i-Sind*, known as *Chachnama*, op.cit, pp. 101-2, hereafter cited as *Chachnama*.
8. Ibid., pp. 32 & 88, also commentary, pp. 29 & 77.
9. Cf. Yohanan Friedmann, ed., 'The Origin and Significance of *Chachnama*', in *Islam in South Asia*, Jerusalem University Press, 1984, pp. 31-2.
10. Cf. Iqtidar Husain Siddiqui, 'Dynastic History of Sind', in *A Comprehensive History of India*, ed. R.S. Sharma and K.M. Shrimali, vol. 4, part 1, New Delhi, 1992, pp. 22-7.
11. Ibn Battuta, *The Travels of Ibn Battuta*, tr. Sir Hamilton Gibb, Cambridge, 1971, vol. 3, p. 597.
12. N.B. Baloch, ed., Commentary, *Chachnama*, Islamabad: Islamic University, 1983, p. 104.
13. Loc. cit.
14. Cf. R. Barnes, *Indian Block-Printed Textiles in Egypt*, Oxford: Clarendon Press, 2 vols. 1997. The New-Berry Collection in the Ashmolean Museum.
15. Elizabeth Lambourn accepts uncritically the erroneous identification by the Ashmolean scholars with textile manufactured in Gujarat and exported from Cambay. This cannot be empirically substantiated. According to the Arabic classical accounts, the rulers of Gujarat were hostile to the Arabs since the Arab conquest of Sind and Multan. They did not allow the Muslim merchants to establish trade relations with their kingdom. It was sometime in the twelfth century that their policy was changed and then the merchants from Arab lands, Iran and Khurasan settled down in Cambay as the details furnished by Sadid uddin Muhammad 'Awfi in his '*Jawami'ul Hikayat wa-Livami'ul-Rivayat*' shows. 'Awfi visited Cambay at the beginning of the thirteenth century. Cf. Elizabeth Lambourn, 'The English Factory or Kothi Gateway at Cambay: An Unpublished Tughluq Structure from Gujarat', *Bulletin of the School of Oriental and African Studies*, (University of London). vol. 65, part 3, 2003, pp. 495-517; see also

S.Maqbul Ahmad, *Arabic Classical Accounts of India and China,* (Indian Institute of Advanced Study, Simla, 1989), pp. 12, 18, 43 & 60; See also N.B. Baloch, Introduction (English) of *Fathnama-i-Sind,* known as *Chachnama,* pp. 20, 51-3, 55, for Daibul port and trade with the outside world.

16. Cf. Nabi Ahmad Khan, *Multan: History and Architecture,* Islamabad: Institute of Islamic History, Culture and Civilization, Islamic University, 1983, pp. 174-6 & 207, Plates, I, II and III.
17. Abul Hasan al-Masudi, *Muruj ul-Zahab,* as cited by Nabi Ahmad Khan, *Multan: History and Architecture,* Islamabad: Institute of Islamic History and Culture, 1983, p. 5.
18. The term *ribat* was replaced by the term *khanqah* in the Persian speaking lands, sometime during the twelfth century. The early writers who migrated to India in the beginning of the thirteenth century use the *khanqah* in place of *ribat* as will be discussed subsequently.
19. Abu Said bin Abdul Hai Gardezi, *Zani al-Akhbar,* ed., Abdul Ha'i Habibi, Tehran: Intisharat-i-Farhang Iran, no. 37, pp. 174-81.
20. Sadid Uddin Muhammad 'Awfi, *Jawami 'ul-Hikayat wa-Lavami 'ul-Rivayat,* ed. Amir Bano Museffa and Mutahir Musaffa, Tehran: Bunyad-i-Farhang-i-Iran, 1971, vol. 3, part 2, pp. 571-5.
21. *Zain al-Akhbar,* op.cit., pp. 179-81.
22. Abul Fazl Baihaqi, *Tarikh-i-ale-Subuktigin,* also known as *Tarikh-i-Baihaqi,* ed. W.H. Mosley, Calcutta: Asiatic Society, 1862, pp. 503-5.
23. 'Awfi has referred to Baihaqi's *Tarikh-i-Nasiri* in his third volume of the *Jawami, 'ul-Hikayat wa-Lavami 'ul-Rivayat,* hereafter cited as *Jawami ul Hikayat.*
24. Firdausi Tusi, *Shahnama,* ed. Said Nafisi, vol. 7, pp. 2238, 2254 & 2298; See also Iqtidar Husain Siddiqui, *Perso-Arabic Sources on the Life and Conditions in the Sultanate of Delhi,* New Delhi: Munshiram Manohar Lal, 1992, p. 15.
25. Muslih uddin Sadi, *Gulistan,* ed. Muhammad Ali Faroghi, Tehran: Intisharat-i-Kovyan, n.d, pp. 104-5.
26. Fakhr-i-Mudabbir, *Muqadimah* of the *Shajra-i-Ansab,* ed., Denison Ross and published under the misleading title '*Tarikh-i-Fakhr al-Din Mubarak Shah Marvarudi,* London, 1927, p. 31. Fakhr-i-

Mudabbir has been confused by the editor with Fakhr uddin Mubarak Shah, the poet associated with the court of Sultan Ghiyas u'ddin Muhammad bin Sam of Ghur in Firozkuh (d.1202). The compiler of the *Shajra-i-Ansab* was a different man, known as Fakhr-i-Mudabbir. The latter resided in Lahore. Therefore, I have referred to this work as *Tarikh-i-Fakhr-i-Mudabbir.*

27. Minhaj-i-Siraj Juzjani, *Tabaqat-i-Nasiri,* vol. 1, ed. Abdul Ha'i Habibi, Kabul: Historical Society of Afghanistan, 1963, p. 405.
28. Hasan Nizami, *Taj-ul-Maasir,* MS. British Library, London, no. Add. 7623, ff. 120a-b; See also *Tabaqat-i-Nasiri,* vol. 2, Kabul, 1964, pp. 163-4.
29. See Juzjani, *Tabaqat-i-Nasiri*, vol. 1, p. 405.
30. Isami, *Futuh us-Salatin,* ed. A.S. Usha, Madras: Madras University Islamic Series No. 9, 1948, p. 408. (hereafter cited as Isami).
31. Iqbal Husain, *The Early Persian Poets of India,* Patna University Publication, Patna, 1937, p. 4.
32. Cf. *Diwan-i-Masud S'ad Salman*, Tehran? 1860, p. 241.
33. Cf. Iqtidar Husain Siddiqui, *Medieval India: Essays in Intellectual Thought and Culture*, vol. 1, New Delhi: Manohar, 2003, p. 29.

CHAPTER 1

The Delhi Sultanate: Political Economy and Public Welfare

The literature produced during the Delhi Sultanate period bearing on the system of governance falls into two categories: one belongs to the genre of the mirror of Princes whereas the other forms the part of episodic historiography. The writers of the first category were generally included among the *ulama* (religious scholars) and they wrote with the intention of enlightening the rulers about the Prophetic tradition and how it was interpreted and followed by the Prophet's immediate successors, the pious caliphs. In particular, the second caliph is portrayed as a role model. Unlike them, the second category of writers were both political thinkers, historians and even courtiers. They wrote on the basis of their own observations, their understanding of history and also of what they thought to be the requirement of changing time, free of all theological restraint. They appear to have considered time as the creator of new conditions. We have to examine their phraseology carefully, in order to know how they met the need of time. Indeed, they were ahead of their time in introducing and popularizing the conceptions of political economy that went a long way in creating conditions for socio-economic growth and material progress in the country. In this chapter an attempt has been made to analyse the ideas that influenced the actual practice and the patterns of political behaviour displayed by powerful sultans.

The early works produced in India are important in more than one way. In them we find clues to the concepts and traditions that evolved in the Ghaznavid Empire, and their impact on the system of governance and economy of the Sultanate of Delhi. For instance, Fakhr-i-Mudabbir's works, the *Muqadimah*[1] (Prologue) of the *Shajra-i-Ansab* and the *Adab ul-Muluk wa-Ki faiyat ul-Mamluk,* the later recension of which is well-known as *Adab ul-Harb wa-Shuja'a*[2] seems to have been compiled for the enlightenment of the sultans, Qutbuddin Aibak and Shams uddin Iltutmish and their nobles. Fakhr-i-Mudabbir, writing on the duties of the Sultan, states that the foremost duty of the ruler is to establish the rule of law and ensure impartial justice to all and sundry; suppress both the pernicious people and social evils and have mosques and madrasas (schools and colleges) constructed in the urban centres; that the bridges, wells and *ribats* (rest houses for the travellers) and forts be constructed along the high ways for protection against highway men. The Sultan is also apprised of his duty to make all possible efforts for creating favourable conditions for the well-being of his *raiyat* (peasantry as well as commonalty).[3] As regards the second work *'Adab ul-Muluk wa-Kifayat ul-Mamluk*, he describes in it the phenomena of political life and culture that developed in Ghazna and Lahore under the Ghaznavid Sultans. Almost all the chapters, with the exception of those that deal with the art of warfare, weapons, war-horses and their treatment, contain detailed exposition of the functions of different ministerial departments at the centre as well as their possible relationship with life in the sultanate of Ghazna. The compiler appears to have described the phenomena as he observed it. He describes the working of the system of governance with a remarkable grasp of the essential characteristics of political power, the stages of its evolution and the intricate relationship of the centralized polity with all aspects of society.

We are here concerned with the seventh chapter that provides us with insights into the role of the state in the regulation of the economy during the time of crisis caused by the scarcity of essential commodities. Writing on the need to select a competent person for the ministerial post of *amir-i-dad* (supreme magistrate), Fakhr-i-Mudabbir includes among his duties the maintenance of public buildings, such as mosques, bridges, the repair of the city walls and gates, the appointment of night-guards to take rounds of the lanes and streets, and protect the houses of the citizens and the shops in the *bazaars* from thieves. Further he states that the *amir-i-dad* has to keep himself well-informed about the conduct of shopkeepers and artisans and safeguard the interest of the public. Thus, the weights of stones used by the shopkeepers should be checked and *bazaar shahnas* (market inspectors) posted in the *bazaars* were to keep a strict watch on prices and inform the *amir-i-dad* through the *rais* (or *shahnas*) about any developments. Further, the heads of artisans and shopkeepers, i.e. their representatives, should be required to enter into formal agreement not to raise prices of essential commodities arbitrarily. The artisans in general and weavers in particular were also to be checked from cheating people by producing under-quality goods such as the weavers mixing rotten and used silk thread in weaving costly fabric.[4] All this is interesting because the *amir-i-dad's* department was situated in the Sultanate of Delhi.

Like Fakhr-i-Mudabbir's work, Sadiduddin Muhammad 'Awfi's *Jawami' 'ul-Hikayat wa-Lavami' 'ul Rivayat* also served as a source of inspiration for the rulers of the Delhi Sultanate. 'Awfi has incorporated in his work interesting details about measures that were taken by the duty-conscious rulers for the welfare of the people and also the development of certain institutions of political and cultural importance in Central Asian lands till his own time. We find in this work allusions to *bimaristan* (hospital) established by the state for the free medical treatment of patients,[5] and the price control of the essential commodities during times of scarcity.[6] In fact, the source of inspiration for the introduction by Sultan 'Ala ud'din Khalji of the price control and rationing system in Delhi lay in Fakhr-i-Mudabbir and 'Awfi's works.

Like the aforesaid writers, Minhaj-i-Siraj, also an emigrant scholar from Ghur writes much for the enlightenment of the ruling elite in his *Tabaqat-i-Nasiri*. He is critical of the wrong policies followed and decadence of the young princes. He dilates on the consequences harmful both for the ruler and people in general. Describing the fall of Sultan Iltutmish's immediate successor, Sultan Rukn uddin Firuz Shah (killed in 1236), he warns the ruling elite that the overindulgence in pleasure and negligence in the performance of kingly duties, such as the administration of justice for the good of commonalty, benevolence towards the armymen and the avoidance of the company of strangers and base people, generally bring ruin upon the empire.[7]

Of the contemporary literature, the documents and epistles, composed by Amir Khusrau for incorporation in the *Ijaz-i-Khusravi* shed interesting light on the political views and concepts of political economy as well as the concern he had for the security and progress of the Sultanate. These documents and epistles provide us with great insight into the complex social and political phenomena during that time. A few of them are futuristic and in composing them Khusrau seems to have visualized the expansion of the Sultanate as well as the problems that would result for the centre in future. Likewise, we also come across Khusrau's critique of State policies followed by Sultan 'Ala ud'din Khalji vis-à-vis the appointment of people belonging to the lower strata of society, to important positions. Khusrau seems to have given thought to certain matters of perennial nature as well as provide solutions for them, such as the Mongol invasion of India; the relationship between the Centre and the hereditary land chiefs; qualifications with regard to the appointment of people to important positions; need for the expansion of the empire; and the treatment to be meted out by the State to the *ulama* and *mashaikh* (sufi saints). His historical *mathnavis* (long poems), *qasidas* (panegyrics) in verse and epistles written in prose display the concern he had for the endurance, defence and the expansion of the Sultanate. I take up for my analysis what has relevance to the problem under study.

The first selection is the specimen record drafted in the form of a *tauqi* (royal mandate), said to have been issued by Sultan 'Ala ud'din Khalji to his son, Prince Farid Khan with regard to his appointment as governor of Ma'abar (present-day Karnataka state) in AD 1312. Its examination in conjunction with the earlier official records shows that Khusrau extends our understanding of the past through elaboration of medieval Indian culture and systems of governance. For instance, the early records of the times of Qutbuddin Aibak and Iltutmish direct the governors designate to act with discretion and sound judgment; abide by the laws, rules and usages; be considerate to the men of religion and learning; administer justice impartially; and make efforts to render the roads safe for the travellers as well as provide protection to merchants who served as liaison between countries and traded in their products.[8]

The following passages are worth considering because they seem to have been written on the basis of the ground reality that existed vis-à-vis the relationship between the state and the non-Muslims. Khusrau writes 'the royal warriors of the army should win over the Hindus… All those who persist in following their ancestral ways and do not give up their old faith, they should be granted the status of protected people with full freedom and security in accordance with the Quranic law. The acceptance by them of the status of protected people ensures the security of life and property and also prevents them from rebellion.'[9]

Like other records, this farman also seems to have been drafted by Khusrau to make a suggestion about the desirability of annexing South Indian territories to the Sultanate, Sultan 'Ala ud'din Khalji was however not interested in establishing his rule but decided to wrest war-elephants and treasures from the southern rulers. For instance, the Sultan's general Malik Kafur, invaded Ma'abar in AD 1312, and only seized the elephants and treasures leaving the rulers free to retain their territories.[10] Nevertheless Khusrau visualized the annexation of the entire region in the near future as the initial victories achieved by Malik Kafur in South India had paved the way for its occupation by the Sultan. Sultan Muhammad bin Tughluq was inspired by Khusrau in this regard as well.

Lastly, we may discuss Khusrau's critique of Sultan 'Ala ud'din's reign, contained in an epistle on *fiqh* (principles of Islamic jurisprudence). It is important in that we are provided with an insight into concepts of political thought and social philosophy of the elite associated with the court. It helps us analyse the political behaviour of the Sultan and the socio-political changes that resulted from it.

Khusrau's critique begins with the praise of the reigning king for his achievements in different fields – military, cultural and economic. Mentioning Sultan 'Ala ud'din Khalji as unequalled in his mastery over economic science (*Ilm-i-ma'ishat*), Khusrau says that he gained precedence over the kings of the past, i.e. by introducing important economic reforms. The allusion, contained therein to *Ilm-i-ma'ishat* tends to suggest that economics formed a part of the political philosophy of the elite in the Sultanate and the standard of education and learning was raised very high.[11] It is also worth recalling that the denunciation by Khusrau and his contemporaries of hoarders and shopkeepers at different places in their respective works casts light on their enlightened and advanced understanding of political economy. They were certainly opposed to the free operation of market economy at all times. In the *Khazain ul-Futuh*, Khusrau glows with pride when he refers to the price control introduced by Sultan 'Ala ud'din Khalji. He states that the Sultan increased the means of livelihood for the general public by reducing the tax on shopkeepers who had been overpricing their wares. He also mentions the posting of an honest and competent *rais* or *shahna*, i.e. bazaar superintendent to safeguard the interest of buyers in the bazaars. The *rais* was charged with the duty to inspect the weights used by the shopkeepers and deal out exemplary punishment to those who cheated people by selling goods underweight.[12] Even 'Isami who does not appear to have had competence in economic analysis is critical of the traders for their fraudulent practices, such as taking to the practice of hoarding in order to create scarcity and then raise the prices of essential commodities.[13] In his account of Sultan 'Ala ud'din Khalji, 'Isami alludes to the reduced prices brought about by the implementation of the price control in these words, 'The rose-water and honey became as cheap as water on account of the prices being very low. The regraters were to be sent to the gallows unless they repented and gave up regrating.'[14]

For Barani, the working of the economy was a very serious matter that could not be left to economic forces. In his *Fatawa-i-Jahandari*, a work on his political thought, he talks about the interdependence of the livelihood of people; both soldiers, commoners and others, and the state revealing an awareness about the economy of Delhi. He also recognized that for the creation of a stable social and political order in the country, the king had to play a crucial role in controlling the prices of essential commodities. He states that the shopkeepers and the *caravanians* (transport-merchants) should not be permitted to hoard food grains and other essentials to make great profits in the days of shortage because hoarders caused the prices to shoot up by stopping supply to the markets. He says further that the prices should be settled by the kings themselves in accordance with the principle of the cost of production; and the officers, *raises* (market superintendents), *shahnas* and *kotwals* (administrators and police superintendents) of the cities should be charged with the duty of regulating the transactions of sale and purchase. Stressing the centrality of such work in the affairs of the state Barani wrote critically about regrating by traders, the *goomashtas* (state agents) of the *mandis* (grain markets), the *shahnas* and *kotwals*. It was suggested that the grains (stock) seized from the regrators (hoarders) be set to fire or they be punished by the confiscation of their goods and exiled. Further shopkeepers and merchants should be kept under control, so that they could not tyrannize innocent buyers. In conclusion Barani stresses the point that people who are supporters of *laissez-faire* in trade and commerce, argue that cheapness is brought about by plenty and refer to the Prophetic tradition in their support. For Barani, deviation from the injections of the Quran, the precepts of the Prophet and the tradition of the early Orthodox Caliphs of Islam was justified on account of the change of time. The passing ages bring men further away from the time of the Prophet and his immediate successors, the pious Caliphs. So with the change of time, not only the requirements of society change but also the psychology of man. Their virtues are transformed into vices and the love of the world has presidence, the precepts of the Prophet are violated. Neither fear of God nor fear of the king prevents the rich from forestalling and hoarding, the poor would suffer. If the king whose duty is to act in the interest of people neglects to exert himself in the control of prices, how can he answer for his negligence on the day of judgement. The king should understand that his efforts in controlling the prices in the capital would go a long way to inspire people and the governors in the provinces. They would also exert in furthering the material welfare of people in the provinces'.[15]

Though Barani's picture of Sultan 'Ala ud'din Khalji in his *Tarikh-i-Firuz Shahi* is that of a ruthless and terrible ruler, he praises him at least for successfully enforcing price control in Delhi during his reign. Sultan 'Ala ud'din is credited for having banned the profession of *dalal* (brokers) who charged commission both from the sellers and buyers in the Delhi *bazaars* and made arrangements for maintaining a regular supply of all goods in demand. The prices of all commodities, food grains as well as merchandise, slaves and cloth, etc. were fixed after their cost of production and margin of profit to the trader had been taken into consideration. The traders were advanced money from the state exchequer to maintain regular supply to the bazaars in Delhi. This was a novel experiment in medieval Indian history. Modern scholars began to write on it from around the beginning of the twentieth century, many questioning its possibility. Of these writers, W.H. Moreland's analysis put to rest the controversy about the successful implementation and the veracity of Barani's account of price control measures. In 1929, Moreland wrote, 'the long and detailed price-regulations [pp.304ff] can be summarized very shortly. The essence was (1) control of supplies, and (2) control of transport, with (3) rationing of consumption when necessary, the whole system resting on (4) a highly organized intelligence, and (5) drastic punishment of evasions'. Further, Moreland comparing it with the introduction of control in war time (modern) England states, 'it will be seen, [it] applies almost precisely to the system of control which was elaborated in England during the years of war, and which was proved by experience to be effective. It is quite inconceivable that a writer like Ziya Barani could have invented these essential features out of his head; but it is quite conceivable that, in the economic condition of the time, a king like 'Ala ud'din, aided, as he certainly was, by competent ministers, should by degrees have arrived at the essentials of the policy he was determined to enforce. He was, it must be remembered, strong just where modern system was weak, for he could rely on an elaborate organization of spies'.[16]

Brief mention should also be made of those who wrote either on 'Ala ud'din's market control or made comments on Barani's account after the publication of Moreland's work. K.S. Lal describes in detail the price control, the area in which it was operative and also the administrative machinery created for its success. Lal's analysis seems to have been based on Elliot's translation of the parts selected from Barani's *Tarikh-i-Firuz Shahi.* At some places Lal's statements are not backed by the text of Barani's work. For example, Barani says that after the enforcement of price control, the brokers were prevented from entering the markets because their profession was banned.[17] Lal misquotes Barani, when he says 'Even after giving due consideration to the exaggeration in which Barani is prone to indulge, the facts that such severe penalties were inflicted on brokers in horse, cattle and slave markets, that even life became so distasteful to them, and they longed for death, clearly shows that the market people must have been disgusted'.[18] On the contrary Barani states emphatically that the people were amazed by the abundance of goods in the market and general prosperity in the metropolis that they had neither heard about nor ever witnessed in the past.[19]

It is also worth noting that Amir Khusrau's *I'jaz-i-Khusravi* that was brought to completion towards the close of 'Ala ud'din's reign has been left by modern scholars untapped, although it contains information of a corroborative and supplementary nature. Khusrau corroborates Barani's account about the abundance of commercial goods in the markets and the supply of foodgrains from the state granaries at the time of scarcity. He states, 'For the sake of the availability of cheap grains, the main source of our life, he (the Sultan) has through the exercise of his imagination, devised such a method that if, for years, the cloud and the sun may not trickle down the dust of their perspiration and the hot-tempered wind may not move its fan and the soil may not cause flowers to sprout on the surface of the earth, and the fire burning sun may not ripen the grains, the common people may still enjoy the fresh and ever continuing supply of food grains from the royal granaries'. As for other commodities in demand, he writes, 'Other requirements of the people, are always more readily available than the yellow-coloured amber and the ordinary cereal. The essential commodities and merchandise are so cheap that one can arrange dowry for the marriage in just ten dirams. The slave and cattle markets (*nakhas*) are like a flowing river, filled with slave girls'. The prices of slave girls are said to have ranged between ten to twelve *tankas*.[20]

B.P.Saxena and Simon Digby have also tried to add significant comments[21] which have been rebutted by Irfan Habib who attempts a fresh indepth analysis of the problem. Habib's analysis is based on a close examination of Barani's account in conjunction with relevant evidence found in other contemporary works, such as Amir Khusrau's *Khazain ul-Futuh,* Isami's *Futuh us-Salatin,* Hamid Qalandar's *Khair ul-Majalis* (the collection of Shaikh Nasir uddin Chiragh-i-Dehli's utterances) and Ibn-i-Batutta's travelogue. In his highly researched article Irfan Habib not only corrects the historiographic errors committed by the above mentioned writers but also does justice to Barani by highlighting his ability for economic analysis.[22]

The price control system was abolished by Sultan Qutbuddin Mubarak Shah, the son and successor of Sultan 'Ala ud'din (reigned:1316-20). By this time the armymen seem to have got richer on account of their share in the booty seized in the conquered territories. The new Sultan is reported to have increased their pay and allowances, in addition to the payment of six months pay in advance as reward at the time of his accession.[23] Moreover the flow of wealth from the conquered territories, in particular south India had given rise to consumerism in the metropolis. The nobles were fond of luxury goods imported from foreign countries. In order to enable the men of means to buy choice goods, the system was dismantled and the traders were given trading freedom. The foreign merchants whom Khusrau recommends for the Sultan's favour must have been pleased. They brought merchandise from the lands of Maghreb (north Africa) and Syria.[24]

It may also be pointed out that the state continued to store foodgrains in the granaries, in order to meet the shortage caused by draught. Food was supplied to the poor free of cost in the days of famine.[25] However, the condemnation by the writers of the hoarders tends to show how the problem of hoarding of essential commodities was largely unresolvable.[26]

Besides the regulatory act with regard to the market economy, the creation of irrigation facilities for the progress of agriculture and the building of *darul-shifa* (hospitals) for health care of the public are also included among the functions of the state.[27] Consequently, the sultans took interest in the construction of waterworks in different regions. Irrigation technology appears to have made great progress. Besides the construction of artificial lakes, step-wells, cisterns and tanks, the introduction of the gearing device for lifting water from the wells, at least since the fourteenth century led to the progress of agriculture. In fact, the diffusion of advanced irrigation technology brought about prosperity and helped the growth of material culture. At least since the reign of Sultan 'Ala ud'din Khalji, the canals were led off from the rivers for the irrigation of the territories that suffered from scarcity of water.[28] The succeeding sultans followed the example set by their predecessors.[29] Even the rich farmers appear to have had canals constructed for irrigating their farms.[30] Sultan Firuz Shah (reigned: 1351-88) turned the arid region of Haryana into a fertile region through the construction of a network of canals. According to Barani, the canals, which were between a 100 and 120 miles long were led off from the rivers the Jamuna and the Ganga. The water flowing through them irrigated the desert and desolate tracts where no well or lake existed before. The depth and width (of certain canals) made the use of boats possible for people to travel long distances.[31]

In short, efforts made by the state helped the cultivators to harvest bumper crops. Amir Khusrau writes in his rhetorical style about general prosperity during the reign of 'Ala ud'din Khalji saying, 'Heaps of wheat surmount so high in the market that the flying birds need not descend to get grains. The balance is deprived of grain as the [exact] rhymes of the [the lines of] verse are due to maneuvering of the wicked, and the empty scale of a balance, looks like a crooked student's gaping mouth. The measuring cups of the hoarders of wheat are full because the ears of wheat have gained the weight of one mound based on shariah.[32] The beggars, seekers, and dervishes fasting indefinitely [i.e. faced starvation] in the past are now observing Idd [festival of feast].'[33]

Lastly, mention is made of hospitals maintained by the state. Shaikh Shihab uddin al-Umari was told by a traveller from India in Damascus that Delhi had seventy *bimaristans.* He writes that the Indians called *bimaristan, 'darul-shifa.*[34] Ikhtisan, the *dabir-i-khass* of Sultan Muhammad bin Tughluq Shah also refers in his work, *'Basatin ul-Uns* to the physicians employed to treat the patients in the *darul-shifa.*[35] According to Barani, the science of medicines was popular and even the members of ruling elite studied and practised it. He writes that Sultan Muhammad bin Tughluq was skilled in the treatment of different maladies. He had authoritative knowledge of Ibn Sina's treatises on medicines.[36] His successor, Sultan Firuz Shah (reigned: 1351-88) who tried to surpass his predecessors in creating the institutions of public utility, is credited with the construction of a colossal structure that consisted of several wings wherein different types of patients were treated and given medicines. There was a separate wing for the treatment of animals and birds.[37]

On the dissolution of the Sultanate of Delhi in the beginning of the fifteenth century, the regional sultans vied with one another in emulating the Sultan of Delhi in every matter. Each one had constructed palaces, mosques, madrasas, hospitals, etc. in their capitals. The description by Shihab Hakim of the *darul-shifa* at Mandu, the capital of Malwa, is graphic. It was constructed inside a beautiful garden and its rooms were decorated with murals so that patients staying therein could benefit from their soothing effect.[38] Efforts were also made to translate Sanskrit classics into Persian, in order to familiarize the Muslim physicians with the indigenous medicines and system of treatment. *Masnad-i-ali* Mian Bhu'a's translation of Sanskrit classics, entitled *Ma'dan ul-Shifa-i-Sikandar Shahi* enjoyed popularity throughout medieval period.[39] The prologue added to this work casts light on Sultan Sikandar's interest also in medicines. Mian Bhu'a writes that he suggested to the Sultan that the *Ilm-i-tib,* i.e. Muslim system of medicines which was based on Greek science did not suit people in the Indian climate. Further, he said that the nature of many herbs was not known and many of them were not available. Unlike it, the indigenous system was suitable and that it was desirable to render the classics of Sanskrit into Persian. The Sultan was pleased to issue the farman and the translation was brought to completion.[40]

In the final analysis it may be stated that the concepts of political economy and public welfare were propounded on the basis of what the writers and thinkers found in the literature about the system of governance that evolved under the Ghaznavid Sultans. It should, however, be admitted that the thinkers of the Delhi Sultanate were also able to make their own contribution. No doubt, the rulers of Central Asia and Iran regulated the prices of certain essential commodities at the time of shortage, but the price control and the mechanism devised for its successful working during 'Ala ud'din's reign was a novel experiment in history.

Endnotes

1. This *Muqadimah,* as mentioned above, is the first work relating to the achievements of Qutbuddin Aibak from his posting as *sipahsalar* (governor) of the territorial unit of Kuhram and Sunam (Haryana) in 1192 upto his accession to the throne in Lahore in AD 1210. I have referred to it as *Tarikh-i-Fakhr-i-Mudabbir* instead of *Tarikh-i-Fakhruddin Mubarak Shah Marvar-rudi.*
2. The comparison of both the recensions suggests that some scribe, probably at the instance of the book trader excluded the first six chapters, copied the remaining ones dealing with diplomacy and the art of warfare and introduced his collection as *Adab ul-Harb wal Shuja'a.* In the year 1346 Shamsi, Ahmad Suhaili Khwansari published its critically edited text from Tehran under the same title *'Adab ul-Harb wal-Shuja'a.*
3. *Tarikh-i-Fakhr-i-Mudabbir,* London, 1927, pp. 16-18.
4. Cf. *Adab ul-Muluk wa-Kifayat ul-Mamluk,* published under the changed title as *Ain-i-Kishwardari,* ed. Muhammad Sarvar Maulai, Farhang-i-Bunyad-i-Iran, no. 212, pp. 40-1.

5. Cf. Iqtidar Husain Siddiqui, *Perso-Arabic Sources of Information on the Life and Conditions in the Sultanate of Delhi,* New Delhi: Munshiram Manoharlal 1992, p. 26. See for English translation.
6. Ibid., pp. 2, 11-12.
7. *Tabaqat-i-Nasiri,* vol. 1, p. 407.
8. Hasan Nizami, *Taj-ul-Ma'asir,* MS. British Library, London, no. Add. 7623, 55b-56a. See also *Perso-Arabic Sources of Information on the Life and Conditions in the Sultanate of Delhi,* op.cit., pp. 168-70, for detailed information.
9. Amir Khusrau, *'Ijaz-i-Khusravi,* Lucknow: Nawal Kishore Press, vol. 4, 1876, pp. 121-40.
10. Zia'uddin Barani, *Tarikh-i-Firuz Shahi,* Calcutta: Bibliotheca Indica, 1862, p. 467.
11. *'Ijaz-i-Khusravi,* vol. 4, op.cit., p. 236.
12. Cf. *Khazain ul-Futuh,* tr. Mohammad Habib, Bombay: D.B. Taraporewala, Sons and Co., 1931, pp. 9-10.
13. Isami states, while mentioning the relief that rainfall brought to people after a severe famine during the reign of Sultan Jalal uddin Khalji (1290-6) that the entire public became cheerful, except the regraters because the *bazaars* were flooded with food grains. Consequently, the prices came down. The foodgrains and cloth came from every direction and the means of livelihood became easy. *Futuh us-Salatin,* ed. A.S. Usha, Madras: Madras University Islamic Series No. 9, 1948, p. 221.
14. Ibid., pp. 301, 314-15.
15. Barani, *Fatawa-i-Jahandari,* ed. Mrs. A. Salim Khan, Lahore: University of the Punjab, 1972; pp. 131-8.
16. Cf. W.H. Moreland, *The Agrarian System of Moslem India,* rpt, Delhi: Oriental Books, 1968, pp. 36-7.
17. Barani, *Tarikh-i-Firuz Shahi,* Calcutta, 1862, p. 313.
18. Cf. K.S. Lal, *History of the Khaljis,* rpt, Delhi: Munshiram Manoharlal, 1980.
19. Barani, *Tarikh-i-Firuz Shahi,* p. 312.
20. Amir Khusrau, *Ijaz-i-Khusravi,* Lucknow: Nawal Kishore Press, 1876, vol. 1, pp. 19-20; See also vol. 4, tr. Iqtidar Husain Siddiqui, Islamic

Thought and Science Institute, 850S. Illinois: Des Plaines Avenue, Suite 102, Forest Park, 4.5.A. 2007, p. 204.

21. B.P. Saxena, *A Comprehensive History of India,* vol. 5 (Delhi Sultanate) ed. Mohammad Habib and K.A. Nizami, Delhi: Peoples Publishing House, 1970; Simon Digby, *War-Horse and Elephant in the Delhi Sultanate: A Study of Military Supplies*, Karachi: Oxford University Press, 1971.
22. Cf. Irfan Habib, 'The Price Regulations of 'Ala ud'din Khalji; A defence of Zia Barani', *The Indian Economic and Social History Review,* vol. 21, no. 4, Delhi, 1984, pp. 398-414.
23. Barani, *Tarikh-i Firuz Shahi,* p. 382.
24. *Ijaz-i-Khusravi;* vol. 4, tr. op.cit., p. 185.
25. Ibn Battuta, *The Travels of Ibn Battuta,* vol. 3, tr. Sir Hamilton Gibb, Cambridge: Cambridge University Press, 1971, pp. 695, 734 & 761.
26. Sharaf Mohammad Alatai, *Fawaid-i-Firuz Shahi,* MS. Patna: Khuda Bakhsh Oriental Public Library, f.281b.
27. Fakhr-i-Mudabbir, *Adab ul-Harb wal-Shuja'a*, Ahmad Suhaili Khwansari, Tehran, 1346 Shamsi, p. 117.
28. Amir Khusrau, *Tughluq nama*, 1933, verses 1201-2, p. 63.
29. Barani, *Tarikh-i-Firuz Shahi,* 1862, p. 442.
30. Ibn Battuta, *The Travels of Ibn Battuta,* vol. 3, op.cit., p. 698.
31. Iqtidar Husain Siddiqui, *Authority and Kingship under the Sultans of Delhi*, New Delhi: Manohar Publishers 2006, pp. 259-82.
32. Here Khusrau's rhetoric style alludes to the tough measures taken by Sultan 'Ala ud'din Khalji against hoarding of food grains.
33. *Ijaz-i-Khusravi,* tr. vol. 4, p. 203.
34. Cf. *Perso-Arabic Sources of Information on the Life and Conditions*, See p. 116, for the English translation of *Masalik ul- Absar.*
35. Ibid., pp. 95-6, for Ikhtisan and his *Basatin al-Uns.*
36. Barani, *Tarikh-i-Firuz Shahi,* p. 464.
37. Anonymous, *Sirat-i-Firuz Shahi,* fascsimile of the manuscript, Patna: Khuda Bakhsh Oriental Public Library, 1999, pp. 235-43.
38. Ali Bin Mahmud al-Kirmani, known as Shihab Hakim, *Ma'asir-i-Mahmud Shahi,* ed. Nurul Hasan Ansari, Delhi: Indo-Persian Society, 1968, p. 64.

39. Shaikh Rizq ullah Mushtaqi states that it was considered the most important work both in standard and value in the entire country during his time (sixteenth century). Cf. *Waqi 'at-i-Mushtaqi*, tr. Iqtidar Husain Siddiqui, New Delhi: Indian Council of Historical Research, 1993, p. 83.
40. Mian Bhu'a, *Ma'dan ul-Shafa-i-Sikandar Shahi* also known as *Tibe-i-Sikandari.* Lucknow: Nawal Kishore Press, 1877, p. 3.

CHAPTER 2

The Process of Urbanization

The establishment of the Sultanate in India in AD 1206 exposed the country to foreign influences. With its rise, the multi-state system created by the Rajputs gave way to a centralized political organization under a bureaucracy, the members of which were transferred from one territory to the other. The new political system enabled the Indian subcontinent to acquire political individuality in course of time. The caste cities were changed into cosmopolitan urban centres as their gates were thrown open to all irrespective of birth or creed. For example, low-caste artisans appear to have built their huts even in the vicinity of the royal palace.[1] Besides the foundation of new cities and towns, the old towns also underwent demographic change on account of the addition of Muslim colonies. These colonies had Muslim emigrants who were highly urbanized and came from different Muslim lands representing diverse cultural traditions. Many important scientific instruments and ideas found their way into India with them. They had an urban ethos, and their mingling with the local people enriched the urban culture on one hand, and paved the way for the establishment of a symbiotic relationship between the followers of anthropocentric and cosmocentric traditions. This relationship was further strengthened by the interaction between Muslim Sufis and Hindu ascetics, or *yogis*.

The progress of foreign trade that resulted from the internationalist attitude of the sultans led to the introduction of new crafts and the modification of indigenous ones. In this chapter, an attempt has been made to draw attention to the factors that helped the process of urbanization, and brought about important change in the social and economic life in the country under the sultans of Delhi.

I begin with a description of the institutions of public utility that helped the development of old towns selected to serve as provincial headquarters, into centres of culture and trade. The first such institution was the *khanqah* (lodge) which at least till the eleventh century, was called *ribat* in the Arab countries and also the Persian-speaking lands. Later, the term *ribat* seems to have been replaced by the term *khanqah* in Khurasan and Central Asia. Some time in the twelfth century AD, Sadid uddin Muhammad 'Awfi tells us about a Ghaznavid noble, posted in Lahore during the later Ghaznavid period, who had a *khanqah* built for travellers.[2] The reference to the *khanqah* in another work compiled by the same writer, casts interesting light on its nature and working. Nizam ul-Mulk Tusi (the celebrated *wazir* of the Saljuqs) had a *khanqah* built in the city of Safahan and posted Amir Saiyid Muhammad, famous for his piety and noble family background to run it. Every year deserving and needy people, Sufis, *ulama* (scholars) and Saiyids came to the *khanqah* from different directions and stayed there. In the month of *Rajab,* Nizam ul-Mulk called Amir Saiyid Muhammad and enquired about the demands of the people (gathered in the *khanqah*) which he met. Some were given stipends, while others got cash, grants (lands) or whatever they deserved, all of them returning home satisfied to observe *ramazan* (the month of fasting).[3] Likewise, Minhaj-i-Siraj Juzjani mentions that *khanqah's* were built with the money of philanthropists outside India, for providing lodging to travellers. In his account of the Shanshabani Prince Ziya' uddin Muhammad, he states that the Prince had a *khanqah* built in Mecca where he had gone to perform pilgrimage. The Prince is also credited with having established a trust for the upkeep of the *khanqah* and entrusted its charge to trustworthy persons.[4] The lieutenants of Sultan Muiz u'ddin Muhammad bin Sam in India also had *khanqahs* constructed in the territories where they were posted as *sipahsalars*[5] (governors) after their conquest.[6] This tradition was continued by the independent Sultans of India after the assassination of Sultan Muiz u'ddin Muhammad bin Sam in 1206.

Before we discuss the interest evinced by the rulers in the construction and maintenance of *khanqahs,* the historiographic error committed by the modern scholars regarding its nature should be corrected. As a matter of fact, the reference to the Multan *khanqah* found contained in the *Fawaid ul-Fuad* led modern scholars to regard it as the property of Shaikh Bahauddin Zakariya Suhrawardi. It was a fortress-like building with a lofty gate.[7] It was actually an official *khanqah,* the charge of which was held by the Shaikh since the reign of Sultan Qutbuddin Aibak.[8] Shaikh Bahauddin Zakariya was responsible for its proper management. The revenue from a number of villages was endowed for its maintenance. All this tends to suggest that the *khanqah,* constructed and maintained by the State was not a Sufi hospice but an institution of public utility, to provide accommodation to travellers, free food and also distribute money and stipends to the deserving persons.

The relevant evidence available in the *malfuzat* (collection of utterances) of the Suhrawardi Sufi, Shaikh Jalal u'ddin Bukhari, known as Jahanian-i-Jahangasht makes it crystal clear that there was no difference between the *ribat* in the Arab countries and the *khanqah* in India. The term *ribat* was still used in the Arab countries for the lodge erected for providing comfort to the travellers. Pointing out the difference between the *ribat* of the Arab lands and the *khanqah* in India, Shaikh Jalal u'ddin Bukhari said that *ribats* were generally built by traders and other philanthropists out of their lawful money, and were endowed with permanent sources of income. Unlike them, the *khanqahs* in India were built and maintained by the state with money collected in the form of taxes not permitted by the *shari'a* (cannon law).[9] At another place the Shaikh repeats that in the region around Mecca, Madina and Gazrun merchants had *ribats* built with money earned through lawful trade. Houses and shops were also built and the income from their rent was endowed for their upkeep and honest men were entrusted with their charge. The King of Yemen was inspired by the example of the Sultans of India and also had a *ribat* constructed for the comfort of way farers. However religious minded people preferred not to stay there for the money spent here came from the royal treasury and was not always collected in accordance with the law of *shari'a.*[10]

The tradition set by Sultan Qutb uddin Aibak was zealously followed by his successors. In Bengal and Bihar, Malik Ikhtiyar uddin Muhammad Bakhtiyar Khalji and Sultan Ghiyasuddin 'Iwaz Khalji had a number of *khanqahs,* mosques and madrasas constructed.[11] The manager of the *khanaqah* was designated *Shaikh ul-Islam* and all state charity in kind and cash was distributed by him among the travellers and other deserving persons on behalf of the Sultan. Income was endowed by the Sultan for the *khanqah's* maintenance, from a number of villages.[12] Ibn Battuta further supplements this information when he mentions that the *khanqahs* were constructed in different provinces on the orders of Sultan Muhammad bin Tughluq Shah, and that the charge of each *khanqah,* and the endowment for its upkeep, was entrusted by the Sultan to a *Shaikh ul-Islam* selected from amongst persons known for their righteousness. Ibn Battutah himself met the *Shaikh ul-Islam* of the state-run *khanqah* in Amroha, the headquarters of the province of the same name. He found the *Shaikh ul-Islam* a man of probity and piety.[13] In the city of Dhar (the provincial capital of Malwa) a spacious *khanqah* was built on a hillock by the order of the Sultan and the entire revenue, accruing from the city of Dhar and the area around it was endowed for its maintenance. Its charge was entrusted to Shaikh Ibrahim Maldibi, a Sufi emigrant to India.[14] Likewise, in the town of Bihar (modern Bihar Sharif) the charge of the newly built *khanqah* was entrusted to Shaikh Sharaf uddin Yahya, the celebrated Sufi of the Firdausi Silsilah.[15] In the region of Sind and southern Punjab, Shaikh Jalal u'ddin Bukhari Jahanian-i-Jahangasht was appointed the *Shaikh ul-Islam* by Sultan Muhammad bin Tughluq Shah. He was entrusted with the charge of forty *khanqahs* scattered in different parts of the region.[16] The official anonymous compiler of the *Sirat-i-Firuz Shahi* credits Sultan Firuz Shah, the successor of Sultan Muhammad bin Tughluq Shah with having surpassed his predecessors in undertaking such projects, i.e. construction of *khanqahs,* madrasas and *darul-shifa* (hospitals) with endowments for public welfare.[17] Like the sultans, the nobles and royal ladies also spent money on the maintenance of the *khanqahs* for the sake of religious merit.[18]

A word may be added here about the reference to *serais,* contained in Zia' uddin Barani's *Tarikh-i-Firuz Shahi,*[19] because it has misled the modern scholars to confuse it with inns meant for the stay of wayfarers. As a result, the meaning and significance of the term has not been explained correctly. During the thirteenth and fourteenth centuries the term *serai* applied to a royal palace or the building owned by a wealthy person. The royal palaces built by Sultan Iltutmish outside Delhi are mentioned by Shaikh Nizam uddin Auliya as *serai Sultani.*[20] It is worth mentioning that long before the foundation of the Sultanate in India, a palatial building belonging to the ruler or any minister or a wealthy man was generally called after him as *sera'i Sultani,* or *sera'i wazir* or *Sera'i Amir-i-dad* outside India.[21] We also find the corroborative evidence in the *Malfuzat* of Shaikh Nasir uddin Chiragh-i-Delhi. Mentioning the visit by Muhammad Khatib to his *Pir,* Shaikh Nizam uddin Auliya, Shaikh Nasiruddin told his visitors, 'one day, he (Khatib) came and having made prostration sat down. The Shaikh enquired: 'Where had he been (for quite some time)?' He replied that he was busy in the (King's) *serai.* He further told the Shaikh: 'Today, the Sultan has rewarded the servants of God (*ulama)* with, more or less, fifty thousand *tankas*'.[22] At another place, the guest house in the compound of the palace of a noble is mentioned as *serai.*[23] Berani also refers to the royal palaces and those owned by the nobles as *serais* in his account of the Khalji Sultans.

Mention is made of the *serai* Jalali and *serai* of Sultan 'Ala ud'din Khalji.[24]

It may also be recalled that the meaning of *serai* seems to have changed since the sixteenth century and began to be used to refer to the lodge meant for the merchants and wayfarers. Sultan Sikandar Lodi is reported to have caravan *serai* constructed for the travellers outside Mathura.[25] This is the first reference to the construction of a caravan *serai* during the Delhi Sultanate period. Subsequently, the writers dropped the prefix caravan and simply referred to such establishments as *serais*. Sher Shah Sur (d. AD 1545) is praised by all the medieval writers for having a number of highways constructed with *serais*, each at a distance of four *kos* (eight miles). The number of such *serais* is said to have reached one thousand and seven hundred. The *serais* had separate quarters for Hindus and Muslims. While Brahmans looked after the Hindus, Muslim employees catered to the needs of the Muslims. Both communities were served with food and also supplied fodder for their animals and horses free of charge. Police posts (*thanas*) were established around the important *serais* that were surrounded by forests. These protected the highways from bandits. Royal villas were also constructed near certain *serais* for the stay of the king at strategic points. The *shiqdars* (military officers) were posted as officers in charge. These sites developed into townships in course of time as businessmen and daily wage earners were attracted to settle down there.[26]

Some words are in order about the origin of the *thana*, for it also helped the process of urbanization in medieval India. Barani's reference to the *thanas* in his *Tarikh-i-Firuz Shahi* occurs in his account of Sultan Ghiyas-uddin Balban's reign (AD 1266-87). It suggests that the Sultan founded the *thanas* in regions abounding in highwaymen and rebels for maintaining law and order. Both Isami and Barani glow with pride when they mention the foundation of the Deopalgir *thana* in the vicinity of Delhi for keeping away the Mewati bandits who had created terror in the surrounding areas. According to Barani, the jungle was cleared and a strong fortification raised in which a strong Afghan garrison was posted. Isami corroborates Barani's argument that the *hisar-i-Deopalgir* (fortification of Deopalgir) made the suppression of recalcitrance in the area easy.[27] Besides, a number of *thanas* were established with Afghan soldiers in different areas around Delhi. One such being Afghanpur where Sultan Ghiyasuddin Tughluq Shah met an accidental death in AD 1324.[28] *Thanas* were also established in other territorial areas where the law and order situation had become acute. Again, Barani referred to the *thanas* established by Sultan Balban at Jalali (district Aligarh), Kampil, Patiali, Shamsabad and Bhogaon, all in the Doab. Each one of them had an Afghan garrison. The *thanas* were studded with mosques and madrasas that had great civilizing impact on the locality.[29] It may be stressed that by the turn of the century each *thana* had developed into an important township, acquiring the status of a *parganah* headquarters. They also provided market facilities to the peasants of the villages that were established around the towns. The *thana* of Kampil[30] acquired so much importance that a strong fortress was constructed there during the reign of Sultan 'Ala ud'din Khalji. Ibn Battuta called it the most impregnable fort in the Doab.[31] Another *thana* worth mentioning, also called Afghanpur, was established at some distance from Amroha, the headquarters of a newly carved out provincial unit in the region of Katehar.[32] Today, this town known as Aghvanpur, flourishes in the district of Moradabad.

These *thanas* also continued to be constructed in the remote areas and along the highways during the subsequent period. With the conquest of the Deccan, a road was built to connect Deogiri with Delhi during the reign of Sultan 'Ala ud'din Khalji (AD 1296-1316).[33] An interesting fifteenth-century *qasidah* (panegyric) composed by 'Aziz-Allah Bistami in praise of Sultan Mubarak Shah Sharqi (d. AD 1501) refers to the *thanadari* of Mohan (in Lucknow district), requesting the royal patron to entrust its charge to his son, 'Abd al-Quddus who was unemployed.[34] Mention should be made of the *thanas* constructed by Sultan Sikandar Shah Lodi in the Chambal valley to keep a check on dacoits. One of his *thanas* was built near the village of Hatkant which developed into an important town by the time of Sher Shah Sur.[35] Sher Shah is reported to have evacuated twelve thousand Tarin Afghans from the *sarkar* of Sirhind and settled them in Hatkant town. With the establishment of the Afghans, the *zamindars* and other contumacious people of the entire region became law-abiding.[36] In fact, the *thanas* and *khanqahs* helped the process of urbanization, the bazaars therein encouraged the peasants of nearby villages to raise cash crops and prosper in consequence. Having come into contact with urban life and members of the ruling elite, the big farmers whom the Sultan had appointed as *khuts* (village headmen) to serve as intermediaries between the state and the peasantry began to emulate the officers' lifestyle.[37] Thus, they wore clothes of fine fabric, rode horses of good breed and employed Muslims from the cities and towns known for their expertise in training horses to act as their horse-keepers.

The institution of slavery also appears to have contributed to the progress of material culture and introduction of fine arts. Slaves brought from foreign countries were trained in different arts and crafts, in fact, the education and training of the slave was seen as a good investment as those with education or skills fetched a higher price. For instance, the *naqshgaran-i-chin* (Chinese painters), mentioned by Isami, were probably the Chinese slaves bought by Sultan Iltutmish to beautify his palaces.[38] These foreign slaves were purchased by the Sultan and the nobles to serve in the army and other departments and were trusted for their loyalty to the master. They came from Turkestan, China, East European countries and Africa.[39] Slave girls even from the Balkan countries were available in Delhi. The slant in the eyes of the Turkish and Chinese girls held great attraction for certain nobles and poets. Besides the thirteenth century immigrant poet, Siraji Khurasani, Amir Khusrau also writes of the, 'beautiful Turkish girls between the ages of 17 and 18 were presented who were so beautiful that they could provide the old sun with a new covering of light by the shade of their faces'.[40] Moreover, the slaves also contributed to the growth of the Muslim population, as they were generally purchased in their childhood and brought up as Muslim.[41]

Following its emergence as an integrative nucleus, in place of Lahore, Delhi promoted an urban ethos in the Sultanate. Minhaj Juzjani describes the sack of Lahore by the Mongols more than once. First, in his account of Sultan Muiz u'ddin Bahram Shah's reign (AD 1240-2), he describes the flight of the governor, Ikhtiyar uddin Qaraqash from Lahore to Delhi. Though Qaraqash was a brave warrior, the residents of Lahore were not cooperative in the defence of their city. Disappointed by them, he decided to leave them to their fate and left one night for Delhi with his followers. The Mongols pursued him unsuccessfully. They however entered the city of Lahore on 22 December, 1241, where they killed Muslims and took away their women and children as captives.[42] The second time Juzjani, has a brief reference to the event[43] and then in the last *tabaqa* related to the rise of the Mongols under Chinggis Khan, we are provided with a detailed account of the event. In 1241, Tair Bahadur of Herat was ordered by the Emperor Ogedi (Persian Chronicler's Ugta'i Khan) to march along with the armies of Ghazna, Garm Sir, etc., across India. At that time Multan was held by Kabir Khan Ayaz and Ikhtiyar uddin Qaraqash who served in Lahore as its governor. First, the Mongols proceeded towards Multan where Kabir Khan well-prepared to face them, raised a strong army for the defence of Multan. He had a royal umbrella unfolded declaring his independence as a ruler. Finding the fortified city of Multan impregnable, the Mongols raised the siege and turned towards Lahore. The fort of Lahore did not have a sufficient stock of food grains and war material, neither were the citizens of Lahore united enough to make a stand against the invaders. Many of them were merchants and businessmen, who travelled in caravans to Khurasan and Turkestan. They acquired permits and *paiza*[44] (plates with official seals) from the Mongol rulers to carry on such trade in the lands under their rule. They were thus unwilling to render any help for the defence of the city. In Delhi, the nobles were angry with the Sultan and did not move to the rescue of Lahore. However, fighting continued for quite some time outside the gates of Lahore. The Mongols installed *manjanigs* (catapults) around Lahore and caused cracks in the walls of the city at several places. Malik Qaraqash continued to resist as long as he could. Disappointed by the indifferent attitude and non-cooperation of the citizens, he came out one night with his loyal followers and dependants, made a surprise attack on the enemy and having thrown its ranks and file into chaos, took the road to Delhi. The Mongols pursued him but failed to catch up. The following day the Mongols however entered the city of Lahore. They met with stiff resistance from the citizens who were divided into two groups under the leadership of Aqsanqur, the Kotwal of the city and Dindar Muhammad, *Amir-i-akhur* (officer-in-charge of the war-horses). A large number of Mongols including their commanders were killed. However, overcoming resistance, the Mongols killed men and took away women and children as captives.[45] Though Sultan Balban (reigned: 1266-87) had the fort of Lahore repaired and placed a garrison, it could not recover its past glory till the Lodi period.

Lastly, our study also calls for a reference to the emergence of Delhi in northern India and Daulatabad in the south as integrative nuclei in radiating urban culture and an ethos, shared with different cities upto Sonargaon in Eastern Bengal and Karnataka and Tamil Nadu in south India. The social phenomena and the political structure at the Centre performed a significant role in shaping the destinies of peoples as well as individuals. In fact, the area around Delhi became the confluence of different cultures as it received settlers from different countries with different cultural traditions. The nobility, colleges (madrasas), sufi *Jama'at khavas* (hospices), the *darul-shifa* (hospitals), bazaars and above all the royal court acted as agents of social change. The towns around Delhi, Panipat, Hansi, Thanesar, Sunam in Haryana and Baran, Kol (Aligarh), Qanauj, Meerut, Badaon and Amroha in western UP, influenced and provided variety and richness to life. The inhabitants of these towns also benefitted from their proximity to Delhi because they adopted its cultural pattern which caused the fusion of different traditions helping the development of India's composite culture.

The following chapters cast light on different dimensions of the cities. Here the important change that took place in the architecture of the country may be mentioned briefly. The skyline of each important city and town was transformed through the introduction of arcuate system, in addition to the indigenous trabeate system. The arch and dome were distinguishing features of mosque architecture in the Muslim countries. Attempts were made to construct them in India. However, the ignorance of the Indian architects and masons of the technical knowledge of the arcuate system led them to create corbelled domes. Constructed in the beginning of the thirteenth century, these were shallow and not durable, compared to the domes constructed through the arcuate system which were lofty, spacious and durable. The services of the architects and masons having technical knowledge and experience of the arcuate system seem to have been available in the Sultanate of Delhi since the last decade of the reign of Sultan Nasir uddin Mahmud (AD 1246-66). Barani's reference to the lofty and spacious and famous *gumbad* (dome) built by the order of Sher Khan Sunqar in Bhatner leaves no doubt about it being a true dome. Barani states that the famous dome in Bhatner and the fortification walls of Bhatner and Bhatinda were constructed under his patronage. Writing in 1357, Barani mentions the dome at Bhatner as a wonderful memorial after the legendary warrior.[46]

It may be recalled that the trade relations between the Sultanate of Delhi and the foreign countries ensured the supply of slaves trained in different crafts and professions including that of masonry. These architects and masons made it possible to construct beautiful mosques, tombs, palaces, water works and the laying out of pleasure gardens. The use of lime mortar was also begun on a large scale. Our sources in fact contain information about the arrival of architects from Iran and Central Asia who supervised the construction of palaces, water works and pleasure gardens. The addition of different features in the monuments erected during different periods of history cast light on foreign influence on the one hand and the fusion of the indigenous trabeate and arcuate systems on the other.[47] Every succeeding Sultan desired to have beautiful buildings constructed surpassing those of his predecessors,[48] a tradition that was emulated and maintained by the regional as well as the Lodi Sultans of Delhi. [49] With the annexation of South Indian regions to the Sultanate of Delhi in the beginning of the fourteenth century, the arcuate system got introduced there also, the towns and cities were studded with beautiful mosques and tombs built inside the gardens. Apart from (metropolitan) cities, less important places like Sagar (in Gulbarga district of Karnataka) hold attraction for the tourist for the Jama mosque, water works tombs and lofty gates of its fort.[50] Not only did the masons and other daily wage-earners profit from this construction work but India's cultural heritage was equally enriched.

Endnotes

1. Mention made by Isami of the huts, owned by the tanners in Lahore in the vicinity of the royal palace, tends to show that in a Muslim town the artisans resided side by side with others and did not suffer from social segregation. Isami, *Futuh us-Salatin,* ed. A.S. Usha, Madras: Madras University Islamic Series No. 9, 1948, pp. 105-6, hereafter cited as Isami.
2. E.G. Browne and Muhammad Qazwini, eds., *Lubab ul-Albab,* London, 1903, part 1, p. 71.
3. Iqtidar Husain Siddiqui, *Perso-Arabic Sources of Information on the Life and Conditions in the Sultanate of Delhi,* New Delhi: Munshiram Manoharlal, 1992, p. 19. See for the English translation.
4. *Minhaj-i-Siraj al-Juzjani Tabaqat-i-Nasiri,* vol. 1, ed. Abdul Ha'i Habibi, Kabul, 1963, p. 341.
5. The term for the governor contained in the contemporary sources of information is *sipahsalar* and not *wali* or *Muqta during the first half of the thirteenth century.* Cf. Iqtidar Husain Siddiqui, *Authority and Kingship Under the Sultans of Delhi,* New Delhi: Manohar Publishers, 2006, pp. 39-40.
6. *Tarikh-i-Fakhr-i-Mudabbir,* London, 1927, pp. 16-18.
7. Mir Hasan Sijzi, *Fawaid ul-Fuad,* Lahore: Malik Siraj Uddin & Sons, 1966, p. 81.
8. Muhammad Bihamad Khani, *Tarikh-i-Muhammadi,* MS., British Library, London, Or 137, f.138b.
9. Ali bin Asad, *Jami 'ul-Ulum,* (*Malfuzat* of Shaikh Jalal u'ddin Jahanian-i-Jahangasht), ed. Qazi Sajjad Husani, New Delhi: ICHR, 1987, pp. 257, 274.
10. Ibid., p. 455.
11. *Tabaqat-i-Nasiri,* vol. 1, op.cit., pp. 427, 436-7.
12. *The Travels of Ibn Battuta,* tr. Sir Hamilton Gibb, Cambridge, 1971, vol. 3, p. 736.
13. Ibid., vol. 3, p. 762.
14. Since Gibb's third volume of his translation comes to an end with Ibn Battuta's departure from Delhi for China and the fourth volume is not available, I have used the Urdu translation by Maulvi

Muhammad Husain. Cf. Ibn Battuta, *Ajaib-ul-Asfar,* vol. 2, rpt, Islamabad, 1983, p. 273.

15. Shu'aib Firdausi, *Manaqib ul-Asfia,* Calcutta: Nurul Afaq Press, 1895, pp. 134-5.
16. Ali bin Asad, *Jami 'ul-ulum,* op.cit., p. 257.
17. Anonymous, *Sirat-i-Firuz Shahi,* facsimile of the manuscript, Patna: Khuda Bakhsh Oriental Public Library, 1999, pp. 142-3, 208-9 & 235.
18. *The Travels of Ibn Battuta,* tr. vol. 3, op.cit., p. 726; See also *Sirat-i-Firuz Shahi,* op.cit., p. 163.
19. Barani, *Tarikh-i-Firuz Shahi,* Calcutta, 1862, p. 56; I have to correct my statement also in which I had identified them with private establishments in my lecture delivered in Symposia: 12, 'Money and Social Change during Medieval Times', 56th Session of the Indian History Congress, Rabindra Bharti University, Calcutta, 29 December 1995, p. 8.
20. *Fawaid ul-Fuad,* op.cit., pp. 74 & 237.
21. Ahmad bin Umar Ibn Ali an-Nizami al-Aruzi as-Samarqandi, *Chahar Muqala,* ed. Muhammad Qazwini Tehran, 1348 Shamsi, pp. 57, 62-3 & 79.
22. Hamid Qalandar, *Khair ul-Majalis,* ed. K.A. Nizami, Aligarh: Department of History, 1959, p. 69.
23. Ibid., pp. 87-8.
24. Barani, *Tarikh-i-Firuz Shahi,* pp. 203, 248.
25. Shaikh Rizq ullah Mushtaqi, *Waqi 'at-i-Mushtaqi,* tr. Iqtidar Husain Siddiqui, New Delhi: ICHR, 1993, p. 17.
26. Ibid., pp. 135-7; See also Abbas Sarwani, *Tarikh-i-Sher Shahi,* ed., Imam al-Din, Dhaka: University of Dhaka, 1964, pp. 216-17.
27. Barani, *Tarikh-i-Firuz Shahi,* p. 452; See also *Futuh us-Salatin,* p. 164.
28. Barani, *Tarikh-i-Firuz Shahi,* pp. 452-3.
29. Ibid., pp. 57-9.
30. Kampil is situated 28 miles north of Fathgarh in UP.
31. *The Travels of Ibn Battuta,* vol. 3, op.cit., p. 722.
32. Ibid., vol. 3, p. 762.

33. Barani, *Tarikh-Firuz Shahi*, pp. 330-1.
34. Saif Jam Harawi, *Majmuah-i-Lataif-e-Safinah-i-Zarraif*, MS. London: British Library, Rieu supplement No. 374, ff. 218b; also Nazir Ahmad, *Fikro Nazar*, Under Quarterly Aligarh, vol. 12 no. 3, 1972, pp. 33-51, for qasidas and the available manuscripts.
35. Ni'matullah Harevi, *Tarikh-i-Khan-i-Jahan*, ed., Imam al-Din, Dhaka, 1960, vol. 1, p. 207.
36. *Tarikh-i-Sher Shahi*, op.cit., pp. 216-17.
37. Barani, *Tarikh-i-Firuz Shahi*, pp. 287-88.
38. Isami, *Futuh us-Salatin*, op.cit., pp. 114-15.
39. Ibn Battuta, *Ajaib ul-Asfar*, op.cit., vol. 2, 1983, p. 260.
40. See Siraji Khurasani's verses in my *Perso-Arabic Sources of Information*, op.cit., pp. 118-119; See also Amir Khusrau, *Ijaz-i-Khusravi*, vol. 4, tr. Iqtidar Husain Siddiqui, Islamic Thought and Science Institute, Illionois, U.S.A., p. 160.
41. *Tabaqat-i-Nasiri*, vol. 2, ed. Abdul Ha'i Habibi, Kabul, Historical Society of Afghanistan, 1964. See the *tabaqa* 22, related to Iltutmish's slave generals.
42. *Tabaqat-i-Nasiri*, vol. 1, op.cit., pp. 465-6.
43. Ibid., vol. 2, p. 20.
44. The *Paiza* was like Chinese P'aitzu, a kind of *Laisse Passer*. Cf. *The Successors of Genghis Khan* [Extracted from *Jami ul-Tawarika*], translated from the Persian... by John Andrew Boyle, Columbia: Columbia University Press, 1971, p. 183.
45. *Tabaqat-i-Nasiri*, vol. 2, op.cit., pp. 163-5.
46. Barani, *Tarikh-i-Firuz Shahi*, p. 65.
47. Cf. Iqtidar Husain Siddiqui, *Authority and Kingship Under the Sultans of Delhi*, New Delhi: Manohar Publishers, 2006, pp. 132, 134 and 143.
48. Ibid, pp. 259-77.
49. Cf. G. Yazdani, *Mandu: The City of Joy*, Oxford: Oxford University Press London, 1929, pp. 51-2; Percy Brown, *Indian Architecture: Islamic Period* 3rd. edition, pp. 27-30.
50. S. K. Aruni, Sagar: Provincial Headquarters of the Islamic Deecan, *Bulletin of the Deecan College*, vols. 56-57, 1996-1997, Pune, pp. 220-229.

CHAPTER 3

Economy and Trade

The bazaar in an urban centre served as an institution of great economic and social importance, as it often attracted merchants from foreign countries carrying merchandise in caravans, who engaged in overseas or overland foreign trade. Once peace was established in the vast region, from Daibul (Sind) and the frontier of Makran in the west up to Lakhnauti (Bengal) in the east, and highways connecting the provincial headquarters and seaports with Delhi, the capital of the Sultanate, the merchants came there from each direction. The import and export of commercial goods depended on their arrival. The choice goods brought by them for sale provided creative initiative to the artisans and craftsmen of the country, and foreign trade led to the introduction of new crafts and the modification of indigenous ones. In the Sultanate of Delhi the bazaars expanded in the cities, and demand and competition brought opportunities, profits and innovation, the latter being more important.

Moreover, the emigrant merchants who came to India as refugees after their homelands of Central Asia and Iran had been conquered and sacked by the Mongols, also played an important role in the progress of trade and commerce. They established *karkhanas* (manufactories) which went a long way to improve the well being of the impoverished Indian artisans. In this chapter an attempt is made to draw attention to the important role played by the bazaar of the Sultanate period in the development of trade and commerce, the economic life of people and promotion of an urban ethos.

Sadid u'ddin Muhammad 'Awfi's description of the Muslim merchants, shows how their activities led in different countries, to the modification of indigenous crafts and introduction of new ones. The bazaars in the metropolitan cities attracted foreign merchants moving in caravans loaded with choice merchandise from different countries. They also brought both male and female slaves, trained in different arts and crafts, from countries as far as the Byzantine empire in the West and China in the east.[1] Thus the merchants and the slaves, brought by them for sale helped the promotion of material culture in the country[2] through the introduction of new profession and crafts. The craft of weaving *hasir* (prayer carpet) was popular in Central Asia and introduced in India. Different dyes were used in its making.[3] Another important craft introduced by the foreign merchants in which slaves and other craftsmen were engaged was that of darning. Any costly damaged fabric was repaired by a darner, with an expert darner charging upto two silver coins for repairing an expensive fur cap.[4]

The emergence of Delhi as the largest city of the entire Islamic world, attracted foreign merchants from both Muslim and non-Muslim countries. Being the capital of the Sultanate since Iltutmish's accession to the throne in AD 1210, it developed rapidly into an emporium of trade and commerce with bazaars thronged with people and beautiful palaces and pleasure gardens. Barring the intervening period between the death of Sultan Iltutmish (AD 1236) and the accession of Sultan Ghiyasuddin Balban to its throne (AD 1266), every powerful Sultan had beautiful palaces erected and pleasure gardens laid out. It may also be added that after Sultan Balban, every succeeding Sultan had a new capital constructed for himself near or at some distance from his predecessor's capital. Over time Delhi thus came to signify a collection of several cities.[5]

As for the important buildings of Delhi constructed under the patronage of Sultan Iltutmish, 'Awfi mentions the beautiful Jama-mosque (congregational mosque) and its lofty minar (Qutb Minar).[6] Incidentally, Minhaj-i-Siraj also refers to the palaces of the same reign. Mention is made of places such as the *Qasr-i-Safed* (white palace), the *Qasr-i-Firuzi* (Green palace), the *Qasr-i-bagh-i-Delhi* (Delhi Garden's palace), *Qasr-i-Loni (palace at Loni), bagh-i-Jun* (garden on the bank of Jamuna), etc.[7]

As for the construction of bazaars in Delhi, Minhaj-i-Siraj's reference to the *bazaar-i-bazazan* (the market exclusively meant for the dealers in cloth) tends to suggest that there were separate bazaars built in large cities. The *bazaar-i-bazazan*[8] was built adjacent to the new fortress, perhaps during the reign of Sultan Raziya.[9]

Similarly, more than one bazaar appears to have been built in the provincial headquarters, both newly-founded and old ones that were expanded owing to the addition of new colonies of immigrants. Mention made by Barani of the bazaar of Lakhnauti is indicative of this fact. Barani refers to it as *bazaar-i-buzurg Lakhnauti,* saying that it was in length more than one *kruh* (more than two miles).[10] Later, new settlements were added with new mosques and bazaars and then the name was changed from Lakhnauti to Gaur. It was then 24 miles long.[11]

Besides Delhi and Lakhnauti, other towns and cities also developed with marts of international fame. Uchh, Multan and Lahore had big bazaars that were found thronged with merchants, Indian as well as foreign. Of them Uchh emerged as a centre of culture after Sultan Nâsir u'ddin Qubācha had made it his capital in AD 1210. It came to he known as *Hazrat-i-Uchh.*[12] In fact, the foundation by the Sultan of a new capital city or selection of any old town for this purpose attracted traders and money lenders, besides artisans and craftsmen from different places. The court-generated trade and the presence of nobles fond of luxurious life provided them with an opportunity to do good business.[13] Uchh made rapid progress under Sultan Qubācha and remained an important city during the following century also. Ibn Battuta found it a large city with fine bazaars and grand buildings. Like Uchh, Multan also had a strong fortification that successfully withstood repeated Mongol attacks. Situated on the frontier of the Sultanate, Multan had become an entrepôt where the merchants came from foreign lands loaded with merchandise and paid custom duty. Ibn Battuta states, 'the goods of all who pass are subjected to a rigorous examination and their baggage searched. Their practice at the time of our arrival (AD 1333) was to take a quarter of everything brought by the merchants, and to exact a duty of seven dinars (*tankas)* for every horse. Two years after our arrival in India the Sultan abolished these duties and ordered that nothing should be taken from people except the *zakah* and the tenth'.[14] We are also provided with interesting information by Ibn Battuta about the conduct of foreign and Indian merchants in profit making, 'As the merchants, Indian and foreign, knew that the Sultan of Delhi would reward the visitor from a foreign country with a huge gift of cash in return for his offering (several times of the offering's value), they sold their gifts to him on credit even in foreign lands on his way to India. The merchants furnished each visitor thousands of *tankas* on loan, the latter would pay off his debts and dues to them in full after he visited the Sultan and got into his favours, so they (merchants) ran a flourishing trade and made vast profits, and it became an established usage amongst them'.[15]

However, the bazaars in the metropolitan city attracted merchants and hummed with commercial activity. The rich people of the city, in particular the grandees and officers bought costly items, silk, weapons, slaves, war-horses, etc.[16]

Furthermore, the expansion of trade relations between the Delhi Sultanate and the foreign countries increased monetization on one hand and helped the growth of old towns and establishment of new ones. The rise of new towns with flourishing marts was not possible otherwise, only the availability of opportunities for the daily workers to earn their livelihood attracted them from the countryside towards the towns. In the desert of Sind many towns owed their growth and prosperity to trade and commerce. For instance, Janani, situated on the bank of the Indus, somewhat to the north of Sehwan, had vibrant bazaars. Sehwan too, though situated in the desert, had bazaars and colleges. The traders who came from abroad both by sea and land routes passed through Sehwan on their way to other parts of India.[17]

Some words are in order about the sea ports of the Sultanate, particularly Lahri Bandar in Sind and Cambay in Gujarat. There is interesting information about them in contemporary sources. With the desertion of Daibul due to silting, sometime during the first half of the thirteenth century, Lahri Bandar (the ruins of which are found on the northern side of the Rao Channel, some 28 miles south-east of Karachi) emerged as a port of call. Ibn Battuta states, 'this is the city of Lahri, a fine town on the sea coast where the river Indus discharges itself into the ocean, and the two seas meet. It possesses a large harbour, visited by men (merchants) from al-Yaman, Fars and elsewhere. For this season its contribution to the treasury and its revenue are considerable; the governor 'Ala' al-Mulk told me that the tax yields from this town amounted to sixty lakhs per annum'.[18]

As regards Cambay, it underwent a complete transformation after its annexation to the Sultanate in 1305-6. Prior to its conquest by the Delhi army, this port city of the kingdom of Gujarat was largely inhabitated by artisans and workers, with small pockets of Muslim traders, Zoroastrians and members of the Hindu business community and aristocracy. Sadid u'ddin Muhammad 'Awfi, the Bukhara-born immigrant who landed in Cambay after 1220 – furnishes useful information about the life and conditions there under the rule of the Rai (Raja) of Gujarat. He was astonished to see that the Rai not only granted religious freedom to Muslims and Zoroastrians but also went out of his way to protect them. However, he called Cambay a city of extremely poor and miserable Indians.[19] Unlike the generality of the city's inhabitants, the Hindu traders of Gujarat were so rich that they are reported by the same writer to have invested their capital in Ghazna. One of them, Salbhir, had invested one hundred million *balutras*[20] (a silver coin) in Ghazna.[21] Incidentally, Shaikh Nizam uddin Auliya corroborates this when he praises the Hindu traders of Gujarat before its annexation to the Sultanate for their fair dealing, in contrast to those of Muslim merchants from Lahore during the first half of the thirteenth century.[22] It is noteworthy that the final conquest of Gujarat and its annexation to the Sultanate of Delhi under Sultan 'Ala ud'din Khalji (reigned: 1296-1316)[23] led to the emergence of Cambay as an emporium of international trade and commerce. Many foreign merchants engaged in overseas trade settled in Cambay and carried on trade inside India as well as with foreign countries which gave fillip to the overseas trade of the Delhi Sultanate. It also brought prosperity to the artisans and workers in Cambay, which, according to Ibn Battuta, was the finest city in the Sultanate. The merchants who are reported to have settled down in Cambay had their establishments in countries ranging from Central Asia to Egypt.[24] Their beautiful fortress-like mansions and the adjacent mosques constructed in the styles of different countries of the Middle East held a great fascination for the visitor. The merchants are also reported to have vied with one another in having their mansions and mosques constructed on a grand scale.[25]

It needs to be pointed out that the Sultan and the nobles, appointed as *walis* (governors) in the provinces (*khittas)* encouraged the foreign merchants to come and settle in India from the very beginning of their rule. In 1196, Malik Baha uddin Taghril, the slave general of Sultan Muiz u'ddin Muhammad bin Sam was entrusted with the governorship of the *khitta* (province) of Bayana. He built the new city of Sultankot (modern Bayana) for his residence and also made it the headquarters instead of the old fortified Tahangarh. He not only invited merchants and scholars from Khurasan and other lands, but also had houses constructed for them, along with essential goods free of cost.[26] The *parwana* (official document) issued by Malik Qutb uddin Aibak to his *naib* (deputy) Malik Hussam uddin Ughalbak in connection with his posting in Kol (modern Aligarh) just after its conquest in 1193-4 also casts light on the state policy towards the foreign merchants and on their importance. The governor was directed to be considerate to them and provide them with protection, 'Every effort should be made to ensure the safety of highways, roads and bridges. The merchants who serve as liaison between the countries and come with the best (products) of each country should be protected and encouraged'.[27] It may be added that the evidence about the merchants being a liaison and source of information between different countries is supplemented by Minhaj-i-Siraj. Much of the last *tabaqa* of Minhaj-i-Siraj's' *Tabaqat-i-Nasiri* is based on what he heard from the merchants. The verbal portraits drawn by him show how inquisitive our historian was about Chinggis Khan and his Mongol generals. Mention is made by him of Khwaja Ahmad Vakhshi and Saiyid

Ashraf uddin, the leading merchants whom people held in esteem in different countries. Saiyid Ashraf uddin was patronized by both Sultan Iltutmish in India and Barke Khan, the Mongol ruler of Eastern Europe, Qipchaq and Khwarazm.[28]

Aware of the importance of the economic and cultural role performed by the merchants, Amir Khusrau is full of praise for them. He is quite different from Barani in this regard. Barani called the merchants 'bazaar people' not worthy of the company of aristocrats.[29] On the other hand the specimen farman drafted by Amir Khusrau during the reign of Sultan 'Ala ud'din Khalji is important in that we are told about India's trade relations with foreign countries as far as Africa and how merchants were advanced money by the state to supply choice merchandise to the Sultan. The port of Cambay along with others is also mentioned.[30]

Sultan Muhammad bin Tughluq Shah appears to have adopted a more friendly policy towards the merchants, in order to promote trade with foreign countries. He entrusted the administration of Cambay to a leading merchant. If any foreign merchant came to Delhi, he was honoured at the royal court and treated as a state guest during his stay in the capital.[31] The first merchant to be entrusted with the government of Cambay was Malik ul-Tujjar from Gazrun (Iran),[32] who was murdered by robbers in Gujarat. Malik ul-Tujjar Taj uddin al-Kawalami, who succeeded him as governor of Cambay, carried on trade with different countries of Africa and Asia, and built a beautiful college in Egypt. He came to Delhi from 'the lands of the Turks with magnificent gifts, including slaves, camels, merchandise, weapons and woven stuffs. The Sultan was highly delighted with his action and gave him twelve laks, though it is said that the value of his gift was not more than one lak, and appointed him to the government of the city of Kanbaya (Cambay)... from Cambay al-Kawalami sent vessels to the towns of Mulaibar (Malabar), the island of Sailan (Sri Lanka) and elsewhere, and valuable articles and gifts came to him in these vessels and he became enormously wealthy'.[33] Likewise, Shihab uddin Gazruni, a merchant from Iran, was given several times the value of the gift that he had brought from his country.[34]

Some of the foreign merchants established endowments at Cambay. For instance, Khwaja Ishaque established a *khanqah* (hostel-cum-charity house) where travellers were served free food and the poor and destitute given money daily. His wealth increased, in spite of the expenditure incurred on the maintenance of the *khanqah*.[35] In short, Cambay became a port city of great prosperity for merchants and of modest well-being for all.

A word may be added about the court generated trade because it gave great boost to trade and commerce and, owing to it, the merchants were attracted to the capital from different parts of India and abroad. Many villages situated along side the route that the merchants passed through in caravans, developed into towns and cities. The merchants from Iran, Khurasan and Transoxiana came by land. It was really because of them that the entire region from Multan was continuously inhabitated.[36] The villagers benefitted by selling fodder and drinking water in pots to the merchants moving in caravans.[37] Towns like Hansi and Sirsuti (modern Sirsa) gradually expanded into cities, with Sirsuti supplying sweet smelling rice of excellent quality to the metropolitan city of Delhi.[38] Under Sultan Ghiyas uddin Balban, the extravagant tastes and habits of nobles indebted them to Hindu money lenders who charged exorbitant interest per month, and acquired great wealth. The nobles repaid these loans with drafts on their *iqtas*.[39] 'Amid Loeki Sunami, the thirteenth century Persian poet tells us that the money lender got twelve for every ten (*tankas*) per month.[40] Thus the rate of interest-charged per month amounted to one hundred and twenty per cent per annum. According to Shams Siraj Afif, the moneylenders of Sirsuti had become so rich that they could also advance loans to the state. The *sarrafs* (bankers), of Sirsuti are said to have offered several laks of *tankas* as a loan to be paid back, to Sultan Firuz Shah (1351-88) when he returned to Delhi after his accession to the throne in Sind.[41] It may also be recalled that the money lenders also benefitted much from the progress of the indigenous banking system in the Sultanate. The legalization by the *ulama* or doctors of Islamic canon law of the use of *hundi* (the bill of exchange) was also to the benefit of the moneylenders. The traders and others could easily transfer money from one place to another through the *hundi* of a *sarraf* (banker) by paying him fee.[42] Likewise, Hansi (in Haryana) which lay along the caravan route running between Multan and Delhi (the supreme centre of consumption), benefitted from the transit trade. It was a large, fortified provincial headquarters, famous for fine buildings, colleges and *dargahs* (shrines) of the leading Chishti Sufis, besides flourishing bazaars.[43] Similarly, towns and villages developed into cities along the highway running between Delhi and Deogiri in the Deccan. For instance, Chanderi, the headquarters of a territorial unit emerged as an important city with bazaars thronged with merchants and others. Ibn Battuta was impressed by its bazaars. According to a later source, besides a strong fort, it had, 14,000 stone mansions, several bazaars, caravan *serais* and hundreds of mosques.[44]

It is also worth noting that outlying provinces too formed the hinterland of the capital city of Delhi and benefited from supplying their choice and quality products to its bazaars. Like Sirsuti, the territorial unit of Kara and Manikpur supplied its farm products to Delhi. Ibn Battuta calls Kara the most fertile unit in the Sultante which produced not only large quantities of wheat, rice and sugar but also manufactured and supplied fine fabrics to Delhi.[45] Besides, the rise of consumerism among the ruling elite in Delhi necessitated the import of luxury goods, including Chinese silk. The gifts distributed by the Sultan on special occasions among the nobles and others, such as the *ulama* and Sufis, comprised choicest merchandise imported through the merchants. The court-generated trade also induced some of the enterprizing foreign merchants to settle down in Delhi and carry on their trade through their agents and servants. They were advanced money by Sultan Muhammad bin Tughluq to supply choice goods from different countries. They had colossal mansions constructed outside the walls of Delhi. For instance, the mansion of the merchant Abu'l Hasan al-Ibadi of Iraq was built outside the city in the lane called Sarapur Khan. This merchant used to trade with the Sultan's money and brought weapons and goods for him from Iraq and Khurasan.[46]

The bazaars and the arrival of merchants with commercial commodities from different countries led to the diversification of the production of essentials in demand. The *karkhanas,* (workshops-cum-storehouses) maintained by the Sultan, high nobles and traders attracted craftsmen and artisans skilled in their arts and crafts. The relevant evidence contained in the *Masalik al-Absar fi – Mamalik al-Amsar* throws interesting light on the important role performed by the *karkhanas* and also the nature of sericulture that developed in the Sultanate during the fourteenth century. In the royal *karkhana* of Sultan Muhammad bin Tughluq Shah, four thousand silk workers wove and embroidered cloth for robes (of honour) and garments. Besides, there were other embroiders who made garments for the Sultan and the royal ladies.[47] The distribution of robes of honour and other gifts twice a year among the nobles and dignitaries made it necessary for the Sultan to maintain these *karkhanas.* Shihab uddin al-Umari was told by a traveller in Damascus, 'The Sultan honours those who are in his service whether people of sword, pen or learning, with costly gifts, wealth, jewels, saddles gilded with gold and silver, golden girdles and cloths of various kinds. The elephants are excluded from his list of gifts because its possession is a royal prerogative'.[48]

In short, the evidence contained in the contemporary sources and impressions of general character provided by the literary sources other than the chronicles tend to show that the role performed by the bazaar, foreign trade and merchants was important. It led to the progress of material culture and improved the well-being of the artisans and craftsmen as well. Barani, who held an elitist view of history writing and considered the role of the man of aristocratic background alone worthy of notice for a historian, was constrained to devote some space to the progress of arts and crafts. He wrote that the artists and craftsmen who flourished in Delhi during the reign of 'Ala ud'din Khalji surpassed their counterparts in other countries in their respective fields. In fact, so many skilled craftsmen and artisans were never found in Delhi in the past. They earned such a distinction in their professions that they became deserving of being mentioned in the history of their age.[49] Many items imported from abroad in the past began to be manufactured in India. In fact, the creative initiative possessed by the Indian craftsmen was such that the like of any imported thing could be easily produced, and hardly differentiated from the original.[50]

As regards the creation of new bazaars in Delhi, in addition to the old ones, in their account of Sultan 'Ala ud'din Khalji, Amir Khusrau and Barani describe the working of the most important bazaars in their description of the price control measures. Amir Khusrau mentions only the construction of the *Sara-i-Adl* bazaar for the sale of goods such as cloths and fruits. The Sultan is said to have ordered that the packages of cloths brought from the provinces and other places were to be opened and sold only there at the fixed price and nowhere else. 'As to the commodities of the '*Sera-i-Adl*' and the cloth which is required by rich and poor', says Khusrau, 'there are all varieties of cloth from *kirpas* to *harir* which hide the body; from *behari* to *Gul-i-baqli,* which are used both in summer and winter, from *Shi'r* to *galim*, which differ greatly in their fibres; from *juz* to *Khuz* (Chinese silk), which are similar in their structure; and from Deogiri to Mahadeonagri, which are an allurement both for the body and the mind'. Khusrau also briefly refers to the sale of fruits and other necessities of the table but does not describe them with their names.[51]

Compared to Khusrau, Barani furnishes a detailed account of two bazaars, the Mandi and the *Sara-i-Adl*. The Mandi was constructed for the sale of food grains. As for the *Sara-i-Adl*, he states that it was constructed inside the Badaon Gate in the direction of the *Kushak-i-Sabz* (Green palace) that remained abandoned for many years. In that place was established the *Sara-i-Adl* for the sale of silk, such as *juz, khuz, Mashru, zarbaft, Kamkhwab, Harir-i-Chini*, besides Deogiri and other varieties of cloth, cooking oils, sugar, etc. It remained open from the morning to late in the evening. Mention is also made of the *bazaar-i-am* but nothing is said about what was sold there.[52]

Perhaps, the *bazaar-i-am* was the *nakhas*, the market meant for the sale of slaves, horses and other animals. This was constructed outsides the walls of the city. The arrival of the foreign merchants in the *nakhas* was a fine spectacle. People rushed from the lanes of the city to enjoy the sight of the slave girls, Tartary and Arab horses and *diba-i-Chin* (China Silk).[53] Foreign horses were coveted by the nobility, and the Sultan distributed such horses with robes of honour to them on special occasions, such as on 'Id festival.[54] The demand for the war-horse during the Sultanate period led the Afghans and the Punjabi's to prosper as they developed good horse-breeding centres in their regions. The climate too was favourable for this development. Of the Indians in the Punjab, the Khokkars, the Jats and Mandahars reared war-horses and maintained a regular supply to the *nakhas* in Delhi.[55] The Afghans also seem to have smuggled Tartary horses from across the border, as their supply to India was not allowed by the hostile Mongol rulers. The provinces of Multan and Sind got Arab horses in good numbers.[56] The *sawars* (horsemen) usually possessed Indian horses and it was beyond their means to buy an imported horse at an exorbitant price, running into hundreds and even thousands of *tankas*.[57]

It is also worth recalling that, with the advent of the Tughlaq Sultan (Ghiyas uddin Tughluq Shah) to power in 1320, the design and architecture of the shops in the bazaars underwent a change under foreign influence. The sites excavated recently reveal the remains of certain important buildings and places in Tughluqabad. According to the surveyors' report:

The *Khass* bazaar (main shopping street) runs at the Western side of the city from the north-Gate of the Fort towards the north, ending in a triangular open area. The triangular area may have been an open market place, where the local farms' products were brought to the town on a daily basis.

The *Khass* bazaar itself seems to have been the main market street of the town, with shops on either side. The ruins of the shops can be found in the middle portion of the street. The shops probably ran alongside the entire length of the street, but the buildings at both ends of the street are in a ruinous state... Although at the *khass* bazaar only the lower parts of the shops have survived, they provide the earliest examples of their kind in India. It seems that, together with the other architectural and urban design features, the form of the shops set on platforms was imported by the Sultan from the region of Khurasan and (now comprising Afghanistan, the present Khurasan province of Iran and the Central Asian state of Turkistan). In cities in India, built a generation later than Tughluqabad, shops with a similar layout have survived, some in better condition, preserving their arched fronts and vaulted ceilings. Early examples of such shops can be found in the fort of Gulburga dating from the early Bahmani period.[58]

Moreover, the new bazaars constructed in Delhi and other cities seem to have been called *bazaar-i-Chaharsu,* i.e. having shopping streets around a square in four directions since the thirteenth century. Mention made by Amir Khusrau of *bazaar-i-Chaharsu* in the *'Ijaz-i-Khusravi* shows how busy they were. He states that the bazaars during the reign of Sultan 'Ala ud'din Khalji, ... 'are so overcrowded that people rub their shoulders (with one another) as rubs the dangling end of a turban... The essential commodities and merchandise are so cheap that one can arrange (to give) dowry for the marriage of four brides in just ten dirhams... Ripe fruits, cooked snakes and dishes of food, as essential for the public as books to students or prayer carpets to a sufi are available in plenty in the shops and streets, and connected shopping squares (*bazaar-i-Chaharsu)* more than the reward of knowledge for the righteous scholars'.[59] The *bazaar-i-Chaharsu* appears to have become a common feature of every newly-founded town under the Delhi Sultanate. When Sultan Sikandar Lodi (reigned: 1489-1517) founded Agra, his new capital near the old city of Agra in 1506, he had the *bazaar-i-Chaharsu* built inside it. This bazaar had shops of costly cloths and merchandise, and separate streets of craftsmen, darners, sarrafs (money lenders and bankers), etc.[60]

Later, the name *bazaar-i-Chaharsu* seems to have been replaced by *Chowk* in the entire country. For example, in his description of Bijapur, the capital of Adil Shahi Sultanate in the Deccan, Nusrati who composed verses in *Hindwi* (called Deccani Urdu) says in praise of the palaces and bazaars:[61]

> Each mansion looks like the city of Kashmir [in beauty],
> Each quarter is by itself Transoxiana [in charm],
> The large city with beautiful *chowks* [shopping squares] thronged with crowds,
> Each *chowk* has four shopping streets in several sectors.

Lastly, mention should be made of export and import items between India and foreign countries. No doubt, we are handicapped by the paucity of evidence as our sources generally focus on political matters. The medieval writers incidentally refer to foreign as well as indigenous products while mentioning the diplomatic gifts exchanged between the rulers or distributed to the nobles on special occasions. The main export items from India besides cotton textile and spices, seem to have been, rice, indigo, honey, ivory and slaves. Ibn Battuta, describes the bazaars of different countries and the commercial commodities available there. He informs us that the famous seaports in the Persian gulf and Arabia had a boom on account of the Indian merchants and products. According to him, the diet of the people of Harmuz and the area around was rice imported from India and Arab traders imported the commercial goods from India. The main port in the Persian gulf was Jerun, the bazaars of which were full of Indian merchandise. This seaport of Jerun, according to Ibn Battuta, was known as that of Hind and Sind on account of the presence of the Indian merchants in large number. From here the Indian products were transported to Iraq, Iran and Khurasan.[62]

Similarly, the residents of the seaport of Aden and other parts of the coast of Yemen lived on rice and trade with India. Ibn Battuta also calls Aden the seaport of the Indian merchants. The chief Qazi (judicial officer) of Aden was Salim bin Abdullah al-Hindi (a man of Indian origin). Most of the ships that came there were from Cambay, Honur, Thana, Sindapore, etc. Besides the Indians, the merchants from Egypt also resided there in connection with their trade. They were wealthy people and owned large cargos that sailed full of commercial goods. Rice was brought from India because nothing except barley was cultivated there. The Indian merchants were held in respect by the local people who received them on their arrival, taking them home as guests. They put on garment made of cotton imported from India.[63] The Muslim merchants are reported to have exported blue-dyed cotton cloths to the countries as far as Mozambique in Africa. Egypt also imported resist printed cloth was from India.[64]

Besides cotton textile and rice, Ibn Battuta also mentions Indian honey that was in demand. That the merchants from different countries including China bought Indian honey for it was considered wholesome in their countires.[65] It is interesting to note that Ibn Battuta is corroborated by other foreign sources. Diplomatic gifts from the Mamluk Sultans to their European counterparts included pots containing 'valuable products such as Indian honey and fine oil'.[66] Sugar also seems to have been an export item. Barbosa found sugar being exported from Bengal to foreign countries. He says, 'great store of this is taken into cargoes and carried for sale to many lands, for it is a principal article of trade'.[67]

Two other expensive export items from India that enjoyed popularity were indigo and ivory. Though necessity made people of different countries grow indigo, none could compete in quality with that from India. It was so profitable that the rulers of the eminence of Sultan Mahmud of Ghazna appear to have invested money in its trade. Sultan Mahmud of Ghazna maintained its stock and had it sold through his servants. At times, he sent it to people as part of gift and reward. Ahmad Nizami 'Aruzi Samarqundi writes that after the departure of the poet Firdausi Tusi, the Sultan decided to bestow honour upon him and sent money and indigo loaded on camels to Tus. The royal messenger however reached Tus after Firdausi Tusi's death and found his bier being carried out to the graveyard. Firdausi's daughter did not accept the royal gift. Informed by the *Sahib-i-barid* (intelligence officer), the Sultan ordered the indigo to be sold and its proceed spent on the construction of a *ribat* and a well between Tus and the city of Marv. The *ribat* existed till the writer's time.[68] Sadid u'ddin Muhammad 'Awfi adds there was a wealthy merchant in Ghazna, named Abu Sahal. His son, Ahmad bin Sahal won the Sultan's favour and was given a stock of indigo for sale. As he could sell only a small part of it, the rest going waste, he was dismissed from service.[69] Abu Raihan Al-Beruni also tells us that the indigo 'masks the defects of ageing', and that it was mixed with henna and used to dye both skin and hair.[70] Allusion to indigo is also made in *Taj-ul-Ma'asir* of Hasan Nizami showing it was in demand abroad.[71] 'Awfi also testifies to the luxurious life led by the merchants on account of trade between different countries.[72]

As for the export of ivory from India to foreign countries, it is one of the ironies of historiography that Indian sources do not mention it even incidentally. The Ilkhanid historian, Rashid uddin Fazlullah suggests that it was an expensive rare item that only the members of the ruling elite could afford to buy. In praising the Mongol emperor Ogedei's consideration towards foreign merchants, Rashid uddin writes:

> He would command their wares to be bought, whether they were good or bad, at the full price paid. And it usually happened that he would give them away without having looked at them... it was his command that whatever it amounted to an additional 10 per cent should be paid. One day the officers of the court represented to him that it was unnecessary to add this 10 per cent seeing that the price of the goods was already in excess of their real value. "The dealings of the merchants with the treasure", said Qaan (the Emperor), "are for the sake of increasing their profit. And indeed they have expenses to pay to you bitichis (state officers). It is their debt to you that I am discharging, lest they depart from our presence having suffered a loss." Some people from India brought him two tusks of ivory. He asked what they wanted and was told 500 (five hundred) *balish*.[73] Without the slightest hesitation he ordered them to be given this amount. The officers of the court made great outcry, asking how he could give so large a sum for so contemptible matter, when these people had come from an enemy country.[74] "None" he replied, "is an enemy of mine. Give them the money and let them go".[75]

As regards the export of slaves, India being a large country like China, both in terms of size and population, was a hub of slave trade. Merchants carried slaves from India to other countries for sale and the city *nakhas* (market for slave and cattle) had Indian and foreign slaves for sale. Amir

Khusrau is not exaggerating when he states about the *nakhas* of Delhi, 'The *nakhas* are like a flowing river, filled with slave girls. They may be likened to the ship of a fisherman,... they (the slave girls) come out as the fish comes out from the river'.[76] Khusrau is corroborated by other contemporary writers. Ibn Battuta while mentioning the female captives, states, 'Even the educated slave girls are cheap, so that no one there needs to buy captives'.[77] No doubt, the ordinary slave girls were cheap, yet beautiful ones fetched high price. Evidence available in the *malfuzat* of Shaikh Nizam uddin Auliya shows that only rich people could afford to buy attractive young female slaves for companionship. The grandson of Qazi Hami uddin Nagauri, the leading thirteenth century Suhrawardy Sufi, brought a young slave girl for one hundred *tankas* while the silver *tanka* was rarely seen in transaction during the thirteenth century. He was the Qazi (judicial officer of Nagaur).[78] According to the same source, Malih, the servant of Hasan Sijzi (the poet) bought an infant slave girl for five *tankas*.[79]

It is also worth pointing out that besides the foreign merchants and the officers of the Sultan of Delhi, some people from the lower middle class also took part in slave trade. A religious scholar who acted as Imam (leader of the prayer in the mosque) sent slaves from Multan to Khurasan for sale.[80] Minhaj-i-Siraj also says that his sister faced financial problem in Khurasan (present-day Afghanistan) and, in order to help her, he sent forty Indian slaves along with money. The slaves were to be sold by his sister.[81]

This was however not one way traffic and foreign slaves from countries as far as China, Africa and Europe were also available in the *nakhas* of Indian cities. Mention is made of foreign slaves by Minhaj in his *Tabaqat-i-Nasiri*. The sultans bought the Turk and non-Turk slaves and had them trained in different professions, particularly in the mode of warfare since the reign of Sultan Qutbudin Aibak.[82] Besides the Turk slaves, the slaves from Rum (Anatolia and parts of Byzantine Empire) and Europe are referred to incidentally. Likewise, the negro slaves holding high positions are mentioned in the details of important events.[83] Isami also mentions the Chinese slaves along with the Indians.[84] In his description of pestilence that broke out in Sultan Muhammad bin Tughluq's army camp in the Deccan, Ibn Battuta states, 'There died black slaves, the mamluk troopers and great amirs'.[85] Similarly, Amir Khusrau describes the Russian soldiers in the military contingent in Dipalpur under Ghazi Malik suggesting that they were originally slaves either purchased by Sultan 'Ala ud'din Khalji or by the Malik himself.[86] Generally the soldiers or nobles of foreign origin were originally slaves from non Muslim countries. They were purchased and trained in the art of warfare or in different crafts. Similarly, slave girls were also brought from foreign countries for sale in Delhi. Shams Siraj Afif provides us with detailed information about the ladies of the *haram* of Khan-i-Jahan Maqbul. They came from different regions of the world including Europe.[87]

Equally important is the description of commercial goods brought by the merchants from different countries to India. The rare commodities sold by the Turks in their homeland (Turkestan) to the merchants were musk (called musk of Tatar, Tibet and Khutan), costly fabrics, Khita'i and Chinese, such as silk painted with flowers, fur, such as that of beaver, fox, precious Bartasi (a land in Turkestan, famous for its fur), that of the Sythian weasel, the ermine, *Sanjab* and the fur of the Tibetan bull, the bows of poplar root, the horn of rhinoceros, hawks, falcons, precious *Yashm* (stone of green colour), horses, and young, hairy and wild camels, the likes of which were not found anywhere else.[88] Likewise, Sadid ud'din Muhammad 'Awfi describes Irani merchants who settled down in Cambay and carried on trade between India and other countries as far as China. They brought silk of different kind from China.[89] The *Taj-ul-Ma'asir* contains references to choice goods of foreign countries which give us insight into the progress of foreign trade just after the foundation of the Sultanate of Delhi. The Chinese mirror and silk, ruby from Badakhshan, Arab horses, Moroco leather, glass cups from Syria and Rumi brocade were in demand in the Indian bazaars.[90] The availability of Chinese silk such as *Khuz*, *Diba*, *Shir* and *Qasab* is described in the work of Isami.[91]

The diplomatic gifts exchanged between the Emperor of China and Sultan Muhammad bin Tughluq may also be mentioned. The former is said to have despatched along with his emissaries to the Sultan of India one hundred slaves, both male and female, five hundred bales of *Kamkhwab* (very expensive and popular silk) and five maunds of musk, besides robes and weapons.[92] In return, Sultan Muhammad bin Tughluq sent one hundred slaves, to China under the custody of Ibn Battuta, 'one hundred dancing girls and one hundred bales of Bairmia, a fine cotton cloth which had no equal in decency and beauty and worth one hundred dinar (gold coin) each. Besides, one hundred bales of silk, called *Juz*. This was woven with threads of five different colours. Four gold Chandeliers and four Chandeliers of silver were in addition'.[93] The exchange of gifts between the rulers of India and foreign countries continued throughout the period under review. In 1467, the Timurid ruler of Khurasan is reported to have sent his envoy Khwaja Jamal uddin Astrabadi to Sultan Mahmud Khalji's court in Mandu (Malwa) with gifts and a request for an elephant. In acknowledgement of his letter, Sultan Mahmud Khalji deputed his courtier, Shaikhzada Alauddin Muhammad to accompany Astrabadi along with costly gifts. The gifts for Abu Said included vases and utensils made of precious metal and studded with jewels and pearls, silk fabric of various type, both Indian and imported from Europe, Ottoman Empire and China, elephants and birds such as rare parrots and peacocks. One of the elephants was trained in performing different styles of Indian dances and playing on musical instruments simultaneously.[94]

It may not be out of place to discuss here briefly the improvement in the position and condition of the artisan class, resulting from the progress of trade and commerce. It is worth recalling that the skilled artisans, being conscious of their position in the country's economy could raise their charges arbitrarily when they thought it necessary. Complaining against their conduct, 'Ainu-l Mulk Mahru says that they charged two or three *jitals* for their work for the whole day during the times of Sultan 'Ala ud'din Khalji. 'A weaver', says he, 'used to charge two *jitals* for weaving a *chadar* (sheet), but, today, he charges thirty *jitals* for it. The tailor who charged four *jitals* for stitching single *yakta* (garment without a lining), today (i.e. Firuz Shah's reign) he is not happy if he is paid thirty *jitals* for the same work. They justify their action complaining about the rise in the prices of foodgrains by way of excuse, although compared to the recent past the prices have again become low. They persist in charging what they charged during the time of famine'.[95] As a matter of fact, the weavers were shown great consideration because their product was included among the important export items that attracted the leading merchants of the world. Likewise, the tailors, skilled in their craft of cutting and stitching were favoured for they catered to the taste of the members of ruling elite, fond of well-stitched garments.

Brief mention should also be made of the urban proletariat in the metropolitan city or in its suburbs, who were attracted by the availability of work. According to Ibn Battuta, the labourers were available in large number in every lane in different towns of Delhi. The *kahars* (palanquin bearers) were engaged by citizens of means and officers to carry them from place to place. The palanquins were possessed by every person of status. Once Ibn Battuta had to engage them. He says that he was carried by eight persons in two lots of four, 'who rest and carry in turn ... it is on them that most people go about on business; if a man has no slaves he hires men to carry him. In the town there are always a number of these men standing in the bazaars and at the Sultan's gate and at the gates of the persons for hire. The *dulas* (litter) of women are covered with silk curtains'.[96] Likewise, people were hired to look after the horses, erect tents, furnish them with carpets etc. The non-military officers and courtiers hired them for they did not maintain slaves or servants. They also had to join the royal expedition for the hunt. Such people were known as *karwaniya*, the *kahars*, the *farashes* and *dawadawiya*. The *karwaniyas* carried the tents and its poles on their shoulders, the *farash* erected the tent and furnished it with carpets. The *kahars* and others furnished with green fodder for the horses, carried utensils and also the master in a *dula* (litter). The *dawadawiya* used to walk ahead of the master, carrying torches at night.[97]

To conclude, it needs to be stressed that the establishment of peace and order along with the unification of the larger part of the country under the centre created favourable conditions for the progress of oversea and overland trade between India and foreign countries. India became open and foreign merchants came with choice merchandise of different countries. The emergence of new urban centres and the expansion of old ones with bazaars led to socio-economic growth as well as the progress of material culture. Moreover the foreign merchandise provided the local craftsmen with creative incentive, new crafts were introduced and indigenous ones modified. All this led to the expansion of an artisan population; and caste restrictions could no longer hamper professional mobility.[98]

Endnotes

1. See Sadid u'ddin Muhammad 'Awfi, *Jawami 'ul Hikayat-wa-Lavami 'ul Rivayat*, in Iqtidar Husain Siddiqui's *Perso-Arabic Sources of Information on the Life and Condition in the Sultanate of Delhi*, New Delhi: Munshiram Manoharlal, 1992, p. 26, hereafter cited as *Perso-Arabic Sources of Information.*
2. In describing the decoration of the royal palaces built by Sultan Shams uddin Iltutmish in Delhi, Isami refers to the Chinese painters in connection with wall-painting. The painters were obviously brought to be sold by the slave merchants from China. Isami, *Futuh us-Salatin*, ed. A.S. Usha, Madras: Madras University Islamic Series No. 9, 1948, pp. 114-15.
3. Siddiqui, *Perso-Arabic Sources of Information*, p. 26,
4. Loc. cit.

5. Ibid., p. 116; also Ibn Battuta, *The Travels of Ibn Battuta,* tr. Sir Hamilton Gibb, Cambridge University Press, 1971, vol. 3, p. 620, hereafter cited as *The Travels of Ibn Battuta.*
6. Siddiqui, *Perso-Arabic Sources of information,* p. 35.
7. *Tabaqat-i-Nasiri,* vol. 1, pp. 463, 468, 472.
8. The reference contained in the *Fawaid-ul-Fuad* to *bazaar-i-Kirbas* in the thirteenth century Delhi either has been used for the same *bazaar-i-bazazan* or it was a different one, exclusively for the sale of cotton, thin fine cotton textile and linen. *Fawaid-ul-Fuad,* Lahore, 1966, p. 112.
9. Minhaj-i-Siraj's reference to the fort suggests that it was a new building constructed during the reign of Sultan Raziya. See also *Tabaqat-i-Nasiri,* vol. 1, op.cit., p. 46.
10. Zia'uddin Barani *Tarikh-i-Firuz Shahi,* Calcutta, 1862, p. 91, hereafter cited as Barani.
11. Shaikh Kabir Batini, *Afsanah-i-Shahan-i-Hind*, rare MS. British Library, London, ff. 100a-b.
12. The capital city of the Sultan was respectfully mentioned as *Hazrat* (exalted). Like Uchh, the capital of Qubācha, Delhi also began to be called *Hazrat-i-Delhi* since the reign of Sultan Iltutmish. Cf. Ali Kufi, *Fathnama-i-Sind,* popularly known as *Chachnama,* ed. N.B. Baloch, Islamabad, 1983, p. 5, for Uchh, hereafter cited as *Chachnama.*
13. Barani writes that on account of the love and loyalty of Delhi's residents towards members of the overthrown dynasty, Sultan Jalal uddin Khalji selected the site near Kilokhari for his capital. The palace of Sultan Kaiqubad was completed. The Sultan had a strong fortification of the *Shahr-i-nau* constructed with gates and lofty towers. Besides the mansions of the nobles, bazaars were also constructed. The shopkeepers, traders and craftsmen are also reported to have moved to the new capital and settled down there. The newly-constructed capital always attracted traders, besides artisans, on account of court-generated trade. Cf. Barani, p. 176; also for the foundation of Ahmadabad, See Mahmud Bukhari, *Tarikh-i-Salatin-i-Gujarat,* ed. A.A. Tirmizi in *Medieval India Quarterly,* Aligarh, 1963, vol. 5, p. 120.
14. *The Travels of Ibn Battuta,* op.cit., p. 604.

15. Ibid., vol. 3, pp. 595-6.
16. Barani, *Tarikh-i-Firuz Shahi*, pp. 26, 28, 113-18.
17. *The Travels of Ibn Battuta*, op.cit., p. 600.
18. Ibid., vol. 3, p. 602.
19. Siddiqui, *Perso-Arabic Sources of Information*, pp. 24-6.
20. The Sanskrit sources mention this coin as *Parutha* which was in circulation in Gujarat. Cf. Dashrath Sharma, *Journal of the Numismatic Society of North India*, Nasik, vol. 1, part 2, pp. 304-5.
21. Sadid uddin Muhammad 'Awfi, *Jawami'ul-Hikayat-wa-Livami'ul Rivayat*, ed. Muhammad Nizamuddin, Hyderabad: Dairat-ul-Ma'arif-il-Osmania, 1965, vol. 1, part 2, pp. 304-5. (Hereafter cited as *Jawami'ul Hikayat.*)
22. Mir Hasan Sijzi, *Fawaid ul-Fuad*, Lahore, 1966, pp. 201-2.
23. It is wrongly held that Gujarat was annexed by the Khalji Sultan in AD 1299, after it had been plundered by the Delhi army under the command of Ulugh Khan. In fact, this expedition was a raid carried out to seize booty. In Cambay the Muslim merchants were also deprived of their wealth. The slave Kafur (later Malik Naib) was also seized from his Muslim master. Cf. Barani, *Tarikh-i-Firuz Shahi*, pp. 251-2; also See Satish Chandra Misra, *The Rise of Muslim Power in Gujarat*, New Delhi: Munshiram Manoharlal, 1982, pp. 63-4, 2nd edition, for the final conquest of Gujarat in 1206.
24. *The Travels of Ibn Battuta*, pp. 730-3.
25. Ibn Battuta, *Ajaib ul-Asfar*, Urdu tr. Maulvi Muhammad Husain, rpt, Islamabad: Institute of Islamic History and Research, 1983, vol. 2, pp. 280-1.
26. *Tabaqat-i-Nasiri*, op.cit., vol. 1, p. 421.
27. The reference to the merchants engaged in foreign trade tends to suggest that the early rulers were aware of the social and economic importance of foreign trade. The foreign merchandise, supplied by the merchants often helped the improvement of crafts and also the progress of commerce. Further, the foreign merchants served as liaison between the rulers of different countries and also transmitted information about new developments in different countries. Hasan Nizami Nishapuri, *Taj-ul-Ma'asir*, MS., British Library, London, no. Add 7623, ff.55b-56a.

28. *Tabaqat-i-Nasiri,* vol. 2, pp. 105-6 & p. 218.
29. Barani, *Tarikh-i-Firuz Shahi,* pp. 33-4.
30. Amir Khusrau, *I'jaz-i-Khusravi,* Lucknow: Nawal Kishore Press, 1876, vol. 4, pp. 141-4; also See appendix, A.
31. *The Travels of Ibn Battuta,* vol. 3, p. 733.
32. Loc. cit.
33. Ibid., vol. 3, p. 734.
34. Ibid., vol. 3, p. 673.
35. Ibn Battuta, *Ajaib ul-Asfar,* vol. 2, p. 231.
36. *The Travels of Ibn Battuta,* vol. 3, p. 607.
37. Shams Siraj Afif, *Tarikh-i-Firuz Shahi,* Calcutta: Bibliotheca Indica, 1891, pp. 124, 126-7. (Hereafter cited as Afif).
38. *The Travels of Ibn Battuta,* vol. 3, op.cit., pp. 595-6, 615-16.
39. Afif, *Tarikh-i-Firuz Shahi,* p. 120.
40. 'Amid Loeki Sunami, *Diwan*, ed. Nazir Ahmad, Lahore, 1984, p. 100; also Siddiqui, *Perso-Arabic Sources of Information*, p. 69.
41. Afif, *Tarikh-i-Firuz Shahi*, p. 61.
42. Cf. Zafar ul Islam, 'The *Fatawa Firuz Shahi:* As a Source for the Economic History of the Sultanate Period', *Islamic Culture,* vol. 60, no. 2, April 1986, pp. 113-14.
43. *The Travels of Ibn Battuta,* vol. 3, p. 617.
44. Cf. Iqtidar Husain Siddiqui, 'Evolution of the Vilayat, the Shiqq and the Sarkar in North India', *Medieval India Quarterly*, vol. 5, Aligarh, 1963, p. 18, for details; See also Zia' uddin Ahmad Desai, The Chanderi Inscription of 'Ala ud'din Khalji, *Epigraphia Indica: Arabic and Persian Supplement,* (EI) 1968, pp. 4-10.
45. *The Travels of Ibn Battuta,* vol. 3, pp. 638-9.
46. Ibid., vol. 3, p. 748.
47. Siddiqui, *Perso-Arabic Sources of Information,* pp. 118-19, for its English translation.
48. Ibid., p. 128.
49. Barani, *Tarikh-i-Firuz Shahi*, p. 365.
50. *The Travels of Ibn Battuta,* vol. 3, p. 755.

51. *Khazain-ul-Futuh,* tr. Mohammad Habib, Bombay: D.B. Taraporewala Sons & Co. 1931, pp. 13-14.
52. Barani, *Tarikh–i-Firuz Shahi,* pp. 304-6 & 309-11.
53. *Futuh us-Salatin,* p. 99.
54. Siddiqui, *Perso-Arabic Sources of Information,* p. 119.
55. Iqtidar Husain Siddiqui, 'Political and Social Conditions in North-Western India during the 13th and 14th Centuries', *Central Asiatic Journal,* Wiesbaden, vol. 27, nos. 3-4, pp. 288-306.
56. Barani, *Tarikhi-Firuz Shahi,* p. 53; also Simon Digby, *War-Horse and Elephant in the Delhi Sultanate,* Karachi: Oxford University Press, 1971, pp. 26-8.
57. Siddiqui, *Perso-Arabic Sources of Information,* p. 119.
58. Cf. Mehrdad Shokoohy and Natalie H. Shokoohy, 'The Dark Gate, The Dungeons, The Royal Escape Route and More: Survey of Tughluqabad', (second interim report), *Bulletin of the School of Oriental and African Studies,* University of London, 1999, vol. 62, part 3, pp. 421-61, See also 'Tughluqabad, the Earliest Surviving Town of the Delhi Sultanate', *Bulletin of the School of Oriental and African Studies,* 1994, vol. 57; pp. 516-50 plates, I XVI.
59. *Writings of Amir Khusrau,* based on *I'jaz-i-Khusravi,* 2008, tr. Iqtidar Husain Siddiqui, Islamic Thought and Science Institute, Illinois, U.S.A. vol. 4, p. 171.
60. Rizq ullah Mushtaqi, *Waqi'at-i-Mushtaqi,* tr. Iqtidar Husain Siddiqui, New Delhi: Indian Council of Historical Research, 1993, pp. 350, 42-4, 62.
61. Mulla Nusrati, *Alinama,* also called *Shahnama-i-Deccan,* (completed in AD 1647), cited by Nasim Faris in 'Decanni Sha'irika Gul-i-Sirsabd', *Nawa-e-Adab, Urdu Quarterly*. Bombay, 2007, vol. 57, nos. 1-2, April-September, p. 53.
62. Ibn Battuta, *Ajaib ul-Asfar,* vol. 1, Urdu tr. Maulana Ata ur-Rahman, Delhi: Rahimi Press, 1348 H, pp. 388-92.
63. Ibid., vol. 1, pp. 359, 360 & 370-2.
64. Jenny Balfour-Paul, *Indigo in the Arab World,* Richmond Surrey: Curzon Press, 1977, p. 125.
65. Ibid., vol. 1, p. 379.

66. Cf. Milwright Marcus, 'Pottery in the Written Sources of the Ayyubid – Mamluk Period, 1171-1517', *Bulletin of the School of Oriental and African Studies,* 1999, vol. 62, part 3, England: Oxford University Press, p. 511; Amir Khusrau mentions aloe-wood oil that might have also been exported. Cf. *I'jaz-i Khusravi,* vol. 4, tr., p. 233.
67. Cf. *The Book of Duarte Barbosa,* tr. Mansel Longworth, 1918, 2 vols, London: Hakluyt Society, vol. 2, p. 146.
68. *Chahar Maqala,* ed. Muhammad bin Abdul Wahab Qazwini, Tehran: Kitab Farosh Ashrafi, 1909, p. 51.
69. *Jawami'ul Hikayat wa-Livami'ul Rivayat,* ed. Bano Musaffa and Mutahir Musaffa, Iran: Bunyad-i-Farhang, 1352 H, Qism 3, part 1, p. 312.
70. Al-Biruni, *Book of Pharmacy and Materica Medica,* tr. and ed. Hakim M. Said, Karachi: Hamdard, 1973, Introduction, p. 229.
71. *Taj-ul-Ma'asir,* tr. op.cit. by Bhagwat Saroop, Delhi, 1998, p. 93.
72. Siddiqui, *Perso-Arabic Sources of Information,* p. 27.
73. The *balish* was a gold ingot, cast in a mould.
74. The countries, the rulers of which did not acknowledge the suzerainty of the Mongol Emperor were regarded enemy and at war.
75. Rashid uddin Fazl ullah, *Jami'ul Tawarikh,* See *The Successors of Genghis Khan* [Extracts from *Jami'ul Tawarikh*], translated from the Persian by John Andrew Boyle, Columbia: Columbia University Press, 1971, p. 83.
76. Khusrau, *I'jaz-i-Khusravi,* vol. 4, tr., p. 170.
77. *The Travels of Ibn Battuta,*, vol. 3, p. 741.
78. *Fawaid ul-Fuad,* 1966, pp. 316-17.
79. Ibid., p. 339.
80. Ibid., p. 15.
81. *Tabaqat-i-Nasiri,* vol. 1, p. 483; See also vol. 2, pp. 38-9.
82. Ibid., vol. 1, pp. 442.
83. For instance, Jamal uddin Yaqut, the negro held the post of *Amir-i-Akhur* under Iltutmish and his successors. Another negro was Ikhtiyar uddin Habshi whom Iltutmish sent as his emissary to the Caliph's court in Baghdad. *Tabaqat-i-Nasiri,* vol. 1, pp. 460-1; See vol. 2, p. 25, for Ikhtiyar uddin Habshi.

84. Isami, *Futuh us-Salatin,* ed. A.S. Usha, Madras: Madras University Islamic Series No. 9, 1948, p. 550.
85. *The Travels of Ibn Battuta,* vol. 3, p. 717.
86. Amir Khusrau, *Tughluq nama,* Hyderabad, 1933, p. 84.
87. Iqtidar Husain Siddiqui, 'Khan Jahan Maqbool', *Encyclopaedia of Islam,* Leiden: E. J. Brill, 1978, vol. 4, pp. 1019a-b. (New edition)
88. *Tarikh-i-Fakhr-i-Mudabbir,* pp. 38, 40;
89. Siddiqui, *Perso-Arabic Sources of Information,* p. 26, f.n.46.
90. *Taj-ul-Ma'asir,* tr. op.cit., pp. 93-4, 103, 116, 135, 212, 216, 258, 268 & 307.
91. *Futuh us-Salatin,* op.cit., p. 550.
92. Battuta, *Ajaib ul-Asfar,* op.cit., vol. 2, p. 243.
93. Ibid., vol. 2, p. 244.
94. Ali bin Mahmud al-Kirmani, known as Shihab Hakim, *Ma'asir-i-Mahmud Shahi,* MS. British Library, London, no. Or. 11, 140, ff.169b-170a. This refers to the manuscript copy because the Printed XI- is an abridged version
95. Ainul-Mulk Mahru, *Insha-i-Mahru,* ed. Shaikh Abdur Rashid, Lahore, 1965, letter no. 20, pp. 47-8.
96. *The Travels of Ibn Battuta,* vol. 3, p. 740.
97. Ibid., vol. 3, pp. 752-3.
98. Cf. *Waqi'at-i-Mustaqi* of Shaikh Rizq ullah Mushtaqi, tr. Iqtidar Husain Siddiqui, New Delhi: Indian Council of Historical Research, 1993, pp. 173-4.

CHAPTER 4

Food and Its Socio-Cultural Significance

With the establishment of the Delhi Sultanate in the beginning of the thirteenth century, Muslim emigrants came to India from different countries, representing different cultural traditions and dietary habits. On their arrival in India they were placed in the civil and military administration of the newly-conquered territories. Consequently, they came to constitute the ruling elite in the Delhi Sultanate. Many began to intermarry regardless of their diverse cultural traditions. This intermixing among the Muslim aristocrats from different countries led to the development of an Indo-Muslim culture which, in due course of time, acquired distinctive features. The majority of the nobles in the Sultanate were emigrants from Central Asian lands. Their culture and life seem to have undergone significant changes following their contact with other foreign Muslims and the local Hindus. The outcome of all this was the growth of a new culture that looked somewhat different in many respects from that of Central Asia, Iran or Arabia. Even the cuisine, popular among the Indo-Muslim nobles, gradually become indigenized and different in taste and flavour from that of other Muslim countries. Visitors to India since the fourteenth century, began to talk about *Hindustani* (Indian) food.

Certain items of food that gained popularity in the early period of the Delhi Sultanate have survived, with new additions through the Mughal period upto modern times. The consumption of meat and sweetmeats (called *halva*) by Muslims, rich and poor alike, led to the setting up of bakeries, restaurants, and the shops of butchers and confectioners (called *dukanha'-i-tabbakhan-o-halva' iyan)* in the cities and towns. The Sultan and the nobles maintained large kitchens (*matbakhs*) while travellers, especially traders, and others bought cooked food from the shops. The Sufi saints and philanthropists spent lavishly on the maintenance of public kitchens called *langars*, where free food was distributed daily among the poor and the destitute. It may also be pointed out that the preparation of most of the delicacies involved the use of imported nuts, dry fruits and herbs, that gave a fillip to foreign trade and to cultivation of certain herbs and plantation of those fruit trees which were naturalized. Notwithstanding its social and economic significance, food in the Indo-Muslim aristocratic culture has not attracted sufficient attention from modern scholars.[1]

In this chapter, I consider evidence, sifted from different sources, historical as well as literary and religious, with regard to feasts hosted by the sultans and nobles that went a long way in popularizing delicacies and setting cultural norms, etiquette and dining manners. The chapter is divided into three parts: the first deals with banquets and their historical and cultural significance; the second with food dishes; and the third with the catering profession and the kitchen-generated trade. The kitchen that served as an institution where people were employed to work in different capacities in large numbers and got training in the art of cooking and serving food has also been discussed; as also the catering profession and the impact of dietary habits of the members of the ruling elite on foreign trade, cultivation of new crops and horticulture.

The banquets hosted by the Sultan and nobles on occasions, social, religious and political, had become an institution of great cultural significance. They went a long way in enriching the cultural heritage of that time as new dishes were introduced periodically, leading to a constant refinement of taste and manners. There is however little information on this in the early thirteenth century sources. The contemporary poet, Taj Reza mentions a royal banquet hosted by Sultan Iltutmish (1210-36) in honour of the visit of an envoy from the Abbasid Caliph of Baghdad to Delhi in AD 1230. The poet tells us in his *qasidah* composed for the occasion that, a grand celebration was held in which all and sundry were entertained.[2] Minhaj-i Siraj's account of the reception accorded to the emissaries of Hulegu (Il-Khanid ruler of Iran) in Delhi (1259) shows that traditions had already been set to make a display of the grandeur and power of the Sultan in order to impress the foreign dignitaries on this occasion. Moreover, the entire population of the capital city was given a chance to enjoy state hospitality.[3]

Barani's account of the reign of Sultan Ghiyasuddin Balban shows how the royal banquets raised the prestige of the Sultan and the grandeur of his court. The Sultan went out of his way to emulate the traditions set by the sultans in Central Asia during the preceding period such as the banquets held at the court of Sultan Muhammad Khwarizm Shah from the senior nobles who had served under him before their migration to India. It was during Balban's reign that the royal banquet became institutionalized and later sultans maintained the norms set by him. The celebrations held in connection with the festivals, religious as well as secular, wedding ceremonies, etc. were marked by and pomp and show. Balban had the banquet hall luxuriously decorated: embroidered carpets and colourful floorings were spread with curtains of *zarbaft* (expensive silk woven with gold threads) hanging all around. The rows were made by artificial trees made of silk of different colours. The trays of food were of different varieties. The food, dry fruits of different kinds, soft-drinks and betel leaves were served in plates, bowls and vessels of gold and silver.[4] The Sultan also appears to have introduced the practice of taking his daily meals along with the *ulama* and *Danishmands* (religious scholars and Muslim Jurists).[5]

Amir Khusrau in the *Dibacha-i-Ghurrat al-Kamal* describes how leading nobles emulated the Sultan in hosting banquets on a grand scale and spent lavishly on entertaining their guests. Some of them, interested in learning and literature, even invited scholars and poets to attend these banquets.[6] A majority of nobles however seem to have been fond of pleasure, and held convivial meetings frequently for the same. The celebration of *Nauroz* (a spring festival) as well as the marriage of their children were also joyous occasions.[7] Describing the weekly celebrations and feasts in the royal palace during the reign of Sultan Jalaluddin Khalji (1290-6), Barani tells us that their highlight was a dance performed by the leading female dancers of that time, Nusrat Bibi and Mehr Afroz, whose beauty, charm and movements could enchant even an ascetic.[8]

It may be noted that like the extravagance involved in the preparation of a large number of food dishes for the banquet, the decoration of the banquet hall or the tent also became institutionalized. The later sultans seem to have attached a great deal of importance to the decoration of the hall or spacious tent where a celebration was to be held. The following details furnished by Ibn Battuta reveal how elaborate the 'Id (Muslim festival celebrated at the end of the month of fasting) decorations had become with the passage of time, and how the art of decorating had become a specialized job, involving large numbers of skilled artists. '... artificial trees are made of silk of different colours, with artificial flowers on them; three rows of them are placed in the hall, and between each pair of trees is placed a golden chair with a covered cushion upon it. The great throne is set up at the upper end of the hall; it is of pure gold throughout, and its legs are encrusted with jewels... upon it there is placed the cushioned seat, and a parasol, encrusted with jewels, is hoisted over the Sultan's head'. After the greetings had been exchanged, the guests were served sumptuous dishes.[9] Over time, profuse use of perfumes for freshening the air in the banquet halls and the demand for expensive decorations led to a refinement of the traditional crafts on the one hand and promoted trade on the other.[10]

The successor of Sultan Muhammad bin Tughluq, Sultan Firuz Shah (1351-88), is said to have surpassed his predecessors in celebrating festivals, hosting ceremonial feasts and making endowments for the upkeep of the *khanqahs* along the highways, madrasas (schools and colleges) in the cities and towns, and the distribution of free food to the travellers, teachers and students.[11] As regards the festivities in connection with the celebration of 'Id*s* (*'Id al-Fitr* and *'Id al-Adha*), *Shab-i Barat* and *Nauroz* (spring festival), the Sultan is believed to have made efforts to increase their traditional gaiety and ėclat. According to Shams Siraj Afif, a spacious tent (mentioned as *bargah-i 'amm)* was elaborately decorated on the occasion of 'Id festivals with tree branches made of costly silk fabric of different colours (*narmina,* etc.,) as well as of wax, and fresh flowers attached to them. The arches of the gates were made of gold and silver. The sides of the tent were also covered with colourful tapestries and expensive curtains.[12] Similarly, the celebration of *Nauroz,* (also called *Jashn-i Bahar*), the reception accorded to the emissaries from foreign countries, and wedding functions also served as joyful events. The *Nauroz* festival seems to have been introduced by emigrants from central Asia at the very beginning of their conquest of north India. The graphic description of *Nauroz* in the *Qiran al-Sa'dain*[13] and other later works shows that people of means celebrated it according to their taste and temperament. Those who were given to the pleasure of the flesh, spent lavishly on liquor, food, dance and music. The religious-minded nobles also celebrated it enthusiastically by hosting a grand feast and arranging *qawwali* programmes (religious or Sufi songs sung by expert male singers).[14] The *Nauroz* celebrations and receptions accorded to foreign emissaries by Sultan Firuz Shah are reported to have been unprecedented in grandeur in the history of the Delhi Sultanate.[15]

Wedding functions held by members of the ruling elite were equally lavish. Even a second-ranked officer performed the marriage ceremony of his children on a grand scale. Once a certain Malik Aitimar Turk spent more than one lac *jitals* on the marriage of his daughter during the thirteenth century.[16] Thus the norms and traditions set by the princes and members of the ruling elite in the thirteenth century continued to inspire the later generations of people. Of the contemporary writers, Amir Khusrau supports our statement in his description of the marriage ceremony of Prince Khizr Khan (son of Sultan 'Ala ud'din Khalji) with the daughter of Alap Khan. The feasts and functions went on for several days. On the final day, the entire city (Delhi) was luxuriantly decorated, spacious tents were installed at various places with golden curtains (cloth woven with gold thread) hanging all around. Beautiful figures of horses and fairies were fixed on the walls in the streets. Every street through which the marriage procession passed was spread with fine silk, called *diba-i-chin* (silk fabric, imported from China), gold and silver coins were thrown among people in the streets and beautiful dancers and musicians entertained the members of the marriage party throughout the day.[17] Ibn Battuta also briefly alludes to the extravagance involved in these functions. According to him, the festivities connected with the marriage of Sultan Muhammad bin Tughluq's sister went on for fifteen days. Two marquees were installed, covering the two audience halls in the Red Palace. Both of these were furnished with fine cushions and carpets. Along with male singers and female dancers, cooks, bakers, roasters, pastry cooks, butlers and betel servers were also employed; animals and birds were slaughtered and people were served food everyday.[18] Barani also refers to the wedding functions but briefly.

The interesting information contained in the official history of the Malwa Sultans, *Ma'athir-i Mahmud Shahi,* substantiates the fact that the fifteenth century sultans, who emerged as the founders of regional kingdoms in the wake of the sack of Delhi by Timur in 1398, not only maintained the traditions set by their former masters but also added much to their cultural heritage. On the occasion of the marriage of Prince Ghiyas u'ddin, son of Sultan Mahmud Shah Khalji, in AD 1412 festivities went on for twenty-two days. The courtyard outside the audience hall was covered by a spacious tent, decorated on a grand scale. The seats studded with precious jewels were placed under twenty-one umbrellas made of costly silk embroidered with threads of gold. Each side of the passages between the rows of seats was decorated with lines of artificial trees. The trees carried colourful flowers and birds, all made of silk of various colours and of wax. Everyday in the evening the guests (the nobles, courtiers and the elite of the city of Mandu) were served with sumptuous food of different kinds and *sharbat* (soft drinks) in gold cups. The betel leaves were served after the dinner in gold plates by immaculately dressed waiters. The dinner was cooked daily under the supervision of expert *chashnigirs* (tasters). As usual, the highlight of the function was singing and dance. On the last day of the wedding ceremony, roads and streets of the city were decorated and the general public was fed.[19]

Likewise, we find a graphic description of the banquet hosted in Mandu, sometime in February 1519, by Sultan Mahmud Shah Khalji II of Malwa in honour of his supporter, Sultan Muzaffar Shah II of Gujarat. On this occasion, the beautiful mansions built by the Sultans of Malwa were decorated in a wonderful manner in connection with the arrangement of the royal banquet. Jewelled thrones were placed in some of the buildings. The surroundings were decorated with artificial trees and flowers of different colours, glittering with pearls, diamonds and other precious stones which were used in making them. The decorators, skilled in their professions, were ordered to decorate the entire city of Mandu. They beautified the bazaar by fixing on either side artificial trees made of wax and costly silk so that every person was amazed to see them. In some buildings the *chashnigirs* (tasters) and *matbakhyan* (cooks) and other employees of the kitchen prepared various kinds of delicious dishes the flavour, smell and taste of which the guests could never forget. Similarly, the *sharbatdaran* (those who served soft drinks) served scented and refreshing drinks of various types in cups made of gold. In the end the *tanbuldaran* (those who served betel leaves) came with gold trays full of betel leaves for the guests.[20]

The sources for the history of the Lodi and Sur periods show that the norms and aesthetic standards set by the early sultans for social gatherings and banquets still prevailed and provided a point of cultural reference. A Lodi Sultan celebrated the festivals of *'Id al-Fitr* and *'Id al-Adha* and the death anniversary of the Prophet of Islam on a grand scale and was emulated by his nobles in the capital and the provinces.[21] For instance, Miyan Zainuddin, the *muqta'* (governor) of Badaon, observed the death anniversary of the Prophet for twelve days, and people were served delicious food on each day. Four thousand *tankas* were spent on food preparation on the first and the last days while two thousand more for other daily expenditure. The poor and rich people were served daily with a variety of food.[22] The Farmuli nobles spent lavishly on the death anniversary of their saintly ancestor, Shaikh Muhammad Salman (a non-Afghan Sufi lying buried in Farmul in Afghanistan), by distributing food and sweetmeats.[23] *Masnad-i 'Ali* A'zam Humayun Sarwani is also reported to have celebrated the 'Id festivals in a lavish manner. Huge amounts of money were spent, three thousand animals, cows, *dumbas* (lamb with thick tail of fat) and camels were slaughtered on the occasion of *'Id al-Adha.*[24] Another occasion on which the kings and the nobles arranged banquets was when foreign dignitaries visited. It is belived that once Rana Sanga hosted a banquet in honour of the rebel nobles of Sultan Ibrahim Lodi at his court, serving food to the guests with his own hands, it being a special mark of honour.[25]

Writing about the generosity of Shaikh Ghuran, a noble under the Lodi Sultans and Babur, Mushtaqi says that beside huge expenditure on items such as clothing and jewellery, he also spent lavishly on entertaining his friends and other people with music and singing for several days in connection with the marriage ceremony of his son. He paid seventy thousand *tankas* to the singers alone. On the final day, he distributed among his men one hundred and fifty horses, four elephants and twenty ass-loads of cloth, including silk fabric.[26] The celebration of *Nauroz* by the Shaikh also seems to have lasted several days, there being no commodity that was not procured by the host for the pleasure and entertainment of his guests. They were invited to the convivial parties arranged in this connection and served with drinks (soft as well as alcoholic according to the attitude of the host) and delicious food, and entertained with music and dance.[27] In some of the parties, poets were invited to recite their fresh compositions. Associated with an aristocratic life and culture, *Nauroz* was also celebrated by orthodox Muslim nobles, who only avoided the use of alcoholic drinks. The religious-minded nobles arranged banquets on a grand scale, with different types of dishes cooked for the guests.[28] In short *Nauroz* had become an institutionalized festival that appealed to all classes in society.

In the Sur period, we find comprehensive information about the banquets hosted by *Masanad-i 'Ali* Khawas Khan, the premier noble of Sher Shah, in connection with the celebration of religious festivals as well as social occasions. Following his death, legends surrounded his large hearted generosity. It is, however, true that it pleased Khawas enormously when a large number of guests ate at his residence.[29] His celebration of the birth anniversary of the Prophet was considered unparalleled. He is reported to have spent whatever money he possessed on this occasion. In the year 1540-1, when he was fighting under the personal command of Sher Shah against the Ghakkars, in the hilly region around Rohtas (Punjab), Prophet's birth anniversary occurred. Although, the Ghakkars had been successful in cutting off the supply of food and cattle to the royal camp creating a shortage of food, *Masnad-i 'Ali* celebrated the function with enthusiasm. He invited all the nobles with their soldiers, numbering about forty to fifty thousand to attend the feast. First the nobles were served with sumptuous dishes, mutton soup, different meat preparations, rice boiled in milk and mixed with sugar candy, and *halvas* (sweetmeats). Separate arrangements were made for the Hindus who also served in Sher Shah's army in large numbers. Astonished by the large number of dishes served there, in spite of scarcity of food stuff in the camp, Haibat Khan Niyazi remarked in joke, 'Today you have performed a miracle'. Khawas Khan retorted, 'It is no miracle. I keep enough in store even while campaigning. Everyone of my ten thousand foot soldiers carries something (of provision). The cows and she-buffaloes form part of the provisions. Likewise, the two thousand horses, camels and elephants are loaded with necessities for the kitchen'.[30]

In passing I also briefly discuss the etiquette expected of the guests at these banquets. The guests had to wait at the dining carpet after the trays of different food preparations had been placed thereon till the *hajib* (in charge of arrangement) gave the signal to eat, saying *Bismillah ar-Rahman ar-Rahim* (in the name of God, Most Gracious, Most Merciful).[31] Shaikh Burhanuddin Gharib, the spiritual successor of Shaikh Nizamuddin Auliya' (d.1325) used to teach his *murids;* 'First help the guests, wash their hands, place loaves of bread on the carpet and then other dishes such as *shorba* (meat soup). People should start eating food after *Bismillah* was recited. Nobody should dip his own spoon in the bowl containing food for a number of guests as it created a feeling of revulsion among others'.[32] The same work tells us that the *khilal* (dental tooth stick) was to be served to the guests after the dinner was over.[33] After it, the ewer-bearers came to help people clean their hands and mouth. The guests were expected to use water carefully so that it might not fall on the carpet. In the end the betel leaf was to be distributed and chewed in a gentle manner.[34]

Of the thirteenth century Indo-Persian works, only the *Qiran al-Sa'dain* contains a somewhat detailed list of the various foods served at a royal banquet, the order in which the dishes were to be served, and the etiquette the guests were expected to observe while taking their meal. In a banquet hosted by Sultan Kaiqubad (1287-90) in honour of the visit of his father, Bughra Khan, from Bengal to his court in Awadh; first, the waiters served the guests with refreshing *sharbats* (soft drinks) made of fruits juices and sugar candy dissolved in water; then different kinds of bread, such as *nan-i tanuri* (dough bread made of fine flour, ghee or clarified butter stuffed with sweet paste and dry fruits and baked in an oven) and *kak* (thin and buttered bread, savoury in taste). After this, the meat and cereal dishes were brought. Here mention is made of the *sambosa (samosa,* triangular in shape and a sort of patty stuffed with minced meat and dry fruits, such as almonds, pistachios, etc.), roasted kid, tongue and head of goat, fried leg of lamb, skinned and stuffed goats, the tail of *dumba,* different kinds of birds and water fowl, chicken, partridge, quail, button quail etc. Beside these, there were various kinds of sweet dishes, particularly, the *halva* and *sabuni* (the latter being of sugar candy mixed with dry fruit and saffron and fried in ghee). In the end betel leaves were served.[35] Two more dishes are mentioned by Amir Khusrau in the *I'jaz-i-Khusravi.* They are, roasted chicken and pudding prepared with cotton seeds mixed with rice and milk.[36] Of the different types of *halvas,* the *halva-i-gajar* (made of carrot mixed with dry fruits, herbs and saffron) was cooked during the winter as this today. The relevant piece of information contained in *Fawaid ul-Fuad,* shows that various ingredients were so mixed in cooking, that a dish could hardly be recognized before one tasted it.[37] In another work we find a reference to *tutmaj* (a preparation of milk, rice and dry fruit cooked and mixed with sugar candy), a sweet dish of the same period. Sultan Kaiqubad seems to have been fond of *tutmaj.*[38]

Incidentally, Zia'uddin Barani also supplies evidence in his brief account of Sultan Balban's *Amir-i-Ariz* (Paymaster-General), Imad al-Mulk, that the Amir used to take his afternoon meal with his subordinate staff in the *Diwan-i-Ariz.* Some members of his staff sat with him on the dining carpet while others (juniors) were served food outside. Beside different types of *nans* (bread) such as *qurs* and *biryan* (fried breads) of fine flour, different preparations of mutton, sweet dishes, roasted pigeons, chicken and soft drinks were supplied from his kitchen daily.[39] Shihab uddin al-Umari who collected information from travellers about India states, 'Here different kinds of food are sold in the bazaars, roast meat, *Mutanjan* (a preparation of rice, sweet and saltish both mixed with meat), fried meat, sweet meats of sixty five kinds, juice of fruits and *sharbats* (sweet drinks) of nice quality that are hardly to be found anywhere else'.[40]

Ibn Battuta, who arrived in India and stayed in the service of Sultan Muhammad bin Tughluq (1325-51) for a number of years, attended dinners at the royal court as well as at the residences of many nobles. In his work, he writes about the maintenance of large kitchens by the Sultan and the nobles and their institutionalized extravagance. Ibn Battuta describes how the members of the ruling elite took their meal daily along with their relations, guests and a number of other associates. He also writes about the order the servants observed in serving the dishes, starting with bread, thin round cakes, 'then they cut up the roasted meat into large pieces four to six to a lamb and put one piece before each man. They served also round dough cakes made with ghee, resembling the bread called *mashrikin* in our country, which they stuffed with the sweet called *saburniya* (modern *sabuni*), and on top of each dough cake they put a sweetcake which they called *khisht* (brick-shaped), made of flour, sugar and ghee. Then they served in large porcelain bowls meat cooked with ghee and onions, and green ginger. After that they served something which they called *sambosa*, made of meat mashed and cooked with almonds, walnuts, pistachios, onions and spices, put inside a piece of thin bread fried in ghee. They put five pieces of these before each person, or perhaps four'. Besides, there was a rice dish, cooked in ghee with chicken (modern *pula'o*) and several sweet dishes, *halva* and pudding.[41]

The Sultan's palace also served two kinds of dinners daily, the private dinner and the public dinner. The private dinner was attended by the Sultan along with a few chosen relatives, nobles and foreign dignitaries whom he wanted to honour, these generally numbering not more than twenty persons. The public dinner was arranged daily in the Council Hall for the *ulama* (religious divines), jurists, nobles, relations of the Sultan, *nadims* (royal associates) and the saintly persons attached to the court. This consisted of various types of bread, round-pieces of bread split and filled with sweet paste, roasted meat, chicken, rice dishes, plain as well as cooked with meat, and *sambosa*. First, the cup-bearers served every person *sharbat* and then a set of all the dishes was placed before everyone. The guests ate from independent plates.[42] Besides these dinners, the Sultan fixed a number of trays of cooked food for his favourite nobles. They were sent from the royal kitchen to their houses daily.[43] The Indian dish of *khhichri* had also become quite popular among the Muslims, who ate it for breakfast like the Hindus. 'They cook,' says Ibn Battuta, '*munj* (moong pulse) with rice and eat it with ghee (clarified butter); this they call *kisri*, (i.e. *khhichri*) and they breakfast on it every day.'[44]

Shihabuddin al-Umari adds on the authority of the Indian travellers to Arabia that the meals were served at the royal palace twice a day, one in the morning and the other in the evening.[45]

The old bits of information available in the *Khair al-Majalis*, the *malfuzat* (collection of utterances) of Shaikh Nasiruddin Chiragh of Delhi (d. AD 1356) supplement Ibn Battuta and the earlier works in respect of the dietary habits of Muslims belonging to different classes, the huge expenditure incurred on the maintenance of public kitchens by rich people and by Sufi saints for distribution of free food among people, as well as restaurants and shops owned by caterers. In this work we are informed that Shaikh Nizamuddin Auliya' (d. AD 1325) used to break his daily fast after sun-set with a piece of *qurs* (large round, stuffed bread).[46] The rich people who had faith in Sufi saints, invited them along with their disciples to dinner and also made arrangements of *sama* (Sufi songs sung by expert singers called *qawwals*) for their spiritual entertainment. Once Shaikh Nizamuddin Auliya' was invited by a resident of Delhi. The Shaikh was accompanied by a large number of people most of whom had joined him on the way. All of them were served *nan, qurs* and meat.[47] At times, the wealthy people served Sufis with *nan* and *maslukh* (skinned and roasted goats).[48] The *qurs* seems to have been baked of different size and weight and could be preserved upto twenty days. Generally, the *nan* was split into two and *qurs* into six pieces. Once Shaikh Nizamuddin Aulia' sent a *qurs* to Shaikh Nasiruddin Chiragh which was about two seers in weight. It was eaten with *halva*.[49] The reference to *Khhichri* suggests that usually people ate it when they suffered from stomach trouble.[50] It was taken with ghee (clarified butter).[51] Another foreign dish among the Muslims was *nahari*, generally made of beef. *Nahari* was eaten with bread for breakfast in the morning.[52]

The sources of information for the reign of Sultan Firuz Shah tend to suggest that the aforesaid dishes, both foreign and Indian that the Muslim immigrants had adopted, became the essential feature of food in Indo-Muslim culture. For instance, *khhichri*, though a common food preparation, was cooked in the royal as well as nobles' kitchen.[53] Of the non-vegetarian dishes, daily served among the Muslims of means, the contemporary poet, Muthar of Kara, mentions the following ones, served on the dining carpet in the *Madrasa-i-Firuz Shahi* (the College built by Firuz Shah): pheasants, partridges, herons, fowl, fish, roasted chicken, roasted kid and beef curry. Besides, there were various sweet dishes including the delicacy, *lauz* (pudding made of rice boiled in milk, mixed with dry fruit, almonds, pistachios, raisin, saffron, now called *firini*). The types of bread heaped on the dining carpet are mentioned as *qurs* and *nans* along with *khisht*, dry and wet. As usual, the *sharbat* of pomegranate and of other fruits was served before food while the *biras* (betel leaves) came at the end.[54]

The *Kitab nama-i-Nāsir Shahi* (compiled towards the end of the fifteenth century or the beginning of the sixteenth century) reveals that new additions were made to the traditional dishes under the impact of new immigrants, particularly from Iran. In this work we find references to certain new as well as old dishes cooked daily in the royal kitchen. The anonymous writer also describes the method of cooking along with the proportion of different ingredients needed in the preparation of a particular dish. The *biryani* (rice coloured with saffron and cooked with meat, dry fruits and spices) is mentioned for the first time, while *shorba, qima* (fried minced meat, mentioned as *Qima-i-Ghiyas Shah* after Sultan Ghiyasuddin Shah, the father of Nāsir Shah of Malwa) and *sambosa* being the traditional old dishes. Besides, a number of *halvas* have also been described.[55] It needs to be stressed here that these dishes are considered today the special feature of Muslim cuisine in South Asia.

Similarly, the works compiled by the writers who had been patronized by the Afghan kings (Lodis and Surs) or their nobles furnish interesting information, bearing on cultural integration in respect of food preparation and dietary habits of the Muslim elite. In the tradition of the great Sultans of Delhi during the fourteenth century, Sultan Sikandar Lodi maintained a big kitchen where a large number of dishes were cooked daily for the members of the royal family as well as for distribution among the courtiers. Mushtaqi says, 'Trays of different kinds of food were set aside by name for various persons (scholars and other royal associates) and were sent daily to their houses accordingly. Whatever dishes Sultan specified in the name of the recipient at the time of his first entry into the royal court, the same dishes continued to be sent to his place till the end. There was no alteration whatsoever'.[56] Emulating the Sultan, the nobles also took their meals along with their associates and also had food distributed among the poor who gathered outside their mansions.[57] In short, the distribution of food among people at the time of lunch and the evening dinner had become a well-established tradition in elitist culture. People considered the distribution of rich food by the nobles among people a virtue and a sign of large-hearted munificence. The more extravagant the noble was in this respect, the greater respect he commanded among people.[58]

Though Mushtaqi does not make mention of dishes in his account of the Lodi period, the brief references to food and kitchen show that generally non-vegetarian dishes were served at the dining carpets. It is only at a few places that he mentions *do-piyaza* (curry made of meat and onion), *khhichri, halvas* and pickles that had become a common feature of food in Indo-Muslim culture.[59] The references contained in the *Baburnama* to Indian food reveal that the dishes of roasted hare, fried carrots and dried meat were delicacies loved by foreigners. It is noteworthy that even the non-vegetarian dishes in India did not strike any similarity with those of Central Asia. Babur calls them Indian dishes.[60] In Kol and Sikandara Rao he was served various dishes at the banquets hosted by Shaikh Ghuran and Miyan Rao Sherwani respectively. He relished the food that he mentions as *Hindustani.*[61]

For the subsequent period, we find comparatively detailed information in contemporary works, both about vegetarian and non-vegetarian dishes, popular among the members of ruling elite during Sher Shah's reign. The Muslim aristocrats seem to have developed a taste for vegetarian dishes in the Indian environment and the Hindu nobles in the service of the Muslim rulers also had no hesitation in attending the feasts arranged by their fellow Muslim nobles. But separate arrangements seem to have been made by the Muslim hosts for their Hindu guests. The cereal and vegetarian dishes were cooked by Hindu cooks for them. For instance, *Masnad-i 'Ali* Khawas Khan, the premier noble of Sher Shah, is reported to have invited all the nobles along with their servants, Muslims as well as Hindus, to the banquets hosted by him on different occasions. The dishes served to the guests were different kinds of bread, *kabab* (resembling hamburger), beef tea (mentioned as *yakhni,* made of meat mixed with certain spices and saffron), roasted lamb, roasted goats (particularly *Khassi,* i.e. castrated), red and yellow mutton *shorba* (curries), chicken, partridge, fowl and various kinds of *halvas.* The Indian cereal and vegetarian dishes cooked in his kitchen are mentioned as *pakvan-i Hindi,* consisting, of *puris* (small fried round bread), vegetables, different pulses, *suhali, gulgulai, gitehndi,* curd curry, *baris, bara, pahluri, manguri* and *mangochhi.*[62]

Malik Muhammad Ja'isi, another contemporary of Sher Shah Sur, is more detailed in his description of the popular dishes among the Hindu and Muslim aristocrats of his age. The Hindu delicacies served on social occasions were: different rice preparations cooked with fragrant ingredients, *jhalars* and *mandas* (both different kinds of breads), *lechui* and *sohari* (cakes of fine flour), that were exceedingly soft and placed on the dining carpet before the cereal and vegetable dishes were brought there. Of the vegetable and cereal dishes, those mentioned are *baris, kohanduris* and different kinds of *achars* (pickles). In the end were brought the sweet dishes such as *murandas* (compounded with milk and curd), *jawari* (a dish made of butter), *puchhiawari* and certain other sweetmeats.[63]

The grandeur and success of such a function among the Muslim elite seem to have been determined by the large number of non-vegetarian delicacies that the host had for his guests. The animals and birds slaughtered for feasts have been mentioned by Jaisi as goats, lamb, black-spotted deer, swamp deer, *sambar* and hares, partridges, quails, button quails, swamp partridge, adjutant birds, painted snipe, green pigeons, jungle fowl, the comb-duck, the teal, whistling teal, etc. Besides these, different dishes of fish were also cooked. Of the various kinds of bread one attracts comparison with the modern *shirmal*. 'They rolled out,' says Ja'isi, 'thin cakes mixed with ghee and afterwards fried them and soaked them in molasses'. These cakes (*shirmal*) and *sohari* (Indian preparation) were soft and so wet that ghee dripped from them.[69]

The above discussion reveals that the Muslims generally took food rich in meat protein. This is true for the poor Muslims also because mutton, beef, chicken, geese and fowl were available in plenty and sold cheaply in the markets.[65]

The last item to be served at dinner or daily meals was the betel leaf, referred to as *bira-i tanbul* or simply *pan* by our sources. The *bira* was made of a few ingredients. First the back of the leaf was smeared with the pastes of lime and *kattha* (catechu) and then rolled. There is evidence to suggest that refined people observed a certain etiquette with regard to its chewing. The work, *Ahsan al-Aqval*, a collection of Shaikh Burhanuddin Gharib's (d.1337) utterances tells us that the guests were made to clean their hands after the meal was over. After it, the servants brought *biras* along with pieces of betel nut in trays. The urbanized guest picked up the *bira*, opened his mouth a little so as not to show the inside of his mouth to others and put it inside carefully. The pieces of betel nut were also put in the mouth one by one.[66] The odd bits of information available in certain earlier works suggest that the distribution of betel leaves among people on certain occasions seems to have acquired symbolic significance in medieval Indian culture as well be discussed later.

The Muslim emigrants in India appear to have developed a taste for betel leaf soon after their arrival. 'Imad al-Mulk, who started his career as a slave under Sultan Iltutmish and attained to the high post of *Amir-i 'Ariz* (paymaster-general of the army) under Sultan Balban, habitually chewed betel leaf at short intervals and always had it distributed among people present at his residence or in the camp.[67] Because of its high demand in the metropolitan city of Delhi, the traders supplied quality leaves from different regions stretching as far as Gujarat.[68] The reason for the popularity of betel leaf among people, poor as well as rich, was the belief that it had digestive properties served as a stimulant in laziness, arrested the decay of teeth and controlled bad breath.[69] It was generally regarded as a substitute for liquor; more or less the same qualities of *pan* were recounted by travellers from India to Shihabuddin al-Umari in Damascus, The latter writes: 'Al-Shibli related: in Delhi wine is not available either in public or in secret, because the Sultan has enforced strict prohibition and can hardly tolerate drunkards. The Indians themselves have no inclination towards it or other intoxicants.

They rather prefer to take betel leaf as a substitute for alcoholic drinks. The betel leaf is clean and free from all harmful properties. Indeed it possesses qualities which are not found in wine. For instance, it sweetens the breath, helps digestion, cheers up the spirit, strengthens the intellect and memory and is delightful in taste. Its components are these: the betel leaf, betel nut and pastes (one made of lime and the other, brown in colour and made of wood) which are prepared in a special way. Al-Shibli said: the Indians think it the most respectable way to entertain (the guest) with betel leaf. If a person entertains his guests with various kinds of eatables, *sharbats* (soft drinks), sweetmeats, perfumes and flowers and does not offer betel leaf to them, it means that he has not been a good host and the guests have not had honour done to them. Similarly, when an important man has to oblige some acquaintance, he offers him a betel leaf'.[70]

The foreign writer is corroborated by the contemporary Indo-Persian historians. For example, 'Afif informs us in his account of Sultan Firuz Shah's weekly visits to his cousin, the daughter of Sultan Ghiyasuddin Tughluq, that after customary exchange of courtesy and entertainment, the betel leaf was offered by her servant to him at the time of his departure.[71] It may also be pointed out that the lime to be used in the *bira* of the betel leaf was made of expensive ingredients. A piece of information contained in the *Malfuzat* of Shaikh Sharafuddin Yahya Maneri (d. AD 1371), reveals that lime was mixed with powder made of pearls and shells. Once the *muftis* (jurists) were asked to give their ruling whether it was lawful from the point of view of Islamic *shari'a* to take this sort of lime as it seemed to be an innovation by the Muslims.[72] Muthar of Kara adds that saffron and the essence of amber were also mixed in the paste.[73]

The *Waqi'at-i Mushtaqi* furnishes detailed information about the symbolic importance of the *bira* or betel leaf. It suggests that the acceptance of the *bira* by a person on certain occasions meant the taking of an oath of loyalty and support to the host. Once *Masnad-i-'ali* Miyan Muhammad Farmuli, known as Kala Pahar (black mountain), had to invade the territory of Bahraich sometime after 1495. He called his followers and informed them about his plan. He told them that everyone of them was free to return to his house with a *bira,* and he would regard all of them as his well-wishers even if they did not join the expedition.[74] The same writer describes with amazement that some nobles were so generous that they had the *biras* distributed among their soldiers to be chewed at the time of muster or on social occasions. At times a touch of musk was added to the betel leaf, probably in the winter.[75] The amazement seems to have been caused by the expensive preparation of *biras* in the establishment of a noble as the ingredients were costly. As regards the trays and bowls in which the *biras* were served at the palace of a noble or in the royal palace, these were made of gold and silver.[76] In short, betel chewing and *bira* making had become an art in medieval India.

As regards iced water, Babur says that there was no ice or cold water in India,[77] possibly because of the dislocation in socio-economic activities in the metropolitan cities of Delhi and Agra caused by his conquest. An earlier lexicon, compiled during the reign of Sultan Sikandar Lodi, does contradict Babur. Explaining the meaning of *barf* (ice) Mahmud bin Zia says that it falls from the clouds like rain during winter. Those who sell ice, bring it in cauldrons which bury they in the ice-places, 'Buried underground, the ice becomes hard like stone and can thus be preserved for years. They dig it out in the summer for sale in the *bazaar*. People use it in *sharbat* of rose, etc. It is very refreshing'.[78] We have evidence about the use of ice in the Sultanate of Delhi, at least since the times of Firuz Shah Tughluq.[79]

Records reveal that it had become a well-established practice by the thirteenth century to employ tasters (*chashnigirs*), cooks, bakers and utensil cleaners in large number, in the kitchen maintained both by the Sultan and the nobles.[80] These servants worked from morning till late in the night. The officer incharge of the kitchen establishment was the chief *chashnigir* whose main function was to ensure that the food for the Sultan was properly cooked and was free from any harmful effects. The chief *chashnigir* was a trusted officer who tasted every dish before it was served at the royal carpet. As he had to accompany the Sultan on his military expeditions as well, he often found the opportunity to impress his master with his courage and received an important post in the royal army as a reward. *Chashnigirs* and cooks often attained high positions in the official hierarchy. For instance, Malik Tajuddin Sanjar Kizal Khan, the slave general of Sultan Iltutmish, served as *chashnigir* in the royal kitchen before he rose to the rank of *amir-i akhur* (the officer incharge of the royal stable).[81] A cook, named Mankah, was elevated by Sultan Muhammad bin Tughluq to a high rank in the nobility.[82] An inscription belonging to the reign of Sultan Sikandar Lodi informs us that the Sultan honoured Miyan Daud *Chashnigir* with the rank of *Malik* in reward for his services. Miyan Daud seems to have been a philanthropic noble.[83]

The royal kitchen not only provided a large number of people with employment, it also generated trade in food stuffs and cattle. The information furnished by Shihabuddin al-Umari is quite interesting where it refers to the number of animals slaughtered daily for the royal kitchen. We learn that 250 cows, 200 goats and, in addition to these, fat horses and different kinds of birds were slaughtered daily.[84] In fact, the intermingling of different cultures in India caused the dishes, brought by the early Muslim immigrants from Central Asia in particular and Middle Eastern countries in general, to change considerably in their taste and flavour.

Babur adds to the information contained in the Indo-Persian works with regard to the large staff and functioning of the royal kitchen. According to him, a number of tasters were employed for their specialization in special delicacies and all of them worked under the chief *chashnigir.* He further informs us that the counterpart of the chief *chashnigir* in Central Asia was designated as *Mir Bakawal.* Babur, having relished certain Indian dishes, decided to retain some of the cooks of Sultan Ibrahim Lodi who had survived the fall of their master. He interviewed sixty of them but employed only four cooks, specialists in cooking a few particular dishes.[85] Mushtaqi also furnishes interesting information about the big kitchens maintained by the members of the ruling elite in pre-Mughal times. His account of the nobles creates the impression that the larger the kitchen a noble maintained the more generous and large-hearted he was considered by the public. One of the leading nobles of Sultan Sikandar Lodi, Miyan Gada'i Farmuli, the *Muqta* of Qanauji, had hundreds of camels to carry foodstuffs, cauldrons and cooking utensils besides the kitchen staff when he accompanied the Sultan on a military expedition.[86]

Mention should also be made of the *langars* or public kitchens maintained by the Sufi saints and other religious-minded people for the benefit of the poor, the travellers and visitors to their *khanqahs.* The evidence contained in the contemporary literature reveals that the rich people considered it an act of piety and virtue to have food cooked for distribution among the poor daily. Shaikh Nizamuddin Auliya is reported to have said that feeding the poor and the destitute had been recommended and praised in all the religions of the world. He also exhorted his followers to make no discrimination against anybody and to feed all irrespective of creed.[87] The leading Sufis maintained large public kitchens with *futuh* (unasked for offering both in cash and kind) while the rich people made endowments for their maintenance. Shaikh Mahmud al-Kuba, a Sufi saint, had every visitor to his *khanqah* served with food daily.[88] Once Shaikh Nasiruddin Chiragh of Delhi, lamenting the scarcity of essential commodities and rise in their prices during the early years of Sultan Firuz Shah's reign, mentioned the big *langars* run by the religious people in Delhi and its suburbs during the reign of Sultan 'Ala ud'din Khalji. Most important of these were the *langars* of Ramazan Qalandar and Malik Yar Paran.[89] In his account of the mother of Sultan Muhammad bin Tughluq; Ibn Battuta informs us that she (*Makhduma-i Jahan*) was 'one of the most virtuous of women and munificent in charity, and has founded many hospices and endowed them to supply food to all travelers'.[90] The later sources show that people devoted to religion and piety established *langars* in charity for the benefit of poor people, travellers and students during the Lodi periods also.[91]

Equally important is the discussion of the flourishing catering profession in the urban centres, cities and towns. The references to the restaurants (*dukanan-i tabbakhan*) and bakeries tend to suggest that this profession must have absorbed a sizeable number of people in medieval India since the thirteenth century.[92] Likewise, the butchers also set up their shops along with the caterers in every shopping centre of Delhi in particular and the bazaars of other cities and towns in general. In the restaurants and bakeries people seem to have bought expensive dishes, including the full roasted kid or chicken.[93] Amir Khusrau writes about the availability of eatables in the bazaars of Delhi, 'Ripe fruits-cooked snakes and dishes of food, essential for the public are available in plenty in the shops and streets, and connected shopping squares'.[94] With the expansion of cities and towns in subsequent periods, the number and the activities of the caterers seem to have increased everywhere. Like other men of means, the caterers lived comfortably and owned slaves to work in their shops.[95] In cities, the caterers, though considered by the elite as socially belonging to the lower strata of Muslim society, seem to have emulated the ways of middle class Muslims.[96] It deserves mention that shops were also set up by caterers, bakers and butchers along the highways through which merchant caravans passed.[97] At times a small town also attracted caterers and others if there was a Sufi saint of eminence among its residents or if it contained the tomb of such a saint for, people came there in large numbers to visit the saint or offer prayer and make vows at his grave. For example, Shaikh Badi'uddin known as Shah Madar (a leading fifteenth century saint) settled down in Makanpur, a small dependency of the territorial unit of Qanauj, and soon people turned to it in crowds to seek his blessings. The caterers also came and set up their shops. Even rich people among the visitors bought food from these shops.[98]

There is little evidence available on the influence of the dietary habits of the Muslim elite on agriculture, trade, internal as well as external, and the growth of indigenous crafts. Efforts seem to have been made from time to time towards growing plants, fruit trees, flowers and medicinal herbs from Central Asia and the region now included in modern Afghanistan, in the royal gardens around Delhi and other metropolitan cities. Our sources create the impression that the immigrants in India continued to get the seeds of delicious fruits from time to time and were successful in farming certain types of grapes, good quality pomegrantes, dates and melons.[99] Likewise, many medicinal herbs used in the Muslim system of medicine (*tibb*) were also introduced.[100] A few of these herbs, such as aniseed, were used in cooking certain dishes or for flavouring them. Moreover, the peasants took interest in raising the crops of quality rice in certain regions as this was in demand for the kitchens of the Sultan and his grandees. Ja'isi mentions the names of various kinds of fine-flavoured rice, *basmati, kajari, ratnari, madhukar, dhela,* etc., but he does not say anything about the regions which produced them.[101] Abu'l Fazl, however, provides us with a comprehensive list of the territories which were known for the production of different kinds of expensive rice and other commodities in demand for the royal kitchen.[102] In fact, the *banjaras,* dealers in food grains, supplied them to the metropolitan cities from different territories from early times upto the Mughal period.

Similarly, the kitchen-generated trade not only led to the modification and development of certain indigenous crafts but also promoted the import of dry fruits, expensive nuts, saffron, different kinds of herbs and spices that were needed in the preparation of non-vegetarian dishes. Besides, green fruits and Chinese wares were also in great demand. The consumption of delicious fruits by the rich people encouraged the traders to supply them from foreign regions as far as Bukhara. The odd bits of evidence pieced together from different sources indicate that even in the thirteenth century one could buy fresh fruits in Delhi imported from the countries of Central and West Asia. Amir Khusrau is not exaggerating when he states with a sense of pride that not only were the fruits grown in India and Khurasan available in Delhi, but also those that no one could have ever seen in Khurasan (the land known for its delicious fruits).[103] Ibn Battuta adds that the sweetest melon was grown in Khwarizm and since the fruit could not be brought to India fresh owing to the long distance, it was cut into strips, dried in the sun and then packed in baskets for export to India. Ibn Battuta further informs us that fruits imported from Khurasan were regarded as great luxuries in India and rich people bought these at quite a high price.[104] We find, 'the couriers put them on (woven baskets like) plates and carry them with great speed to the Sultan'.[105] The yellow plums, fresh melon, grapes of different varieties, dry fruits, such as almonds, pistachios and raisins, were supplied by the merchants from Bukhara, parts of modern Afghanistan and Iran to India. Shihabuddin al-'Umari supplements the information available in the work of Ibn Battuta in this respect, 'People of Bukhara come (to India) with yellow melons, which are available there (in Bukhara) till the winter. They present them to the Sultan who bestows considerable gifts upon them. I am acquainted with a person who started with two camel loads of melons for the Sultan. But the greater part of them went bad on the way, only twenty-two melons were found in a presentable condition. The Sultan rewarded that man with three thousand *mithqals* of gold'.[106] Sultan Muhammad bin Tughluq used to distribute fruits supplied to him by merchants from foreign countries among his favourites.[107]

Another important item in demand and connected with the kitchen establishment was the porcelain chinawares. We do find a brief reference to chinawares in the Indo-Persian sources. In his account of Sultan 'Alu ud'din Khalji, Barani mentions the flasks made in China as *Batakhha-i-Chini* (Chinese flasks resembling ducks).[108] Isami refers to the visits of the Chinese merchants to Delhi since the reign of Sultan Iltutmish. They supplied Chinese products along with slaves, trained in different and arts crafts.[109] In *Waqi'at-i-Mushtaqi* we find evidence about the profuse use of Chinese wares, especially trays, bowls and plates, at the establishments of the nobles during the Lodi and the Sur periods.[110] The archaeological finds in Delhi, belonging to the fifteenth century, corroborate Mushtaqi in this regard.[111]

Like the foreign trade in Chinese wares, the indigenous craft of making cups, vases, goblets, and platters of gold, silver and precious stones also received impetus during the Delhi Sultanate period. The sultans, nobles and other rich people were served drinks and betel leaves as well as food in gold or silver wares besides the chinaware.[112] Consequently, the trade in these articles increased considerably; their possession was regarded a sign of aristocratic living. According to Muthar of Kara, beautiful vases, called *bargdan* (bowls for betel leaves), were made of gold and silver.[113] It is worth recalling that of the great Sultans of Delhi only Firuz Shah is said to have prohibited the use of gold and silver wares at the royal dining carpet out of respect for the Islamic Shariat (religious law) which does not allow it. 'Afif tells us that their use was prohibited and food and drinks were served in the palace in porcelain or stone crockery instead.[114]

The industry of metal and stone wares developed so much that the Indian products seem to have acquired world-wide fame during the fourteenth and fifteenth centuries. They were considered niceties the possession of which could be coveted by aristocrats outside India. The relevant piece of evidence available in *Masir-i Mahmud Shahi* reveals that in the year AD 1467 Sultan Mahmud Khalji of Malwa sent to Abu Said, the ruler of Herat, in response to his request, besides elephants, silk fabrics, gold and silver vases, the vessels and jars made of precious stones: one *jam* (goblet) of cornolian, a large spoon of ruby (of brilliant luster), a bowl of agate, cups of other precious stones, a tray of turquoise and an ewer, all of them the *'amal* (work) of Indian craftsmen.[115]

In the final analysis it may be said that a study of the royal banquets, food habits of the ruling elite, and the catering profession in pre-Mughal India helps us in understanding the cultural interaction between the Muslim immigrants from Central Asian lands, in particular, and other Muslim countries, in general, and the Hindu aristocracy. The introduction of new dishes, combining the Indian and Muslim ways of cooking food, and the foreign trade in fruits and other commodities certainly led to diversity in our national culture. The royal as well as public and private kitchens provided job opportunities to a large number of people in urban centres. The patronage extended by the rulers and nobles to expert cooks made cooking a highly specialized art. The origin of catering shops where people took their lunch or dinner or bought cooked food for consumption at home may be traced to the Delhi Sultanate period from the thirteenth century onwards. Most of the popular dishes in Indo-Muslim culture, introduced during the times of the Sultans of Delhi, have survived through the Mughal period upto modern times. Moreover, Indian cuisine, popular in European and American countries, consists generally of non-vegetarian preparations introduced by the Muslims in medieval times. The profession of decorators as well as the craft of manufacturing utensils and perfumes also flourished as a result of the banquets hosted by members of royalty and aristocracy.

Endnotes

1. S.M. Jaffar and Kunwar Muhammad Ashraf have made general remarks about food and table manners in their works. None of them, however, could study the socio-economic aspect of food in medieval Indian culture. Similarly the kitchen and the state of catering profession also do not find mention in their respective works. Cf. S.M. Jaffar, *Some Cultural Aspects of Muslim Rule in India*, 2nd edition, Peshawar: Muhammad Sadiq Khan, 1950, pp. 182-3; See also

K.M. Ashraf, *Life and Conditions of the People of Hindustan,* rpt, New Delhi: Munshiram Manoharlal, 1970, pp. 218-19.

2. Taj Raza says: 'There is rejoicing and festivity in the city, for they have brought a special robe from the Amir al-Mu'minin for the king'. Cf. Agha Abdul Sattar Khan, 'Sultan Iltutmish ke Daur men 'Ilmi-o-Adabi Tahrikat,' Lahore: *Oriental College Magazine* (Urdu), May 1939, p. 26.
3. *Tabaqat-i Nasiri,* tr. Major Raverty, vol. 2, Calcutta, 1897, p. 857.
4. Zia'uddin Barani, *Tarikh-i Firuz Shahi,* Calcutta: Bibliotheca Indica, 1862, p. 32, hereafter cited as 'Barani'.
5. Barani, *Tarikh-i-Firuz Shahi,* p. 46.
6. Khusrau, *Dibacha-i Ghurrat al-Kamal,* MS. British Museum Library, London, Add. 21, 104, ff. 177a-178a.
7. Barani, *Tarikh-i-Firuz Shahi,* p. 114.
8. Ibid., p. 199.
9. Ibn Battuta, *The Travels of Ibn Battuta,* tr. Hamilton Gibb, Cambridge University Press, 1971, vol. 3, pp. 666-7. (Hereafter cited as '*The Travels of Ibn Battuta.*)
10. The references to the use of perfumes in purifying the air show that besides '*itr* (scents), aloe wood and amber were burnt. The early sixteenth century work *Kitab Ni'matnama-i Nāsir Shahi* describes the preparation method for *chuva,* a fragrant paste of four ingredients. Mushtaqi also states that Miyan Walid, a petty official during the Lodi period, supplemented his income by manufacturing perfumes and the *chuva* produced by him was regarded of excellent quality. The whole locality was filled with its fragrance when it was produced. Anonymous, *Kitab-i-Ni'matnama-i Násir Shahi*, MS. India Office Library, no 2775; Rizq ullah Mushtaqi, *Waqi'at-i Mushtaqi,* tr. Iqtidar Husain Siddiqui, New Delhi: ICHR, 1993, p. 273, Hereafter cited as *Waqi'at-i-Mushtaqi.*
11. Anonymous, *Sirat-i Firuz Shahi,* MS, Patna: Khuda Bakhsh Oriental Public Library, ff. 106b, 120a, 123b; *Diwan of Muthar of Kara*, Lahore: *Oriental College Magazine,* May, 1935, vol. 2, no. 3, p. 132; Shams Siraj 'Afif, *Tarikh-i Firuz Shahi,* Calcutta: Bibliotheca Indica, 1891, pp. 278, 365-6 (hereafter cited as 'Afif').
12. 'Afif, *Tarikh-i Firuz Shahi,* p. 365.

13. Amir Khusrau, *Masnavi Qiran us-S'adain,* Aligarh College Institute, 1918, pp. 73-86.
14. *Waqi'at-i Mushtaqi,* op.cit., p. 119.
15. 'Afif, *Tarikh-i Firuz Shahi,* p. 278.
16. Sijzi, *Fawaid ul-Fuad,* p. 134.
17. Amir Khusrau, *Deval Rani Khizr Khan,* Aligarh, 1917, pp. 152-72.
18. *The Travels of Ibn Battuta,* vol. 3, pp. 686-7.
19. Ali bin Mahmud al-Kirmani, known Shihab Hakim, *Ma'sir-i-Mahmud Shahi,* ed. Nurul Hasan Ansari, Delhi: Indo-Persian Society, 1968, pp. 50-2.
20. Anonymous, *Tarikh-i Muzaffar Shahi,* Unpublished manuscript MS, British Museum Library, London, Add. 262, 70, ff. 45b-50b.
21. *Waq'at-i Mushtaqi,* 1993, p. 74-5, 79, 84, 118-20.
22. Ibid., pp. 74-5.
23. 'Abbas Sarwani, *Tuhfa-i Akbar Shahi,* known as *Tarikh-i Sher Shahi,* ed. Imam al-Din, Dacca: University Publication, 1964, p. 98.
24. *Waqi'at-i-Mushtaqi,* 1993, tr., p. 91.
25. Ibid., pp. 198-9.
26. Ibid., p. 119.
27. Shaikh Jamali, *Mathnavi-i Mahr-wa-Mah,* ed. Husamuddin Rashidi, Karachi: Institute of Central and West Asian Studies, 1974, pp. 155-6.
28. *Waqi'at-i Mushtaqi,* 1993, p. 79.
29. Ni'matullah Haravi, *Tarikh-i Khan-i Jahani,* ed. Imam al-Din, Dhaka, 1960, vol. 1, pp. 339-40, 42.
30. *Waqi'at-i Mushtaqi* 1993, pp. 160-1.
31. *The Travels of Ibn Battuta,* vol. 3, p. 608.
32. Hammad bin 'Imad Kashani, *Ahsan al-Aqval,* (Unpublished manuscript) MS, University Collection, Maulana Azad Library, Aligarh *tasawwuf,* no. 318, f. 16a.
33. Ibid., f. 19b.
34. Ibid., f. 20a.
35. Amir Khusrau, *Qiran us-S'adain,* Aligarh, 1918, pp. 183-5.

36. Amir Khusrau, *I'jaz-i Khusravi,* vol. 4, tr. Iqtidar Husain Siddiqui, Illinois, USA: The Islamic Thought and Science Institute, 2007 pp. 158 & 165.
37. Sijzi, *Fawa'id ul-Fuad,* op.cit., p. 189.
38. Anonymous, *Surur al-Sudur,* MS, Habib Ganj collection, Maulana Azad Library, Aligarh, p. 48 (folios are not marked).
39. Barani, *Tarikh-i-Firuz Shahi,* 1962, pp. 116-17.
40. Siddiqui, *Perso-Arabic Sources of Information on the Life and Conditions in the Sultanate of Delhi,* New Delhi: Munshiram Manoharlal, 1992, p. 115.
41. Ibn Battuta, Travels of Ibn Battuta, vol. 3, pp. 607-8.
42. Ibid., pp. 670-1.
43. Ibid., pp. 680-1.
44. Ibid., pp. 611-12. *Khhichri* is an Indian dish. It is cooked with rice and pulses mixed and eaten by all Indians.
45. Siddiqui, *Perso-Arabic Sources of Information,* op.cit., p. 120.
46. Hamid Qalandar, *Khair al-Majalis,* ed. K.A. Nizami, Aligarh, Department of History, The Aligarh High University, 1959, pp. 10-11.
47. Loc. cit.
48. Ibid., pp. 19-20.
49. Ibid., pp. 186-7.
50. Ibid., p. 187.
51. Muhammad Akbar Husaini, *Javami al-Kalam,* (*Malfuzat* of Shaikh Gesudaraz) Kanpur: Matba Intizami, A.H. 1356, p. 341.
52. Ibid., p. 186.
53. Ibid., p. 216.
54. Muthar, *Diwan-i-Muthar,* Lahore: May, 1935, vol. 2, no. 3, pp. 136-8.
55. *Kitab-i Ni'matnama-i Nāsir Shahi,* rare MS, India Office Library, London, f. 3a-b.
56. *Waqi'at-i Mushtaqi,* tr. op.cit. 1993, pp. 63-4.
57. Ibid., pp. 74-5, 83, 87.
58. Ibid., pp. 97, 99, 163.

59. Ibid., pp. 70-1, 75, 87.
60. *Baburnama*, tr. Mrs A. Beveridge, rpt, New Delhi 1975, vol. 2, p. 54.
61. Ibid., pp. 587-8.
62. *Waqi'at-i Mushtaqi*, pp. 160-5.
63. *Padmavat*, tr. A.G. Shirreff, Calcutta: The Royal Asiatic Society of Bengal, 1944, p. 174.
64. Ibid., pp. 312-13.
65. Siddiqui, *Perso-Arabic Sources of Information*, pp. 114-15.
66. *Ahsan al-Aqval*, op.cit., f. 20a.
67. Khusrau, *Dibacha-i Ghurrat al-Kamal*, op. cit., f. 177a.
68. Khusrau, *I'jaz-i Khusravi*, Kanpur: Nawal Kishore, vol. 3, pp. 249-51.
69. Khusrau, *Qiran al-Sadain*, p. 186.
70. Siddiqui, *Perso-Arabic Sources of Information*, p. 131.
71. 'Afif, *Tarikh-i-Firuz Shahi*, pp. 101-2.
72. Zain Badr 'Arabi, *Khan-i-Pur Ni'mat*, Patna, AH, 1321, p. 41.
73. 'Muthar's poem', *Oriental College Magazine*, op.cit., p. 138.
74. *Waqi'at-i Mushtaqi*, tr., op.cit., pp. 99-100.
75. Ibid., p. 86.
76. 'Muthar's *Diwan*, op.cit., p. 138.
77. *Baburnama*, vol. 2, p. 518.
78. *Tuhfat al-Sa'adat*, also known as *Farhang-i Sikandari*, MS, Raza Library, Rampur, no. 2483, ff. 50b-51a.
79. Ashraf, *Life and Conditions of the People of Hindustan*, pp. 218-19.
80. Ibn Battuta incidentally mentions the large number of cooks, bakers, roasters, pastry cooks, butlers and betel servers all of whom belonged to the staff of the royal kitchen. Cf. *The Travels of Ibn Battuta*, vol. 3, pp. 686-7.
81. *Tabaqat-i Nasiri*, vol. 2, op.cit., pp. 3-4.
82. Barani, *Tarikh-i-Firuz Shahi*, pp. 505-6.
83. *Epigraphia Indica, Arabic and Persian Supplement*, ed. Z.A. Desai, (Epigraphical Survey of India) EI, Calcutta, 1968, p. 37.

84. Siddiqui, *Perso-Arabic Sources of Information,* p. 120.
85. *Baburnama,* vol. 2, p. 541.
86. *Waqi'at-i Mushtaqi,* tr. 1993, p. 87.
87. *Fawaid ul-Fuad,* 1966, pp. 21, 28, 63.
88. *The Travels of Ibn Battuta,* vol. 3, p. 626.
89. Qalandar, *Khair al-Majalis,* op.cit., p. 185.
90. *The Travels of Ibn Battuta,* vol. 3, p. 736.
91. Miyan Bhu'a, the *Wazir* of Sultan Sikandar Lodi, is said to have endowed money for a *langar* attached to the mosque built by him. Cf. Shaikh 'Abd al-Quddus Gangohi, *Maktubat Quddusi,* Delhi: Ahmadi Press, AH, 1287, letter no. 62. pp. 49-51.
92. Sijzi, *Fawaid ul-Fuad,* op.cit., p. 112.
93. Hamid Qalandar, *Khair al-Majalis,* op.cit., pp. 51, 226.
94. Khusrau, *I'jaz-i-Khusravi,* op.cit., tr. vol. 4, p. 171.
95. *Javami' al-Kilam,* p. 176.
96. *Waqi'at-i Mushtaqi,* op.cit., p. 284.
97. Ibid., p. 17.
98. 'Abdul Qadir Badaoni, *Najat ur-Rashid,* ed. Syed Moinul-Haque, Lahore: Idara-i-Tahqiqat-i-Pakistan, Danishgah-i-Punjab, 1972, pp. 147-8.
99. Both Zia'uddin Barani and Ibn Battuta refer to the availability of delicious melons grown in and around Delhi; the difference between the flavour and taste of the Delhi and Khurasan melons was not much yet the former was smaller in size. The evidence contained in the later sources tends to show that their quality deteriorated after a few years. The supply of the seeds from Khurasan might have been maintained. According to Mushtaqi, the trees of pomegranates became naturalized and bore fruits comparable to those imported from Khurasan or Afghanistan. See Barani, pp. 222-7; *The Travels of Ibn Battuta,* vol. 3, 1971, p. 624; Anonymous, *Sirat-i Firuz Shahi,* MS, Patna: Khuda Bakhsh Library, ff. 80a-82b, for the royal gardens and orchards; Also see *Baburnama,* vol. 2, 1975, pp. 532-3; *Waqi'at-i Mushtaqi,* 1993 ff. 93b-94a; *Tarikh-i Daudi,* Aligarh, 1969, p. 76.
100. *Sirat-i Firuz Shahi,* 81a-82a.

101. *Padmavat,* op.cit., 1944, pp. 174-312.
102. *Ain-i Akbari,* tr. H. Blochmann, New Delhi: Oriental Books, 1977, rpt, vol. 1, pp. 59-60.
103. Khusrau, *Qiran us-Sadain,* p. 34.
104. *The Travels of Ibn Battuta,* vol. 3, p. 547.
105. Ibid., vol. 3, pp. 594-5.
106. Siddiqui, *Perso-Arabic Sources of Information,* p. 125.
107. *The Travels of Ibn Battuta,* vol. 3, p. 547; *Khair al-Majalis,* p. 220, for pomegranates.
108. Barani, p. 485.
109. Isami, pp. 144, 550.
110. *Waqi'at-i Mushtaqi,* pp. 87, 126.
111. The porcelain pieces excavated at the Purana Qila (Old Fort) in Delhi bear inscription of the Ming dynasty, especially Cheng Hua era (1465-87). They are available in the Museum at the Old Fort.
112. Barani, *Tarikh-i Firuz Shahi,* p. 32; *The Travels of Ibn Battuta,* vol. 3, p. 608.
113. Muthar's *Diwan,* op.cit., p. 138.
114. 'Afif, *Tarikh-i Firuz Shahi,* p. 374.
115. *Ma'sir-i Mahmud Shahi,* MS., ff. 169b-170a, printed text, pp. 128-9.

CHAPTER 5

Pyrotechnics and the Growth of Firearms

The study of the history of pyrotechnics is important so far as it led to the production of gunpowder weapons that resulted in changes and innovations in war technology, military tactics and strategy, affecting both society and economy. The technique of gun-casting and producing gunpowder introduced new crafts as well as provided the traders with incentive to trade in the essential constituents of gunpowder, such as saltpetre, sulphur, charcoal, etc. Since India was rich in all the constituents, Indians faced no difficulty in producing gunpowder. With the proliferation of gunpowder weapons, India became a main exporter, at least of saltpetre to Europe.[1] In this chapter an attempt is made first to analyse the evidence available in medieval sources about the beginnings of gunpowder use and then the introduction of artillery and its technology in India during medieval times.

Information about gunpowder reveals that it was first used in the production of pyrotechnics from the last decades of the thirteenth century. We come across references to fireworks in a *qasida*, composed by Amir Khusrau in praise of Sultan Jalal u'ddin Firuz Shah Khalji (AD 1290-6). On each festive occasion a display was made of fireworks that appear to have become part of royal celebration. Of the fireworks mentioned by the poet in the *qasida*, *hawa'i* (missile) and *fatila-i-gardan* (stone-shaped toy) are important because the gunpowder was used as the main ingredient in their making.[2]

The reference to the *hawa'i* in the couplet is interesting because, when it was ignited, it flew into the air and burst with noise scattering fire flowers. As for the *fatila-i-gardan* (stone-shaped toy), it turned round while burning. In his *I'jaz-i-Khusravi* also, Amir Khusrau refers to fireworks in connection with the celebration of *shab-i-barat,* the night of 15th *Shaban* of the Islamic calendar, basically meant for the Muslims to offer supererogatory prayers till the dawn. Influenced by the Hindu festival of Diwali, the Muslims turned *shab-i-barat* into a festival of lights. As the Hindu temples were illuminated at the night of Diwali festival, the mosques began to be illuminated on the occasion of *shab-i-barat.* Amir Khusrau's description is worth quoting:

> Everyone is fetching lamps to the mosque in accordance with his means. But this humble servant (Khusrau himself) wishes to light his house with the lamp of *namaz* (prayer).[3] because such darkness prevails in his heart that no lamp can dispel it. He wishes that his house too is lit up by the lamp of prayer tonight, as its darkness cannot be removed otherwise by any means.

Khusrau has also mentioned the display of fireworks by the children in connection with the celebration of *shab-i-barat,* saying 'Little children, who shall be the inhabitants of paradise and whom the fire of hell can never touch, are playing with fireworks, thinking that it is fair on their part to do so. With the fireplay the entire town has transformed into the garden of Ibrahim'.[4]

By the time of Sultan Firuz Shah (1351-88), the use of fireworks seems to have become widespread in the Sultanate. On the occasion of *shab-i-barat,* besides the mosques, the royal buildings in the capital of Firuzabad were illuminated with innumerable lamps and candlelight. Besides four sites were fixed on the wall of the *kushak-i-nuzul* (palace of alighting) for such illumination that turned the night into day. The display of fireworks was done each night from the thirteenth to the fifteenth Shaban. The Sultan used to come out, in order to enjoy the display of pyrotechnics. He had the *tir-i-atishin* (fire arrows) shot that burst into the air splitting flowers (of fire). It became a three-night entertaining festival and people came from far and near to enjoy the scene.[5]

In the *malfuzat* of Shaikh Jalal uddin Bukhari, the leading Suhrawardi sufi, popularly known as *Jahanian-i-Jahangasht* (globetrotter), we find that the Islamic orthodoxy was opposed to the display of pyrotechnics and condemned it as nothing short of sinful innovation. The Shaikh was asked by a *murid* (disciple) about the legality of the display of fireworks from the religious point of view. The Shaikh is reported to have remarked in reply that bursting *turaq* (crackers) or igniting *mushang* (toy mice filled with gunpowder) or shooting *hawa'i* (toy missile) in the air was all sinful. There is also a reference to the *tir-i-atshin* calling it the practice of *Nimrud* (symbolically known as tyrant and the enemy of God).[6] Though pyrotechnics is opposed here, such evidence leaves no doubt about the availability of gunpowder.

Equally interesting is the corroborative evidence about pyrotechnics available in the Central Asian sources, compiled since the time of Amir Timur. Mention made by the Timurid historians of *atish bazi* (pyrotechnics) used by the Indians, reveals that it was still not an effective war weapon that could do considerable damage to the enemy.[7]

Likewise, the relevant evidence contained in the *Maasir-i-Mahmud Shahi,* the fifteenth century official history of the Malwa Sultans tends to suggest that by this time considerable progress had been made in pyrotechny. A class of professionals, called *atishbazan* (fire work makers) had come into existence and its members catered to the need of the Sultan and his nobles by providing fireworks of different kinds. In the details of the festivities, arranged for twenty-two days in connection with the marriage ceremony of the son of Sultan Mahmud Khalji I in AH 846 (AD 1442) Shihab Hakim, the compiler states that when it grew dark in the evening the *atishbazan* fired arrows in the air and when they burst, the fire-splitting wheels were scattered with contrived images of giraffe, elephant, tiger, etc., they also danced in the air.[8] We also find evidence in the same work about the use of *tir-i-antishin* (fire arrows) and *tir-i-ra'd* (thunder arrows) in warfare. Sultan Mahmud Khalji I is reported to have employed experts to manufacture *tir-i-ra'd* and used them in capturing the forts considered impregnable.[9] These arrows seem to have been pipes or balls filled with gun powder and shot through an iron pipe as the *atishbazan* do even today.

By the fifteenth century gunpowder seems to have been used all over India in the form of pyrotechny. The rulers of Bengal are reported to have used fire-arrows as a war weapon as well. Babur in his account of his campaigns in East India during the year 1528-9 informs us, 'Bengalis have a reputation for *atishbazi* (fire-shooting); we tested it now, they do not fire counting to hit a particular spot, but fire at random'.[10]

As for the introduction of firearms, such as cannons and matchlocks, in India, there seems to have been resistance to any change in conventional war technology. Changes came following Babur's invasion and the first battle of Panipat in AD 1526. Babur recognized the importance of artillery after the defeat of Shah Ismail Safavid of Iran by the Ottoman Sultan Salim in the battle of Calderan in AD 1514.

The view that the existence of close cultural and trade relations between India and the countries of Middle East led to the introduction of artillery in the Deccan and Gujarat during the fifteenth century is not supported by authentic historical sources. It is believed however that the Ottoman Turks used cannons in battles since AD 1389, while other Muslim countries lagged behind the Ottoman Empire in possessing artillery till the close of the fifteenth century. Even the Mamluk rulers of Egypt and Syria do not seem to have acquired artillery pieces during the first half of the fifteenth century. Although they possessed certain type of firearms which could hardly have had any significant impact on the outcome of their battles.[11] Indo-Persian and Portuguese sources support this view. For instance, the Mamluk Sultan of Egypt entered an alliance with Sultan Mahmud Begada of Gujarat and then directed the governor of Jedda Amir Hussain in AD 1597 to lead a naval expedition and destroy the Portuguese power in the Indian Ocean. On Amir Husain's arrival in the Arabian Sea, Malik Aiyaz, the Gujarati governor of Diu and Mustafabad territorial units joined him to battle the Portuguese. The Portuguese were defeated with heavy losses both in man and material in AD 1508. The Portuguese commander who was the son of Francisco Dalmeida, the Portuguese Viceroy in India, was drowned while many Portuguese soldiers who survived were made prisoners. In reward for this grand victory achieved on the Portuguese navy, Amir Hussain was accorded a reception at Sultan Mahmud Begada's Darbar and showered upon with royal favours.[12]

In an attempt to retrieve his nation's prestige, the Portuguese Viceroy in Cochin decided to lead a naval expedition in person, and defeated the combined naval fleet of Egypt and Gujarat. Sultan Mahmud Begada was forced to make peace with the Portuguese, although the Sultan of Gujarat was powerful enough to defend his territory on land. Peace was, however, concluded between him and the Portuguese also through the intervention of the Gujarati Hindu *Wazir*, Gopi.[13] It is clear that in their details neither the compiler of the *Zamima-i-Ma'asir-i-Mahmud Shahi* (an official history of Gujarat) nor the Portuguese sources make any mention of the use of artillery or firearms in the above-mentioned battles. As a matter of fact, it was only after the defeats of the overwhelming armies of Sultan Ibrahim Lodi in the first battle of Panipat in AD 1526 and Rana Sanga in the battle of Khanwa in AD 1527 by Babur that the Indian rulers felt pressured to acquire the services of the Ottoman craftsmen to have cannons and matchlocks cast for their defence.

As for Babur, recognizing the importance of artillery following the battle of Calderan in 1514 AD, though lacking resources, Babur employed the Ottoman craftsmen Mustafa Rumi and Ustad Ali Quli to cast field pieces and matchlocks for him. Though he could not afford to have more than a small number of cannons and a few hundred matchlockmen, Babur defeated large and powerful Indian armies with the help of limited firearms,[14] forcing the Indian rulers to recognize the role of artillery for their defence.

Of the Indian rulers, Sultan Bahadur Shah of Gujarat and Sher Shah Sur seem to have been the first in having built artillery and adopted Ottoman mode of warfare. Sultan Bahadur Shah employed an emigrant from the Ottoman Empire, conferred upon him the title of Rumi Khan and also entrusted him with the governorship of the territorial units of Mahim and Diu. Rumi Khan helped the Sultan in possessing such a powerful park of artillery that he could defeat the Portuguese in the Arabian Sea and keep Humayun in fear of his aggression against him. Mut'i, the court poet of Sultan Bahadur Shah, does not exaggerate the facts when he describes in his historical *mathnavi, Gunj-i-Ma'ani* the destructive potentiality of the gigantic mortars and cannons possessed by his royal patron. The *Gunj-i-Ma'ani* also provides us with interesting information about Bahadur Shah's victory over the Portuguese at Diu, the seaport and island. Muti'i also mentions the names of the cannons in the details of the battle fought against the Portuguese. He praises a large cannon in these words, '*Ra'd-i-Bahadur-Shahi* (a large cannon, named after the king), your fortune caught hold of auspiciousness so that it might destroy the *Firang* (i.e. Portuguese)'. At another place, while mentioning other cannons, named Laila and Majnun, imported from the Ottoman Empire, he says that the Portuguese were intent upon taking possession of the island of Diu and were planning day and night to achieve their end for quite some time. Ultimately, once they attacked the island in large number, in ships, Majnun belched out fire which kindled flames in the ranks of the enemy, and so much fire enveloped the boats and ships that it appeared as if water and fire had mixed together; the Portuguese were defeated, some having died and the rest put to death.[15] Moreover, the large field pieces are described as having been cast in different shapes, such as that of a dragon. Laila was the name given to the cannon originally cast by Amir Salman Reis (an Ottoman craftsman). Another Ottoman craftsman, Mustafa is credited with having cast the cannon called Majnun.[16]

Like Sultan Bahadur Shah of Gujarat, Sher Shah Sur the leader of the Afghans who liberated India from the Timurid ruler Humayun in AD 1540, and laid down the foundation of the Sur empire, acquired artillery pieces for the defence of the Chunar fort even before his rise to sovereign status in AD 1540. He was able to employ skilled Ottoman craftsmen to build a strong arsenal of artillery for the defence as well as expansion of his arms. A few cannons discovered in Bengal with inscriptions on them show that Sher

Shah Sur acquired the services of the Ottoman craftsmen well acquainted with the technology of casting. They cast cannons of bronze which were less subject to corrosion. Being muzzle-loaders they were also stronger and safer. Further, they could take more gun powder for the calibre shot and greater penetration in consequence. One of Sher Shah's cannons found in Malda (West Bengal) is made of bronze and measures 4 feet 5 inches in length and weighs 132 pounds. The muzzle is shaped like a tiger's head, and there are two small trunnions in the middle. According to the inscription, this cannon was cast in Gaur in 1541-2 by Saiyid Ahmad Rumi, an emigrant from Ottoman Turkey. Similarly, two other cannons found in the same province were also field pieces and cast under the supervision of Saiyid Ahmad Rumi who seems to have been entrusted with the charge of the *top-khana* (arsenal) in Bengal as the inscription contains the name of Janatabad (Gaur) as the place of casting.[17]

Malik Muhammad Jaisi, Sher Shah's contemporary poet furnishes a graphic description of the artillery used by Sher Shah on the battle field in his celebrated Hindi poem, *Padmavat.* Writing during Sher Shah's time, he says, 'The guns advanced, cannon balls in their mouths, and as they came advancing the whole earth quaked. They were fixed on wheels ... the gun carriages shone, all plated, with-gold-upon these the enormous cannons were placed: they were made of all the light metals, cast in moulds. These cannons swallow one hundred mounds of the powder, which is their wine, at a time: where they strike, mountains are broken up. They lie upon their carriages drunk (with this wine), but they rise up and stand among their enemies'.[18]

The artillery placed by Sher Shah in important forts in every territory was so large that upon the breakup of the Empire after Islam Shah Sur's death in AD 1553 Hemu was never short of guns. On the occupation of Delhi by Humayun in AD 1555, Hemu, the commander of 'Ādil Shah Sur's army, moved from Chunar with a artillery. He defeated Tardi Beg who held Delhi after Humayun's death in AD 1555. Hemu occupied Delhi in January 1556. The Mughals were driven away to the Punjab where Bairam Khan had declared Akbar as Humayun's successor to the throne.[19]

As for the second battle of Panipat fought fiercely between the Mughals and Hemu on 5 November 1556, the rival armies suffered heavy losses but without the use of gun fire. Hemu's strong artillery that was dispatched from Delhi in advance under the weak guard, commanded by Mubarak Khan and Bahadur Khan was overwhelmed by the Mughals who destroyed the guard and captured the entire artillery. Probably, the Afghan guard set on fire the gun powder, rendering the field pieces unfit for use. That is why no gun shot is reported to have been fired in this battle.[20]

To conclude, the introduction and proliferation of Ottoman firearms in India also had significant economic and social consequences. With this development, a new system of fortification had to be evolved against gunfire or bombardment. The old forts and the openings in the existing fortifications had to be strengthened with new additions and alterations so that heavy mortars could be set up thereupon for defence purpose. The gunpowder factories and cannon foundries were raised to meet the demand of artillery. As all this involved huge expenditure, only very resourceful rulers were able to keep pace with this development. However, the rising demand for the components of gunpowder, such as saltpetre and sulphur led to the enrichment of certain petty businessmen, enabling them to rise socially. For example, Hemu, the hero of twenty-two victories, is reported to have dealt in the trade of saltpetre before he entered state service during Sher Shah Sur's reign.

Endnotes

1. Cf. K.N. Chaudhuri, *The Trading World of Asia and the English East India Company,* 1660-1760, Cambridge: Cambridge University Press 1978, pp. 337-8.
2. Cf. Khusrau's *qasida*, edited and cited by Mahmud Khan Shirani, in *Maqalat-i-Hafiz Mahmud Shirani* vol. 7, ed. Mazhar Mahmud Shirani, Lahore: Majlis-i-Taraqi-i-Adab, 1976, pp. 290-1.
3. Amir Khusrau being an orthodox Muslim was opposed to the adoption of innovations.
4. The allusion is to conflagration of fire into which the Prophet Abraham was thrown by the order of Nimrud (the ruler) which was miraculously turned into a garden. Cf. *I'jaz-i-Khusravi,* vol. 4, op.cit., tr. pp. 270-1; also Persian Text, p. 324-5.
5. Shams Siraj 'Afif, *Tarikh-i-Firuz Shahi*, Calcutta: Bibliotheca Indica, 1891, pp.365-7.
6. Anonymous, *Siraj-ul-Hidaya* (collection of the utterances of Shaikh Jalaluddin *Jahanian-i-Jahangasht*) ed. Qazi Sajjad Husain, New Delhi: ICHR, 1983, pp. 211-12.
7. The late leading scholar of Persian literature points out in his highly researched article that gunpowder was never used in mining the

enemy fortification till Timur's time. Besides the works of Nizam uddin Shami, Sharaf uddin Yazdi and Abdur Razzaq Samarqandi, contemporary Arabic sources have also been used to show that since the rise of Mongol power in the thirteenth century, tunnels and *manjaniqs* were used but not gunpowder for the conquest of forts. Cf. Mahmud Khan Shirani, 'Atishbar Alat aur Timur', *Maqalat-i-Hafiz Mahmud Shirani*, ed. Mazhar Mahmud Shirani, Lahore: Majlis-i-Taraqi–i–Adab, 1976, vol. 7, pp. 261-9; Iqtidar Alam Khan's statement that the Mongol invaders of India during the thirteenth and fourteenth centuries used mining technique cannot be substantiated, neither any Arabic nor any other source contains positive evidence. Cf. Iqtidar Alam Khan, *Gunpowder and Firearms in Medieval India*, New Delhi: Oxford University Press 2006, p. 31.

8. Ali bin Mahmud al Kirmani, known as Shihab Hakim, *Ma'sir-i-Mahmud Shahi*, ed. Nurul Hasan Ansari, Delhi: Indo-Persian Society, 1987, p. 51.
9. Ibid., pp. 38, 62.
10. *Baburnama*, tr. Mrs. Beveridge, New Delhi, 1975, rpt, vol. 2, p. 672.
11. Cf. David Ayalon, *GunPowder and FireArms in the Mamluk Kingdom: A Challenge to a Medieval Society*, London: Vallantine, Mitchell, 1956. pp. 2-3, 98; also Stephen Christensen, '*European-Ottoman Military Acculturation in the late Middle Ages*', in War and Peace in the Middle Ages, ed. Brian Patrick McGuire, Copenhagen, 1987, pp. 233-4; Bernard Lewis *Islam: Politics and War*, New York, 1975, vol. 1, pp. 26.
12. 'Ataullah, *Zamima Ma'sir-i-Mahmud Shahi*, transcribed copy of the manuscript in the India Office Library, available in the Centre of Advanced Study, Department of History, Aligarh Muslim University, Aligarh, pp. 123-5.
13. Cf. M.S. Commissariat, *A History of Gujarat*, Bombay: Orient Longman, 1938, vol. 1, pp. 246-51.
14. *Babur Nama*, 1970, pp. 550, 564 & 667.
15. Mut'i, *Ganj-i-Ma'ani* edited with portions translated by Z.U. Desai, in Iran Society's Silver Jubilee Souvenir, *Iran Society*, Calcutta, 1970, pp. 75-7.
16. Loc. cit.

17. Abdul Karim, *Corpus of the Arabic and Persian Inscriptions of Bengal,* Dhaka: Asiatic Society of Bangladesh, 1992, pp. 383-8.
18. Malik Muhammad Jaisi, *Padmavat,* tr. A.G. Shireff, Calcutta: The Royal Asiatic Society of Bengal, 1944, p. 295.
19. Abul Fazl, *Akbar Nama,* ii/40; Ni'matullah, *Tarikh-i-Khan-i-Jahani,* Dhaka, 1960. vol. 2, p. 485.
20. Iqtidar Husain Siddiqui, *Sher Shah and His Times,* 2nd revd edn. Jaipur Publication Scheme, 1955, pp. 210-13.

CHAPTER 6

Social Mobility and Emergence of New Social Groups

The treatment by modern historians of the Delhi Sultanate has often been confined to rather narrow concerns, such as the chronology of important battles or the centralizing efforts of individual sultans. At best there has been an analysis of the nature of kingship under individual sultans or dynasties, concerned, for example, with how far the sultans were able to suppress factions within the ruling elites. Adequate attention does not seem to have been paid to any analysis of the patterns of political behaviour of successive sultans and the socio-economic changes accompanying reforms in state policies and royal institutions. Undoubtedly, part of the limitation of modern research has been due to the paucity of evidence in conventional historical sources.

Recently, attention has been drawn to hagiographic literature, epigraphic material, and literary works that supplement the meagre information available in historical works about socio-economic conditions in India during pre-Mughal times. Information pieced together from the chronicles, supplemented by other miscellaneous source material, will hopefully enable a fuller portrait of society and social mobility under the Delhi Sultanate. I briefly refer to demographic mobility as well, as the meagre source material discourage a detailed investigation.

Following the establishment of Turkish rule in Delhi, several factors induced a large number of people to migrate from Central Asia. The conquest of large territories and the need to consolidate their rule led the sultans to welcome such immigrants to India. Attracted by the opportunities in the newly established Sultanate, people from the region of Ghazna seem to have turned to India in large numbers in order to seek their fortunes. This seems to have been the case with the Khaljis and the Afghans, both of whom are reported to have lived at the level of bare subsistence in their ancestral lands.[1] The Khaljis who had served in the army of the rulers of Ghazna as *sawars* (horsemen) and petty officers[2] established themselves rapidly and emerged as a new social group within the first decade of their arrival.[3] Unlike the Khaljis, the Afghan immigrants from the tribal lands took longer to gain positions of influence and authority in state service. Strangely enough, the Afghans lagged behind even the Hindu converts to Islam in this regard, for soon the sons of neo-Muslims were able to raise themselves socially.

The condemnation by Minhaj-i Siraj[4] and Zia'uddin Barani of Indian converts to Islam, or those who were descended from the early converts, suggests that they had started competing with members of the aristocratic families of early immigrants from Central Asia and other Islamic countries for posts in state service. Advocating that the sultans employ people with aristocratic backgrounds, Barani advises that the children of low-born converts to Islam should not be admitted into madrasas because this education would qualify them for government jobs. Further, he implies that only noble families had been chosen by God to rule mankind, and that their existence was necessary for the maintenance of justice and stability in society.[5] He also praised Sultan Ghiyasuddin Balban for his considering noble birth a prerequisite for state service, citing the case of a certain Kamal Mahiyar whom the nobles took to the Sultan as a candidate for the *khwajgi* (post of accountant) of Amroha district. The Sultan rejected him because his father had been a low-caste convert to Islam.[6] It is interesting to note that Sultan Balban's son, Prince Muhammad, who held the trans-Sutlej territories under his charge, valued knowledge and talent more than noble birth.[7]

Balban's immediate successor, his grandson, Sultan Kaiqubad (1287-90), also seems to have had no prejudice against people on the grounds of birth, for Barani includes Kamal Mahiyar's son in the list of the high nobles of his reign.[8] In fact, the social stratification that had resulted from the political domination by Muslim immigrant families, which monopolized key positions both in the civil and military administration, could not last long. The progress of learning, expansion and consolidation of the central authority, cultural influences such as those of the *sufis* (Muslim mystics), and the employment of skilled craftsmen in the royal *karkhanas*, paved the way for the rise of people from unprivileged families in society. This was because the consolidation and expansion of the Sultan's authority in the provinces created the need for a large number of educated people to carry on administrative work and old aristocratic families could no longer supply sufficient officers to meet these needs.

With the advent of the Khaljis to power in Delhi, far-reaching changes took place in state policies with regard to the recruitment of officers. The Khalji Sultans had no pretensions to noble lineage or past glory. During their period, the doors of official opportunity were thrown open to all, and race, birth and even creed ceased to be all-important criteria.[9] Under Sultan Jalaluddin Khalji (d. 1296), a Hindu chief who belonged to the Mandahar tribe was honoured with the post of *vakil-i dar* (minister charged with the responsibility of arranging ceremonies at court).[10] Sultan 'Ala ud'din Khalji (1296-1316) continued and even extended the policies of his uncle. Dividing 'Ala ud'din Khalji's reign into three phases, Barani says that the last phase was dominated by low-born officers and 'lasted for four of five years. In these years the Sultan remained unwell, and the whole administration was conducted by Malik Naib (Kafur). All the important posts were held by indecent and low-born persons. With the ascendancy of low-born *shiqqdars* and officers, the whole administration was disturbed and people suffered.'[11]

Even ministerial posts of a religious and quasi-religious nature, such as those of the chief *qazi* (chief justice), called *Qazzat-i-Mamalik,* and *Sadr-us-Sudur* (minister for theological affairs), called *Sadr-i Jahan,* could be entrusted to the charge of those educated people who had no claim to noble descent, although these posts had been the exclusive privilege of the members of certain old respectable families of Shaikhs and Saiyids. Criticizing Sultan 'Ala ud'din Khalji's policy with regard to the appointment of officers, Barani suggests that the offices of *Qazzat* and *Sadr-i Jahan* could only be held by learned men belonging to certain noble families who commanded respect in the country for their piety and learning. According to Barani, Sultan 'Ala ud'din Khalji had followed this tradition in the beginning of his reign; Qazi Sadruddin Arif, the father of Daud Malik and grandson of the daughter of *Sadr-i Jahan* Minhaj Siraj Juzjani (author of the *Tabaqat-i Nasiri)* was given joint charge of both offices. The office of *Qazzat* and *Sadr-i Jahan* acquired lustre and prestige thereby. Even if the incumbent was not considered a distinguished scholar, being from a noble family, he commanded respect and discharged his duties properly. He was succeeded by Qazi Jalaluddin Livalji in the office of chief *qazi* and Maulana Zia'uddin of Bayana as *Sadr-i Jahan.* The latter had served as *qazi-i Lashkar* (*qazi* in the army). Since both of them lacked high family status, the departments lost much of their influence and prestige. Barani says, 'During the last phase of Sultan 'Alauddin's reign, the *Qazzat* of the empire that was in every way an important and lofty position and for which no one but the member of a well-established family of noble descent, traditionally known for learning and religiosity could be considered fit, was entrusted to *Malik-ul-Tujjar* (chief of merchants), Hamiduddin Multani. The latter had served in the royal household as *Pardabar* (incharge of curtains) and *Kuliddar* (keeper of the keys). Any mention of this *Malik-ul-Tujjar* (Hamid Multani) is not worthy of space in history. Nobody had courage to point out to the Sultan that only education and knowledge were not sufficient grounds for appointment to this position.[12] It is of interest that Shaikh Nasiruddin *Chiragh-i Delhi,* the contemporary Chishti Sufi had a different and better opinion of the same minister's good qualities. Hamiduddin is said to have been helpful to scholars and other deserving persons as *sadr,* and to have performed the functions of chief justice with honesty and integrity.[13] In short, the spread of education helped to undermine the social barriers created by Muslim immigrant families in the early days of the Delhi Sultanate.

It is also noteworthy that elevation of members of unprivileged families and slaves to high positions in the army and administration created conditions favourable for the entry of others of the same class. For example, the appointment of Khusrau Khan Parwari as the *Naib-i Sultanat* under Sultan Qutbuddin Mubarak Shah Khalji (1317-20) paved the way for the short-lived ascendancy of the Hindu *Parwaris* of Gujarat at the imperial court.[14] Though the murder of Sultan Mubarak Shah Khalji by the *Parwaris* brought about their downfall, no reaction seems to have occurred against the appointment of Hindus and low-caste people to government posts. Sultan Ghiyasuddin Tughluq Shah came to power with the slogan of punishing Khusrau Khan and his supporters, and so made use of the obvious advantage in condemning the religious affiliations of the *Parwaris.* Yet he himself already had Hindu *khokkars* as officers and *sawars* in his service in his *iqta* of Depalpur. They supported him in his struggle for the throne of Delhi against Khusrau Khan.[15]

The most important period in this respect, marked by a remarkable example of upward mobility in the nobility, was the reign of Sultan Muhammad bin Tughluq (1325-51). Both Ibn Battuta and Barani mention many low-born persons whom Sultan Muhammad bin Tughluq raised to important positions in the empire. The nature of the officers and the posts assigned to them indicates that many of them were educated people. Ibn Battuta's reference to Ratan, a Hindu, who was a barber by caste, is of great significance. Despite his lowly origin, Ratan was a scholar of mathematics.

Impressed by his knowledge and competence, the Sultan appointed him *wali* (governor) of the *vilayat* of Sind with permission to have drums and flags, a privilege accorded only to prominent nobles.[16] The following passage in the *Tarikh-i Firuz Shahi,* shows how social mobility resulted from the Sultan's attitude, 'Najib the musician of obscure origin was so much honoured that he superseded in position and status many of the (old) nobles. He was assigned the charge of Gujarat, Multan and Badaon (territories perhaps held in succession). Like him, 'Aziz Khummar and his brother were favoured, *Firuz,* the barber, Mankah, the cook, Mas'ud Khummar (liquor brewer), Ladha, the gardener, and many other base and mean people were elevated to important posts and assigned *iqta's.* Shaikh Babu, son of Nayak, the weaver, was made a royal associate and thus the scoundrel became an influential man in society. Pira *Mali* (gardener), who was the meanest and most ignoble person in India, was honoured with the charge of the *diwan-i wizarat* and raised in this way over and above the *maliks,* nobles, *walis* and *muqtas.*'[17] Further he says: 'Kishan Bazran of Indri who was mean of the meanest got the governorship of Awadh. Maqbal, the slave of Ahmad Ayaz, was entrusted with the governorship of Gujarat, an office meant for high nobles and prominent ministers, although he possessed no qualities outwardly or inwardly.'[18] Isami would have us believe that the Sultan favoured Hindus because he was the enemy of Islam, and, therefore, subjected Muslims everywhere to tyranny.[19]

Of the low-born nobles mentioned by Barani, Ibn Battuta also mentions a few showing how much they had risen because of the Sultan's regard for their competence. Aziz Khummar successively held the governorships of Amroha and Malwa, while Maqbal ruled over Gujarat as the *naib* (deputy) of the *Wazir,* Khwaja Jahan. Ayaz is described as a man of violent temper[20] but Maqbal had no such shortcoming. Ibn Battuta found him a cultured and hospitable person.[21]

It will not be out of place to discuss here the role of a few cities that had definite social and economic functions to perform, in the rise of social mobility. I analyse here the role of the port city of Cambay and the metropolitan city of Delhi. The former underwent a complete transformation after its annexation to the Sultanate in 1306, while the latter developed into a centre of international culture during the reign of Sultan Iltutmish (1210-1336).

Like foreign merchants, many scholars and Sufi saints came from neighbouring countries and settled down in Cambay. Ibn Battuta states that of the Sufi saints Shaikh Ali al Haidari (qalandar) '...was held in high respect, well-spoken of, and of wide reputation. The sea traders used to vow to give large sums to him, and on arriving in Cambay they would go first of all to salute him. He would show them that he knew what was in their minds; often one of them would make a vow and then repent of it, but when he came to salute the Shaikh, the latter would tell him first how much he had vowed and order him to fulfil it faithfully.'[22] At another place Ibn Battuta mentions two other Sufis of eminence, Qazi Nasr from Diyarbakr and Khwaja Ishaque. The former lived in a cell near the Jama mosque while the latter maintained a *khanqah* where travellers got food daily and the poor and needy, money. All of them catered to people's needs, material as well as spiritual.[23]

In short, Cambay under the Sultanate of Delhi became a city of enrichment for its residents. It was really its prosperity and grandeur of its beautiful buildings that impressed the Indian and foreign visitors alike. 'Ainul Mulk Mahru, one of the nobles of Sultan Muhammad bin Tughluq, who visited Cambay in connection with some official work, called it *Shahr-i-Mu'azzam* (a great city) having all around it high and beautiful buildings, surrounded by beautiful gardens.[24] Likewise, the extent of Cambay's prosperity impressed Barbossa, an early European traveller.[25]

As regards the metropolitan city of Delhi, contemporary sources naturally provide us with much greater information than they do for Cambay. Before its conquest by Qutbuddin Aibak, Delhi was a mere local military post and a small *pargana* headquarter.[26] It developed into a magnificent city after Iltutmish made it his capital in 1210. It received large numbers of immigrants from Central Asia and Persia, who were driven hither by Mongol invasions. Among these refugees were many celebrities of the Persian speaking world. As a result, Delhi became the repository of the best of Islamic culture that had developed in Persia, Khurasan and Central Asia. Early thirteenth century writers refer briefly to the exodus of people from foreign countries;[27] the later historian, Isami, however, gives a graphic description of the categories to which these foreigners belonged, saying 'Many genuine descendants of the Prophet arrived there from Arabia, many artisans from Khurasan, many painters from the country of China, many *'ulama* [learned men], born in Bukhara, many saints and devotees from every quarter of the world. There also came craftsmen of every kind and every country, many experts knowledgeable in precious gems, innumerable jewel merchants, philosophers and physicians of the Greek School. In that happy city they gathered like moths around a burning candle'.[28]

Again Isami refers to the immigrants from foreign lands and also from different parts of India settling in Delhi and other cities and towns when he praises Sultan 'Ala ud'din Khalji's concern for the welfare of the people. He states, 'Anyone who arrived from the foreign land or any part of India to this 'garden of happiness' developed so much predilection for it (Delhi) that he hardly even remembered his native land. World travellers, who did not stay at any place even for a month, settled down in India overcome by its charm.'[29]

Isami also supplies interesting information about the large population, the numerous artisans adept in different crafts, and the supply of essential as well as luxury goods in plenty in the bazaars of Delhi.[30] According to him, Delhi had become the largest of the cities of India during 'Ala ud'din Khalji's time. None of its quarters, says he, would look empty of people even if a hundred divisions were raised there and went out. Many of its scientists and men of arts and learning had acquired fame in foreign countries.[31] Barani corroborates this in his praise of the progress of arts and crafts in Delhi during the Khalji period.[32]

Of the important institutions of foreign origin that served as important factors for social mobility, the *karkhanas*[33] (discussed above) and madrasas (schools and colleges) deserve special mention. The sultans and the nobles appear to have evinced interest in maintaining *karkhanas* and having madrasas constructed. Nobles posted in the provinces as governors maintained *karkhanas* like the sultan,[34] and made efforts to employ master craftsmen to work there. Of all the sultans, Sultan Firuz Shah (reigned: 1351-88), is said to have surpassed his predecessors in maintaining a large number of *karkhanas* in Delhi. Goldsmiths, gem cutters, perfumers, artisans skilled at making different types of weapons and armour, were all employed in large numbers. Master craftsmen trained thousands of slave boys in different crafts.[35] Many slaves trained in the *karkhanas* attained important positions and took active part in the politics of the Delhi Sultanate. They ultimately emerged as a powerful group after the death of Sultan Firuz Shah in 1388.[36]

Like the *karkhanas,* educational institutions maintained or aided by the state during the period under review also played an important role in this respect.

It is possible that education spread through the madrasas was responsible for a certain amount of social tension in Delhi and other cities. The few details furnished by Barani and Isami of the rebellion by Haji Maula (a liberated slave) in Delhi in 1301 show how resentful people belonging to the lower cadres of state service had become over the inequitable distribution of state patronage. Haji Maula, who served in Ritol[37] as *shahna* (police inspector), decided to take advantage of the situation; he came to Delhi, won over soldiers and others and led a revolt against 'Ala ud'din Khalji. Tirmizi, the *kotwal* of the old city, was treacherously killed and the royal stables, and the treasury and armoury were seized. The entire force of the *kotwali* men (*kotwalryan),* the *lashkar* (soldiery) and the *khalq* (commoners) rallied around Haji Maula.[38] Isami's condemnation of them as *mard-i kam-maya* (penniless fellows) suggests their plebeian background.[39] Similarly Haji Maula's selection of an 'Alavi (descendant of Ali, the fourth Caliph of Islam) as king, suggests that the rebels wanted a different kind of state. Haji Maula's rebellion was brutally suppressed.[40]

It was the fear of antagonizing public opinion in Delhi that served as a check on the sultans from time to time. The transfer of population from Delhi to Daulatabad in 1327 did not take place only on account of Sultan Muhammad bin Tughluq's desire to develop the newly-founded city of Daulatabad in the Deccan into a leading centre of Muslim culture, in order to have a base for local support for the consolidation of his power. He also wanted to get rid of Delhi's population before he began to pursue his radical policies and religious goals.[41] Both Isami and Ibn Battuta corroborate each other when they say that the Sultan did not trust the people of Delhi and forcibly shifted them to Daulatabad by way of punishment.[42] The relevant evidence contained in Barani's account of Ghiyasuddin Tughluq's reign clearly indicates that people in Delhi were hostile to the Sultan for his niggardliness in distributing money among people even on occasions of social significance.[43] It would not be incorrect to say that Delhi was never abandoned as the first capital for after the evacuation of the entire population, people were brought from the neighbouring towns and cities to inhabit the empty city. Obviously many of these newcomers in Delhi, whom Isami dubs rustic fellows having no cultural background, got the opportunity to take to professions or even occupy posts that previously they could not have hoped for.[44]

The main reason for the transfer of population from Delhi to Daulatabad (Deccan) was Sultan Muhammad bin Tughluq's fear of popular opposition to his state and religious policies – people who lived in provincial cities and towns were thought to be more docile. Nevertheless an important outcome of this measure was that Daulatabad received a large number of the old capital's highly cultured citizens, and came to rival Delhi, as a city.

Ibn Battuta's description of Daulatabad shows that its rise to being the second metropolitan city of the Sultanate benefited the Deccan, as it began to serve as an integrative and cultural nucleus in south India. The establishment of *karkhanas* and other institutions, cultural as well as political, led to social mobility. Daulatabad soon compared with Delhi in both size and grandeur.[45] However, it ceased to be a place of significance when for political reasons, the founder of the Bahmani dynasty shifted the capital to Gulbarga. In Daulatabad, the powerful Afghans and other supporters of Makh Afghan, who had assumed the title of sultan were antagonistic to the Bahmani sultan and soon Gulbarga was replaced as a seat of culture and learning.[46]

It is also worth recalling that, with Firuz Shah's accession to the throne of Delhi, a reaction started against the state policy of Muhammad bin Tughluq yet the appointment and promotion of the officers of ordinary family background to high positions was not stopped. Writing after 1357, Barani laments that by that time the *ajlaf* and *lutran* (people of low origin and base stock) dominated the entire world.[47]

The emergence of the Afghans, Kalals and Araqians (liquor-brewers), Jains, Khatris and Kambos of the Punjab as prominent communities during the period of the Delhi Sultanate also provides us with insights into the social processes at work. The Afghans who seem to have settled in large numbers in the frontier region to the north-west of Punjab long before their conversion to Islam and the annexation of their homeland by Sultan Mahmud of Ghazna, were a tribal people given to plunder. They began to enter the fold of Islam during the reign of Sultan Mahmud (reigned: 998-1030), and by the close of the twelfth century almost all the Afghan tribes seem to have converted to Islam. The only reference to their presence in Delhi contained in the *Tabaqat-i-Nasiri* is indicative of the fact that they were known for their ferocity and rustic ways. They served the nobles as soldiers till the second half of the thirteenth century.[48] The lack of culture and sophistication apparently retarded their upward mobility.

During the reign of Sultan Ghiyasuddin Balban, a new generation of Afghans, brought up in the environment of the Delhi Sultanate, came on the scene. Sultan Balban entrusted them with the charge of newly-established *thanas* (police posts) around Delhi and other territories, and in the provincial armies also the number of Afghan soldiers increased considerably.[49] This improvement in their position seems to have encouraged them to impart education to their children. As a result, the Afghans rose to the status of high nobles during the reign of 'Ala ud'din Khalji.

Amir Khusrau, who mentions the Afghans as uncultured people not fit to reside in the midst of civilized people in his *diwan, Tuhfat-ul-Sighar*,[50] had to change his tune in the reign of 'Ala ud'din Khalji. As the Afghans got used to aristocratic ways and competed with members of the old aristocratic families, Amir Khusrau now simply called them 'boastful persons bereft of excellence'.[51] Khusrau, being an aristocrat and opposed to change, was clearly not free from prejudice against Afghans and others who had risen from below. The details furnished by Ibn Battuta, Isami and Barani about the Afghan nobles of their time, show that by then many of them had become cultured aristocrats and commanded respect in society for their services to the Empire.

During the Tughluq period their number increased considerably, and they held important administrative posts in every province. By the time Sultan Muhammad bin Tughluq came to the throne, the Afghans had emerged as a new social group in the Sultanate. In Multan, Gujarat and the Deccan, they became so powerful that some of them began to aspire to kingship. Even the suppression of their rebellions against Sultan Muhammad bin Tughluq in different provinces did not weaken their strength in India, and they continued to hold important *iqta's* and posts in the Delhi Sultanate as well as the regional kingdoms that arose after Timur's sack of Delhi in 1398.[52] Mention may be made of Malik Khurram Nuhani (Afghan), who was the first Afghan to found an independent principality, that of Jalore in Rajasthan, at the beginning of the fifteenth century. His descendants continued to rule over it till the next century.[53]

The *Kalals* (liquor brewers) seem to have prospered particularly because of the introduction of liquor distillation, which is mentioned by Barani. He describes them as *khummars* (wine makers) and *araqis* (distillers). Later medieval writers refer to them by their Hindustani caste name, *Kalal*. The wealth and prosperity acquired by members of this caste seems to have led some of them to embrace Islam. This tends to suggest that they had abandoned their hereditary profession and were educated Muslims who acquired prominent positions through merit. Ibn Battuta and Barani mention Aziz Khummar who was notorious for his harsh dealings with people, and enjoyed the confidence of Sultan Muhammad bin Tughluq. The Sultan first appointed him controller of revenue in the territorial unit of Amroha,[54] and later governor of Malwa.[55]

Traditions which seventeenth-century writers incorporated in their works about the origin of the founders of the regional dynasties of Nagaur and Gujarat in the beginning of the fifteenth century not only shed light on the social mobility of low-caste converts to Islam but also hint that close contact with the Muslim elites could have attracted some Hindus towards

Islam. According to these traditions, Zafar Khan, founder of the Sultanate of Gujarat and his brother, Shams Khan Dandani (who founded the principality of Nagaur) were the sons of Saharan, a member of the *Kalal* caste. According to Shaikh Kabir Batini, Saharan married his sister to Firuz Shah, sometime during the reign of Sultan Muhammad bin Tughluq and this marriage was followed by the family's conversion to Islam. Saharan and his brothers were honoured with high ranks and titles.[56]

Our sources for other regions also show that alcohol was in demand in every city,[57] as many among the ruling classes had cultivated a taste for liquor. Liquor-sellers and manufacturers were still predominantly Hindus and came to acquire aristocratic habits on account of their prosperity. An inscription dated 24 February 1436 mentions Bhola Maharaj *Khummar* who spent money on the construction of a step-well in Jahtra for the benefit of the people at large.[58]

In the kingdom of Malwa, certain *Kalals* are said to have changed over to other trades. Mushtaqi in his narrative of the love-affair between Sultan Nâsiruddin Shah Khalji and a *Kalal* girl says that her family traded in utensils. It is said that Nāsir Shah became enamoured of the girl, and, when approached, the girl's mother gave her to the Sultan in marriage. In the case of this family also the matrimonial alliance paved the way for the rise of its members to a rank in the nobility. The brothers of the girl were assigned titles, ranks and *iqta's.*[59]

Like the liquor-brewers, the Jains, a community of merchants and tradesmen, moved upward socially. The Jains are reported to have attained high positions in the Sultan's service from the reign of Sultan 'Ala ud'din Khalji. For instance, Pheru Jain, an expert gemologist, was appointed superintendent of the royal mint in Delhi by Sultan 'Ala ud'din Khalji. He retained his position till the reign of Sultan Muhammad bin Tughluq, and had so much influence that he could recommend men of his community to the Sultan.[60] Samar Singh Jain held an important position during the reign of Sultan Qutbuddin Mubarak Shah Khalji.[61] In the provinces of Gujarat and Nagaur as well, Jains rose in the social hierarchy under the patronage of Muslim governors. Sultan Muhammad bin Tughluq (1325-5) went out of his way to befriend the Jain community along with other non-Muslims. The traditions set by the fourteenth-century sultans in conferring favours on the Jains seem to have been followed by the regional sultans and chiefs who rose into prominence after the dissolution of the Delhi Sultanate in the fifteenth century. The Kambos originally belonged to a Hindu caste of the Punjab and were mostly peasants.[62] In Multan they embraced Islam under the influence of the Suhrawardi saint; their association with Shaikh Bahauddin Zakariya of Multan led to their descendants being seized with a passion for learning.[63]

A document in the *Insha-i Mahru,* a fourteenth century collection of epistles, reflects the social mobility owing to which people once belonging to the lower strata of society could manoeuvre for position through what may be termed as their ability to create a nuisance. By the time of Sultan Firuz Shah, the Kambos of Multan had become so influential that they could intervene with the governor and could even approach the royal court and be heard by the Sultan.[64] They emerged as an influential group in the fifteenth century. In 1443, they supported Shaikh Yusuf Qureshi, a descendant of Shaikh Bahauddin Zakariya, and declared him Sultan of Multan.[65] By now many of the Kambos of Multan had distinguished themselves as *ulama* (scholars) and *mashaikh* (Sufi saints). One of the eminent Suhrawardi Sufis, Shaikh Samauddin Kambo, became the patron saint of the Lodi dynasty in Delhi.[66] Shaikh Samauddin Kambo's son-in-law, Shaikh Jamali, was elevated to the status of poet laureate at the court of Sultan Sikandar Lodi,[67] and many other Kambos occupied important ranks and positions in the Lodi Empire.[68] One of the ministers of Sher Shah Sur was Imadul Mulk Kambo, who headed the department of *Amir-i Ariz.*[69]

Like the Kambos of Multan, the Khatris, who resided mostly in the Punjab and Delhi, also appear to have emerged as an important new social group in the Sultanate during the fourteenth century. Having acquired proficiency in accountancy and arithmetic, they were employed in the revenue department. Many of them went to the provinces as finance officers along with the governors. Barani and Isami mention them incidentally in the details of rebellions in south India.[70] When Sultan Muhammad Shah II appointed Zafar Khan and Dilawar Khan Ghori as governors of Gujarat and Malwa respectively between 1391 and 1392, both took their Khatri *diwans* with them. Their sons and relations also gained important positions through their influence at the provincial courts. Upon the decay of the Delhi Sultanate, the Khatri nobles began to play an important role both in Gujarat and Malwa.[71] Most prominent among the Khatri nobles in Gujarat were Malik Shahpidar Khatri, Jivan Khatri and Rai Das Khatri. They were among the trusted nobles of Sultan Muzaffar Shah, founder of the Gujarat kingdom.[72]

In the Sultanate of Delhi the revenue department was heavily manned by Khatri officials. Under Khizr Khan Saiyid and his successor, Sultan Mubarak Shah, the Khatris enjoyed high positions at Delhi.[73] Similarly, they supervised the financial administration at the Centre and in the provinces during the Lodi period. Babur was surprised to see that all revenue officials were Hindus.[74] Hindu domination of the revenue department seems to have caused resentment among the Muslim land grantees, for they were not expected to show any leniency in collecting state revenues at the time of harvest. For this reason, Shaikh Abdul'l Quddus Gangohi, a prominent Chishti saint, suggests in a letter to Babur that Hindus should not be entrusted with the work of collecting revenue.[75]

Social mobility increased in certain regions under the provincial rulers after the dissolution of the Delhi Sultanate in 1398. Local rulers took a keen interest in the economic development of their kingdoms and cemented their relations with the local people by constructing large tanks, step-wells and other buildings of public utility.[76] In the fifteenth century, under the fostering care of its rulers, Nagaur developed from a small town into an important centre of learning and commerce.[77] Its fame attracted people from distant parts who were patronized by the local rulers. The evidence in the contemporary literature shows that the Chishti Sufis of Nagaur were also responsible for increasing social mobility. They admitted disciples (*murids*) from different strata of the society and many of them were able to rise in social status because of their association with the *dargah* of Shaikh Hamiduddin Nagauri, a thirteenth-century Chishti Sufi of great eminence.[78]

Mention should be made of Shaikh Husain Nagauri Chishti, who flourished during the fifteenth century, and whose disciples included nobles, traders and even untouchables. One of his *murids,* a sweeper who had converted to Islam, performed religious exercises under his master's guidance and turned into a devout Sufi. Later on, many traditions developed about his spiritual powers.[79] Rich people brought him gifts and sought his blessings. He would undoubtedly otherwise have lived and died an untouchable. Indeed, the activities of genuine Sufis often led to social mobility in the cities and towns; their *khanqahs* served as seats of learning because lectures were delivered daily on the religious sciences followed by discussions relating to literary and spiritual matters. Often, unlettered people were seized with a passion for learning and serving mankind. Another advantage they offered was that the poor *murids* of an eminent sufi could get help from the richer *murids* of the same *pir.* Many disciples of Shaikh Husain Nagauri were members of the ruling elite in different regions. Ahmad Khan Lodi Sarang Khani, governor of Jaunpur under Sikandar Lodi, was one of his *murids,*[80] as was Sultan Ghiyasuddin Khalji, who is said to have offered him great treasure on his visit to Mandu. The Shaikh spent some part of it on constructing buildings at Ajmer and Nagaur; the remainder was given away to the poor.[81] Like Shaikh Husain Nagauri, other Sufi saints also admitted low-caste people into the circle of their *murids*. Some of them belonged to the weavers' or dyers' communities and gained prestige as dervishes.[82]

The improvement of trade and commerce in the principality of Nagaur also deserves attention. Situated along the trade route linking Gujarat with Delhi and other centres in north India, Nagaur was frequently visited by merchant caravans. The details Mushtaqi gives about Mian Mahmud Farmuli's career show that Nagaur had become famous for its trade in war horses of good breed, weapons, and fine cloth.[83] This trade seems to have given a boost to indigenous crafts as well.

Epigraphical sources indicate that among the business communities of Nagaur, the Jains were prominent. They had close and friendly relations with members of the Muslim elite, and both communities appear to have co-operated with each other in social matters. Like the Muslim aristocrats, the Jains spent money on constructing schools where children were instructed in the traditional sciences. Once, when a school building was acquired by the government during the Sur period (1552), the Jains approached Shaikh-ul Mashaikh Sulaiman to intercede with the Afghan governor for its restoration, which was done.[84] The land grant made by Sultan Sikandar Lodi (1488-1517) to a Jain saint, Jambuji, earlier also tends to suggest that the Jain community had acquired great importance in western Rajasthan.[85]

I cannot go into details here of social mobility in Gujarat. It may, however, be pointed out that the system of social stratification here was further weakened after the establishment of the independent Sultanate. Those gifted with talent and determination appear to have escaped from their traditional caste occupations into those bringing prestige and dignity. Fortunately, we are given interesting information about cases of this kind in the *Mirat-i Sikandari*. Describing the beginning of the construction of pleasure gardens with fountains, artificial waterfalls, and channels of running water during the reign of Sultan Mahmud Begara, Sikandar bin Manjhu informs us that once an immigrant from Khurasan said to the Sultan, 'I have got sufficient experience of designing, the plans and supervising the construction of gardens and buildings.' He then built for the Sultan a beautiful garden with a cistern in its centre, fountains, artificial waterfalls, and channels of running water all around. During its construction the foreign architect allowed only illiterate workers to enter the enclosure so that his art could not be learnt by the Gujarati architects. One of the local workers, a carpenter named Bailu, however, observed every technique employed in constructing the garden and then applied for royal permission to build another garden like the one designed by the Khurasani architect. Being permitted to do so, Bailu succeeded in constructing a yet more magnificent garden. Highly impressed by Bailu's intelligence and achievement, the Sultan showered favours upon him, presented him with the *khilat-i khas* (special robe of honour) and raised him to the status of a grandee.[86]

Like skilled artists and craftsmen, capable slaves are also reported to have been appointed to important positions at the royal court. The career of Malik Sha'ban, the *wazir* of Sultan Mahmud Begara, is a case in point. He was purchased as a boy by Sultan Muhammad Shah II (son of Sultan Ahmad Shah), and was trained for state service along with other slave boys, after which he made rapid progress in the official hierarchy. Ultimately he rose to be a *wazir* during the reign of Sultan Mahmud Begara.[87] In most cases, the slaves, being local people, they would help their relations and caste people in obtaining state favours and gaining social advancement.

There were also those, belonging to low-caste families, who entered the royal army as soldiers or petty officials and rose in the official hierarchy by dint of merit and hard work. Such officers offer an important illustration of social mobility.

References to Muslim *biradaris* in most sources suggest that by the fifteenth century, the Indo-Muslim community had been divided into numerous *biradaris* (brotherhoods), a term of sociological significance. If anywhere it is in the formation of a *biradari* that the influence of the Hindu caste system seems to have been quite strong. The Afghans in India were also divided into *biradaris.*[88] A case can be made out that the *biradaris,* like artisan guilds, came in the way of an artisan wishing to take up a profession other than his hereditary one, as Babur would have us believe.[89] Yet there is no dearth of evidence to show that people changed their professions if they knew that the change would benefit them. People in the urban centres seem to have enjoyed considerable freedom in this matter. In fact, education, talent, trade, and also the institution of slavery in certain cases, contributed in elevating social status. During the Sur period, members of the weaver and Banya communities attained high rank in the nobility. As in the past, Sher Shah's slaves and their sons also occupied key positions in the Empire.[90]

As regards men of low-caste, the examples of Iqbal Khan, a Muslim weaver, and Hemu Bagal, who belonged to the Dhusar caste (a sub-caste of the Banyas) in Rewari, may be cited. Iqbal Khan (formerly Karamullah) started his career under Sher Shah as a soldier and ultimately rose to the command of 5,000 *sawars* (horsemen) under Islam Shah (1545-53). The latter is said to have honoured him with a high position at his court.[91] Likewise, Hemu started his career as a market inspector during Sher Shah's reign, but rose to the rank of the premier noble under Sultan 'Ādil Shah Sur (1553-7).[92]

During the period of his ascendancy, members of Hemu's caste rose in society: Rizq ullah Mushtaqi, a contemporary of Hemu, states that he destroyed the *chaudhris* and *muqaddams* in the territory of Rewari (probably for their recalcitrance) and replaced them with Banyas (*baqqals*).[93] Mushtaqi's testimony suggests that the Dhusar *zamindars* mentioned by Abu'l Fazl in the *sarkar* of Rewari during Akbar's reign were the creation of Hemu.[94] Hemu's relations, such as Taharpal, Rajya and Bhagwan Das were also entrusted with important positions in the army and administration of the Empire.[95]

The revival of trade and commerce in the Sultanate of Delhi during the Afghan period seems to have contributed towards greater social mobility. Trade attracted enterprising people from the higher as well as lower strata. Some members of aristocratic families preferred trade to state service, whereas petty officials enriched themselves by engaging in commerce. Two examples may be cited: the brothers of Malik Adhu Kansi (the latter being an important noble of Sultan Sikandar Lodi), who belonged to the town of Shikarpur in Punjab, travelled to Iran and Central Asia with a merchant caravan taking Indian products abroad and returned loaded with foreign merchandise.[96] Unlike the brothers of Malik Adhu Kansi, Mian Walid, a non-Afghan army man in the contingent of Khan A'zam Lad Khan Lodi Sarang Khani, the *Muqta*' (governor) of Jaunpur under Sultan Ibrahim Lodi, amassed wealth by dealing in perfumes and glassware. Himself a master craftsman, he trained his servants and slaves in manufacturing glassware and extracting perfumes of fine quality. He also purchased quality goods, stored them and then supplied them to the market when they fetched high prices. With this additional income, he was able to live like an aristocrat, holding banquets for friends and giving money to his relations.[97]

Finally, it may be stressed that demographic mobility in India during medieval times was closely linked with the process of urbanization. The expansion of old towns and construction of new metropolitan centres first in the Delhi Sultanate and then in the newly-founded regional kingdoms in the fifteenth century led artisans, artists, craftsmen and merchants to move there in the hope of better prospects. In his account of the reign of Sultan

Jalal uddin Khalji, Barani says that when *Shahr-i-nau* (Kilokhari) was made capital in place of (old) Delhi, the palace of Sultan Muiz u'ddin Kaiqubad which was still in process was completed and a pleasure garden laid out by the order of the new Sultan on the bank of the river Jamuna. The nobles also had their palaces and mansions constructed. Soon the traders and shopkeepers, started their business in its bazaars. This *Shahr-i-nau* was surrounded by the lofty fortification built with stones.[98] Similarly, in his description of the foundation of Ahmadabad in 1410, the author of the *Tarikh-i Salatin-i Gujarat* mentions the arrival of masons, craftsmen and *baqqals* in large numbers, who took permanent abode in the new capital. The bazaars and quarters of Ahmadabad are reported to have hummed with commercial activity, on account of the many foreign traders they attracted.[99]

In 1506, when Sultan Sikandar Lodi made Agra the capital of his empire, the royal *karkhanas* attracted skilled workers from different parts of India. There are references to ironsmiths from Rapri[100] and stone-cutters from Nagaur[101] who are said to have settled down in Agra and other places in the Lodi empire. The *sarrafs* (bankers and money-changers), artisans such as skilled darners and cloth-merchants, were attracted by trade and settled in the new capital.[102]

To conclude, it may be stated that the institutions (both political and social) of the Sultanate, the process of urbanization, and the enlightened policies followed by certain sultans were important factors making for social change in the Sultanate. In addition, the royal *karkhanas*, madrasas, the *khanqahs* of Sufi saints, and the institution of royal slave-households helped the emergence of important new social groups in the urban centres during pre-Mughal times.

Endnotes

1. See Minhaj-i Siraj, *Tabaqat-i Nasiri*, ed. Abdul Ha'i Habibi, Kabul, 1963, vol. 1, pp. 426-7 & 435, for the poverty-stricken Khalji emigrants, Cf. also Iqtidar Husain Siddiqui, 'The Afghans and their Emergence in India as Ruling Elite during the Delhi Sultanate Period', *Central Asiatic Journal*, Wiesbaden, 1982, vol. 26, nos. 3-4, pp. 241-61 and 246-50.
2. Minhaj-i-Siraj, *Tabaqat-i Nasiri*, vol. 1, p. 399.

3. Iqtidar Husain Siddiqui, 'The Nobility Under the Khalji Sultans', *Islamic Culture*, vol. xxxvii, No. 1, Hyderabad, January 1963.
4. *Tabaqat-i Nasiri*, vol. 1, p. 489; 2, pp. 69-70.
5. Zia' uddin Barani, *Fatawa-i Jahandari*, tr. Afsar Begum and Muhammad Habib, *Medieval India Quarterly*, Aligarh, 1958, nos. 3-4, p. 172.
6. Zia' uddin Barani, *Tarikh-i-Firuz Shahi*, Calcutta: Bibliotheca Indica, 1862, p. 36. (hereafter cited as Barani).
7. Ibid., p. 68.
8. Ibid., p. 126.
9. Cf. Siddiqui, Islamic Culture, 1963, op.cit., p. 55.
10. Barani, *Tarikh-i-Firuz Shahi*, pp. 195-6.
11. Ibid., pp. 336-7.
12. Ibid., pp. 351-2.
13. Hamid Qalandar, *Khair ul Majalis*, ed. K.A. Nizami, Aligarh, The Department of History, The Aligarh Muslim University, 1959, pp. 88 & 241.
14. Barani, *Tarikh-i-Firuz Shahi*, p. 409.
15. Amir Khusrau, *Tughluq Nama*, ed. S. Hashmi Faridabadi, Matba-i-Urdu Aurangabad, 1933, lines 2, 522, p. 131.
16. Ibn Battuta, *The Travels of Ibn Battuta*, vol. 3, tr. Hamilton Gibb, Cambridge University Press, 1977, p. 599. (hereafter cited as *The Travels of Ibn Battuta*).
17. The spelling *muqta* is preferable to *muqti*, which was not in vogue.
18. Barani, *Tarikh-i-Firuz Shahi*, pp. 505-6.
19. Isami, *Futuh us-Salatin*, p. 515.
20. *The Travels of Ibn Battuta*, vol. 3, p. 762.
21. Ibn Battuta mentions Malik Maqbal first in his account of the rebellion of Jalal Afghan and then in his account of his visit to Cambay on the way to China. In Cambay he enjoyed his hospitality. Since Gibb's volume comes to a close before Ibn Battuta left for the Deccan and the fourth volume is not available, we have to utilize the Urdu translation for information about the cities in the Deccan and

Gujarat. Agha Mahdi Husain's translation of Ibn Battuta's account of India seems to be faulty at places. Ibn Battuta, *The Travels of Ibn Battuta* vol. 3, op.cit., p. 730; *Ajaib-ul Asfar* (Urdu tr.) Maulvi Muhammad Husain, 2nd edn. Islamabad, 1983, vol. 2, pp. 280-1.

22. *The Travels of Ibn Battuta,* vol. 3, pp. 705-6.
23. Ibn Battuta, *Ajaib-ul Asfar,* vol. 2, op.cit., p. 281.
24. *Insha-i-Mahru,* ed. Shaikh Abdur Rashid, Lahore, 1965, p. 133.
25. *The Book of Duarte Barbossa,* tr. Mansel Longworth Dames, London: Hakluyt Society 1918, vol. 1, pp. 112, 120 & 140.
26. Isami, *Futuh us-Salatin,* p. 108, lines 7 and 8.
27. A contemporary poet who left Bukhara for India and was attached to the court of Iltutmish, says 'People sought refuge at your court against the tyranny perpetrated by the infidels of China (Mongols)'. (*Qasida* contained in Muhammad Bihamad Khani's, *Tarikh-i Muhammadi,* MS British Library, London, Or. 134 f. 345 b). Minhaj-i Siraj states 'This city through the number of grants and unbounded munificence of that pious monarch (Iltutmish) became the retreat and the resting place for the learned, the virtuous and the excellent of the various parts of the world'. He goes on to state that everyone who fled from the tyranny of the Mongols, sought refuge in India and was helped by the Sultan (*Tabaqat-i Nasiri,* vol. 1, pp. 440-1).
28. Isami, *Futuh us-Salatin,* pp. 114-15.
29. Ibid., pp. 300-1.
30. Ibid., pp. 451-2.
31. Ibid., pp. 445-6.
32. Barani, *Tarikh-i-Firuz Shahi,* p. 365.
33. *Jawami'ul-Hikayat,* vol. 2, part 3, Iran, 1353 Shamsi pp. 467-8, for its foreign origin.
34. Barani, *Tarikh-i-Firuz Shahi,* pp. 30, 60, 92.
35. Shams Siraj' Afif, *Tarikh-i-Firuz Shahi,* Calcutta, 1891, pp. 270-2, 307.
36. For example, towards the end of the fourteenth century, *Malik-us-Sharq* Khwaja (the founder of the Sharqi kingdom of Jaunpur) was Firuz Shah's slave and had been assigned, at the beginning of his

career, the duty of a water-bearer. Cf. Shaikh Kabir Batini, *Afsana-i Shahan,* MS, British Library, London, Add, 24, 409, f. 90b.

37. The printed text of Barani's *Tarikh-i Firuz Shahi* mentions Ritol as Ritank but the manuscript copy of the first recension, released by its author in the 5th year of Firuz Shah's reign, correctly mentions the place as Ritol (district Meerut, UP). The first recension was revised by Barani in the 7th year of Firuz Shah's reign. In the revised recension, the didactic element becomes preponderant in the author's approach to the history of the Delhi Sultans. Hence the qualitative difference between them. The copies of the first recension are available in the Raza Library, Rampur, and the Bodleian Library, Oxford. See *Tarikh-i Firuz Shahi,* MS, Raza Library, Rampur, cat. no. 1846, f. 106 b. The reference to the folio indicates the first recession, i.e. manuscript.

38. Barani, *Tarikh-i-Firuz Shahi,* pp. 279-80.

39. Isami, *Futuh us-Salatin*, p. 277.

40. Barani, *Tarikh-i-Firuz Shahi,* pp. 279-80.

41. The evidence available in Barani's first recension calls for a reappraisal of the history of the so-called transfer of the capital under Sultan Muhammad bin Tughluq. In this recension Barani informs us that first the Sultan sent the wives, children and other dependents of the nobles in Delhi, along with his mother, to Daulatabad. Soon afterwards he ordered the Saiyids, *mashaikh* (Sufi saints), *ulama* and other notables (of Delhi) to be brought to Daulatabad. All of them left the city (Delhi) with their dependents. In the third phase, after the rebellion of Kishlu Khan had been quelled, the entire population of Delhi was shifted to Daulatabad. Thereafter, according to Barani, people were brought from the neighboring towns and settled in Delhi. Cf. (*Tarikh-i Firuz Shahi* MS, Raza Library, Rampur, cat. no. 1846, f.106 b: Bodleian Library MS 173, Elliot, 353, f. 292 a).

42. Cf. *Futuh us-Salatin*, p. 446, Travels of Ibn Battuta, tr. vol. 3, pp. 707-8.

43. Barani, *Tarikh-i-Firuz Shahi* pp. 434 & 436-7.

44. Being hostile to the Sultan, Isami criticises the Sultan's policy regarding the evacuation of the old residents and settlement of people from other places in Delhi in these words: 'This was like replacing nightingales and parrots with crows and ravens'. *Futuh us-Salatin,* pp. 446, 450.

45. Battuta *Ajaib ul-Asfar*, vol. 2, pp. 275-7.

46. Isami, *Futuh us-Salatin*, pp. 558-9, 570.
47. Barani, *Tarikh-i-Firuz Shahi,* p. 366.
48. Iqtidar Husain Siddiqui, 'The Afghans During the Delhi Sultanate Period', *Central Asiatic Journal,* 1982, vol. 26, Nos. 3-4, Wiesbaden, pp. 242-3.
49. Barani, *Tarikh-i-Firuz shahi,* pp. 57-9.
50. Amir Khusrau, *Tuhfat-ul Sighar,* cited by Wahid Mirza, *The Life and Works of Amir Khusrau,* Delhi: reprint, Idarah-i-Adabiyat, pp. 51-2, rpt, 1974.
51. *Aina-i Sikandari*, ed. Muhammad Said Farooqi, 1917, Aligarh College Institute, lines 29-30, p. 37.
52. Siddiqui, *Central Asiatic Journal,* 1982, vol. 26, nos. 3-4, pp. 253-6.
53. Cf. M.S. Commissariat, *A History of Gujarat,* Bombay: Orient Longman 1938, vol. 1, pp. 50-2.
54. *The Travels of Ibn Battuta,* vol. 3, p. 762.
55. Barani, *Tarikh-i-Firuz Shahi,* pp. 501-2.
56. *Afsanah-i Shahan,* MS, British Library, London, Ad. 24, 409, ff. 90b-91a. The early official historians of Gujarat are silent on the origin of Zafar Khan. Sikandar bin Manjhu is the first Gujarati historian to deny the validity of the traditions about his low origin. He corroborates Shaikh Kabir in so far as the details of the marriage of his sister with Firuz Shah are concerned but twists the facts about Saharan's social background. According to him, an ancestor of Saharan was expelled from the Khatri caste because of his weakness for wine. Since then the family had been fond of wine and its members were called *nayak* (Sikandar bin Manjhu, *Mirat-i-Sikandari,* Bombay, AH 1308, p. 56).
57. Rizq ullah Mushtaqi, *Waqi'at-i Mushtaqi,* tr. Iqtidar Husain Siddiqui, New Delhi: ICHR, 1993, p. 247.
58. *Epigraphia Indica, Arabic and Persian Supplement,* (EI) 1953-4, pp. 39-40.
59. *Waqi'at Mushtaqi,* tr., pp. 228-9.
60. Cf. *Thakura Pheru's Parikha,* ed. and tr. S.R. Sharma, Aligarh: Viveka Publications, 1984, pp. 3-12, (Introduction).
61. (Agha) Mehdi Husain, *Tughluq Dynasty,* rpt, New Delhi, 1976, pp. 315-16, 363-4.

62. William Crooke, *The Tribes and Castes of North-Western India,* rpt, Delhi: Cosmo Publications, 1975, pp. 118-21.
63. Shaikh Farid Bhakhari, *Zakhirat-ul Khwanin,* vol. 1, ed. S. Moin-ul Haque, Karachi: Pakistan Historical Society, p. 148.
64. Ain-ul Mulk Mahru, *Insha-i Mahru* ed. Sh. Abdur Rashid, Lahore, University of the Punjab, 1965, Letter 29, pp. 65-7.
65. Nizamuddin Ahmad Bakshi, *Tabaqat-i Akbari,* vol. 3, Calcutta: Bibliotheca Indica, p. 53.
66. Shaikh Jamali, *Siyar-ul Arifin, Matba-i-Rizvi*, Delhi, H. 1311, p. 177; also Ahmad Khan, *Shajrah-i Suhraward,* MS, Raza Library, Rampur, ff. 15b-17a.
67. Nimatullah Herevi, *Tarikh-i Khan-i Jahani,* ed. S.M. Imam al-Din, Dacca: Asiatic Society of Pakistan, 1960, vol. 1, pp. 225-7.
68. See Iqtidar Husain Siddiqui, 'The Composition of the Nobility Under the Lodi Sultans', *Medieval India- A Miscellany*, Aligarh, 1977, vol. 4, pp. 20, 23, 62, for Kambo nobles under the Lodi Sultans.
69. Iqtidar Husain Siddiqui, *Mughal Relations with the Indian Ruling Elite-16th Century,* New Delhi: Munshiram Manoharlal, 1983, p. 94.
70. Cf. Iqtidar Hussain Siddiqui, *Authority and Kingship under the Sultans of Delhi,* New Delhi: Manohar Publishers, 2006, pp. 140-1.
71. Shaikh Kabir Batini, *Afsanah-i Shahan,* op.cit., MS Add. 24, 409, British Library, London, ff. 33a-b.
72. *Mirat-i Sikandari,* op.cit., p. 22.
73. Cf. Yahya Sirhindi, *Tarikh-i Mubarak Shahi,* Calcutta: Bibliotheca Indica, 1931, p. 234.
74. *Baburnama*, tr. Mrs. A. Beveridge, vol. 2, rpt, New Delhi, 1975, p. 518.
75. *Maktubat-i Quddusi*, Delhi, AH 1287, Letter to Babur, pp. 53-6.
76. Cf. Z.A. Desai, 'Inscription of the Khanazads of Nagaur', *Epigraphia Indica, Arabic and Persian Supplement,* (EI) 1970, Calcutta, 1975, pp. 16-20.
77. Cf. M.A. Chaghtai, Nagaur: A Forgotten Kingdom', *Bulletin of the Deccan College and Research Institute,* Poona, 1940, vol. 2, nos. 1-2 pp. 166-83.

78. Anonymous, *Surur-us Sudur,* MS Habib Ganj Collection, Maulana Azad Library, Aligarh, folios unmarked.
79. Abdul Haque Muhadith, *Akhbar al-Akhyar,* p. 209.
80. *Waqi'at Mushtaqi,* ... op.cit., p. 93.
81. Abdul Haq Mubaddis Dahlavi, *Akhbar al-Akhyar,* Delhi: Matba-i-Mujfabai, H 1309, p. 253; Shaikh Ruknuddin, *Latif-i Quddusi,* Delhi, AH 1311, pp. 57-8, for the low-caste *murids* of Shaikh Abdul Qudus of Gangoh (d.1535).
82. *Akhbar al-Akhyar,* p. 225; *Lataif-i-Quddusi,* pp. 57-8.
83. *Waqi'at-i-Mushtaqi,* tr., p. 102.
84. *Epigraphia Indica, Arabic and Persian Supplement,* 1955-6 as cited by W.H. Siddiqui, 'Religious Tolerance as Gleaned from Medieval Inscriptions', *Proceedings of the Seminar on Medieval Inscriptions,* Aligarh, 1970, p. 56.
85. *Jambu Sagar,* Shlok no. 29, pp. 319-20. For this reference, I am indebted to Munshi Sohan Lal who has cited the Jambu Sagar in his Urdu work, *Tarikh-i-Bikaner.*
86. *Mirat-i Sikandari,* pp. 109-10.
87. Ibid., p. 132.
88. *Waqi'at-i-Mushtaqi,* p. 27 where the term *biradari* occurs for the first time; also Shaikh Abdul Haq Muhaddis Dehlevi, *Zadul Muttaqin wa Saluk-i Tariqal-yaqin,* MS personal collection of the author, ff. 149b, 150a, for the division of Muslims into *biradaris* in Gujarat.
89. *Baburnama,* op.cit., vol. 2, p. 518.
90. *Masnad-i-ali* Khawwas Khan, the premier noble under Sher Shah, was the son of Malik Sukha, a slave of Sher Shah. Haji Khan was also Sher Shah's slave and continued to serve as the governor of Bayana, Mewat and Eastern Rajputana till the fall of the Sur Empire in 1555. Cf. Iqtidar Husain Siddiqui, *History of Sher Shah Sur,* Aligarh, 1971, pp. 66, 68, 149 (endnote 3).
91. *Waqi'at-i Mushtaqi,* tr., p. 205; Abdul Qadir Badaoni, *Muntakhab-ut Tawarikh,* Calcutta: Bibliotheca Indica 1869, vol. 1, p. 411.
92. *History of Sher Shah Sur,* pp. 149-58.
93. In medieval times the Dhusar caste (grocers) was considered to be the lowest Banya caste, because most of its members dealt in food

grains and other commodities on a small scale. *Baqqal* is a word normally used in Indian Persian for Banya. See Abul Fazl, *Akbarnama*, Calcutta: Bibiotheca Indica, 1886, vol. 1, p. 337, tr., Beveridge, Calcutta: Bibliotheca Indica, 1939, pp. 616-17; also I.H. Siddiqui, *History of Sher Shah*, pp. 149-50.

94. *Waqi'at-i-Mushtaqi*, p. 210, also See Iqtidar Husain Siddiqui, *History of Sher Shah Sur*, p. 157.
95. There are references to the Dhusar *Zamindars* in the Persian text of the *Ain-i Akbari* but Jarrett has translated *Zamindars* as castes which is incorrect.
96. *Waqi'at-i Mushtaqi*, pp. 283-4.
97. Ibid., pp. 272-3.
98. Barani, 1862, p. 176.
99. Mahmud Bukhari, *Tarikh-i Salatin-i Gujarat*, ed. A.A. Tirmizi, *Medieval India Quarterly*, Aligarh, 1963, vol. 5.
100. *Waqi'at-i Mushtaqi*, p. 196.
101. *Epigraphia Indica, Arabic and Persian Supplement*, Calcutta, 1953-4, pp. 3-4.
102. *Waqi'at-i Mushtaqi*, pp. 35, 40-1, 44, passim.

CHAPTER 7

Scientific Developments in the Delhi Sultanate

Many important scientific instruments found their way into India along with elite emigrants from the neighbouring Muslim countries in general, and Central Asia in particular, after the foundation of the Sultanate at the beginning of the thirteenth century. The growth of the natural and applied sciences and scientific instruments in pre-Mughul India is however largely unexplored. Nevertheless, available evidence, both in the conventional and non-conventional sources, helps piece together a portrait of intellectual life as well as the progress of creative astronomy, astronomical instruments and time-keeping devices, and a scientific temper in India during the period of the Delhi Sultanate. This chapter analyses evidence found in contemporary sources.

It is worth mentioning that Delhi, which was earlier a *pargana* town of no importance,[1] emerged as a repository of the highest cultural achievements in the Persian, speaking lands of the Islamic world, for following the conquest of Central Asia and Iran by the Mongols in the thirteenth century, men of talent and learning who survived the massacre came to seek refuge in India. Many of these men played an important role in enriching the culture of India. According to Sadid u'ddin Muhammad 'Awfi, a Bukhara-born refugee, the Sultan (Shams u'ddin Iltutmish) helped those who fled the tyranny of the Mongols and entered India.

> The power, grandeur and magnanimity of the religion sustaining monarch turned his dominions into a safe haven for the Muslim refugees. The Sultan went out of his way to help those who fled tyranny and oppression of the infidel Tatars [i.e. Mongols]. He takes care of the refugees. By the grace of God, he has been able, like Alexander to defend [his people] against the hordes [of Mongols]. During these days when the World

> of Islam has been sacked by the fire of their sword, thousands of mosques and pulpits have fallen in disuse, neither *khutbah* [Friday sermon] is read nor congregational prayer offered there. Thousands of houses have been levelled to the ground and the residents disappeared. The Sultan [Iltutmish] granted them shelter and made arrangements for their comfortable living. Every Muslim is safe and free from worry and fear.[2]

'Isami supplements the earlier source with regard to the emergence of Delhi as a metropolis during the reign of Sultan Iltutmish (AD 1211-16). He mentions in some detail the arrival of men of learning, scientists, artists, artisans physicians and others from different civilized countries during the region of Iltutmish. They turned Delhi into a centre of art and learning.[3]

> In that city one splendour became evident, yes, there is delight in the new city. Many genuine descendants of the Prophet (PBH) arrived from Arabia, many traders from Khurasan, many painters from China, many learned men natives of Bukhara, many ascetics and devotees from every clime, from every kingdom and of every sort, artisans from every town and every race,...Many assayers, knowledgeable in precious gems, numberless sellers of jewels, scholars versed in greek sciences [*hakiman-i-yunan*] and physicians from Rum [Anatolia or Asia minor], many learned men from every part. In that city they came like moths gathering around a candle.[3]

Since the source of the scientific knowledge and instruments introduced in the Sultanate by the refugees lay in the Arab-Persian lands or Central Asia, I first discuss the history of the progress of the science of astronomy in the classical lands of Islam.

While Islamic civilization acquired knowledge of natural and applied sciences from different countries, the Muslims made advances on these subjects through their own researches. They also invented instruments useful in scientific applications. In fact, various sciences, and scientific instruments became the necessary accompaniments of civilized life and generated new components of elite culture.

By about the eleventh century AD, the science of astronomy, including astrology, had gained popularity among the elite in Central Asia. Growth of intellectual curiosity among the scientist-philosophers led to the questioning of accepted truths concerning the universe. Al-Beruni (d. AD 1048) and others even suggested 'the possibility of the centrality of the sun in a solar system, with the earth both revolving around it and turning on its own axis, but, for various reasons, this did not then seem the most likely hypothesis'.[4]

An intellectual culture developed under the patronage of the rulers of the lands of higher culture, such as Khwarazm, Ghazna and Qarakhanids of Samarqand, and inspired the Shansabani rulers of Ghur who were otherwise portrayed by the early eleventh century writers as 'nominal Muslims lacking culture'. Amir 'Abbas bin Shis, a tyrannical ruler, is credited with having invited skilled architects and scientists from different places for the construction of a fort with an observatory at Sangah in the Valley of Mandesh. Minhaj-i-Siraj says:

> The walls, after the manners of a parapet, were carried from that castle, on two sides, to the strong ground on the summit of the mountain, on a knoll, a lofty *qasr* [palace] was directed to be raised, with twelve towers, and in every tower, like the zodiacal circle in the firmament, there were six towers towards the east and north, and six others towards the west and south, marked out; and these were so arranged that, every day, the sun would shine through one of those openings and approximately turned to the position of its rise. By this means, he used to know in what degree of what sign of zodiac the sun was on the particular day.[5]

The followers of Al-Beruni in India held fast to the view that the earth moved round the sun. In his celebrated historical *mathnavi, Qir'an us-S'a'adayn* (long poem), composed during the reign of Sultan Mu'iz uddin Kaiqubad (AD 1287-90), Amir Khusrau says:

> The movement of the earth has been linked with the time, hence the day and night, the seasons of Spring and Autumn. These changes constitute the source of life and comfort for the living beings.[6]

Again, Amir Khusrau expresses the same view in his prose work, *I'jaz-i-Khusravi,* brought to completion towards the close of Sultan 'Ala ud'din Khalji's reign (AD 1296-1316). He says that people moved around the man in authority as the earth moves around the sun.[7]

Amir Khusrau's view does not seem to have been buried with him. The relevant evidence, available in a later source tends to suggest that many astronomers in India subscribed to the same view. Commenting on Khusrau's above-quoted verse, Shaikh Nur al-Haqq, the compiler of *Zubdat al-Tawarikh,* says that some of the *hukama'* (scientist scholars) hold that change in time is owing to the movement of earth. That the earth rotates from the west to the east.[8]

Other works, composed by Amir Khusrau such as *Nuh Sipihr* and *Tughluqnama* show that he possessed good knowledge both of astronomy and astrology. His interest in astronomy seems to have encouraged him to gain familiarity with the achievements made by Hindus in scientific fields during ancient times. Extolling their achievements, he wrote that physics, mathematics, astronomy and divination of the past and the future were known to Hindus. Khusrau also became conversant with the subtleties of these sciences to some extent[9] and also appears to have evinced interest in creative astronomy. References contained in his writings to 'astrolabe' show that he possessed technical knowledge of the instrument.[10]

A word about the popularity of astrology among the ruling elite of the Sultanate of Delhi may be added. The early writers who came from Khurasan and Central Asian lands to India do not seem to have been sceptical about the scope of the influence of stars on the earth and its inhabitants, although it was contrary to the teachings of Islam. The *ulama* (orthodox scholars) considered it blasphemous impertinence. Unlike them, the social elite both in Central Asia and India patronized the astrologers and astronomers practised astrology as a livelihood by preparing astrological tables and horoscopes. It may also be recalled that astrology had already become an integral part of astronomy in Central Asia long before the foundation of the Delhi Sultanate through Buddhist influences. For example, Hasan Nizami who came from Nishapur to Delhi during the reign of Sultan Qutb u'ddin Aibak (AD 1206-10) and wrote the historical work, *Taj al-Ma'asir,* mentions the zodiac, the seven planets and the constellation of the stars, displaying his faith in the roles of the stars and planets over man's destiny. Muhammad 'Awfi calls Nizam al-Mulk Junaidi *Sahib-i-Qira'an* (fortunate one born at the time of the meeting of two auspicious stars).[11] But the pursuit of astrology was condemned by the Muslim orthodoxy. Amir Khusrau also writes that the practice of astrology was seen as nothing short of blasphemy by the Islamic orthodoxy.[12]

Shams Siraj 'Afif wrote in defence of astronomy and astrology stating, 'Astronomy is one of the fourteen sciences known to the scholars. But its study has been forbidden by the Prophet (PBH). The *ulama* (orthodox scholars) also disapprove of it. It is, however, permissible to know the rules, concerning the shadow of the sun and that in a particular month in what degree of what sign of the zodiac the sun would be, the hours of the short night and the long night and when it (the night) turned into the day.'[13]

As regards Zia u'ddin Barani, he not only informs us about the famous astronomers of Delhi of his time (thirteenth and fourteenth centuries) but also provides us clues about the interaction and co-operation between the Hindu and Muslim astronomers. According to him, there was considerable observation and experiment. The sultans patronized the men of talent and knowledge and promoted the cause of different sciences, natural as well as applied. Here I confine the discussion to the progress of astronomy and astronomers only. Barani says that Mawlana Hamid u'ddin Mutriz could be compared with the famous Greek scientists of ancient times in his knowledge of medicines *(tib)* and astronomy.[14] Writing on the efflorescence of learning and culture during the reign of Sultan 'Ala ud'din Khalji (1296-1316), he tells us that many scientists, men of learning and talent, having been attracted by India's fame, came from different countries and took abode in Delhi, with the result that Delhi surpassed Baghdad and Cairo as a centre of culture and became the rival of Constantinople (the centre of Greek sciences and philosophy). Many expert astronomers gained fame on account of their knowledge of and experience in calculating the astronomical tables. Barani adds that the science of astronomy and astrology was so popular among the elite of Delhi that none of its quarters was found without an astronomer. They received gifts and rewards both in cash and kind, from the King, the grandees and other important persons of the city. Many of them received villages and stipends from Sultan 'Ala ud'din Khalji and many Hindu and Muslim astronomers were also held in great favour, owing to their fame. According to Barani, 'the elite of Delhi could not start any work or undertake any project without consulting the astronomer. Even the wives of Sultan 'Ala ud'din Khalji patronized them'.[15] All this tends to suggest that astrology and astronomy had come together and had the makings of a 'shared interest' for the Hindu and Muslim elite of India.

The official history of Sultan Firuz Shah's reign, *Sirat-i-Firuz Shahi* (compiled in AD 1370), also provides us with interesting information about the Sultan's interest in astronomy and astrology. According to it, royal inquisitiveness promoted research into the particulars of astronomy and a number of treatises were composed in consequence. Some of them were dictated by the Sultan himself. We are also informed that the ancient Sanskrit works on astronomy were translated into Persian and the *Dala'il-Firuz Shahi* that dealt with the systems of rainfall, eclipses, conjunction of stars and the impact the stars had on the earth and its inhabitants was also compiled.[16] This work has in fact survived. It was compiled by 'Abd al-'Aziz Shams Thanesari and it is significant in so far as it casts light on Sultan Firuz Shah's belief that the heavenly bodies influenced the earth and its inhabitants.[17]

The following section examines information contained in our sources about astronomical instruments that found their way into India during the Sultanate period. The magnetic compass and astrolabes in particular became known in India through the immigrants. Muhammad 'Awfi, a widely-travelled man gives an eye-witness description of the magnetic compass in his magnum opus, *Jawami' al-Hikayat wa-Liwami' al-Riwayat* (completed in AD 1230). This magnetic compass was used by seamen, voyaging through the Arabian Sea and the Indian Ocean. The following is his description, 'Once I was on a voyage through the sea when all of a sudden a storm burst. It became dark and cloudy and the waves were violent. The people, being seized with panic, started clamouring. Much disturbed, the captain lost direction. However, he quickly brought out a hallow (instrument) of iron, resembling a fish in shape, and put it in a dish full of water. The (instrument) revolved and became fixed in the direction of *qiblah* (i.e. Makhah).[18] As a result, the captain obtained the correct direction. Being amazed, I made enquiry about it; he told me: "This is the Lode-stone *(sang-i-maqnatis)*; when it is placed in the dish, it revolves, owing to its magnetic property and becomes fixed as soon as the particular direction is reached. I actually found it to be so. God knows the truth".'[19]

The astrolabe (*ustarlab* in Arabic), another important astronomical instrument that was used by seamen as well as astronomers, seems to have been introduced by the immigrants about the beginning of the thirteenth century. Since it was the name given to a set of astronomical instruments that served various theoretical and practical purposes, such as the demonstration of many problems of spherical astronomy, the measuring of altitudes, determination of the hour of the day and the night, etc., the history of its origin in the classical Muslim lands needs to be briefly discussed.

The Arabs began to take interest in Greek sciences during the 'Abbasid period (ninth century) and had ancient Greek works on astronomy and other sciences translated into Arabic. They were also inspired to have astronomical instruments, such as the astrolabe[20] constructed. The references to *ustarlab-i-Shumali* (northern astrolabe) and *starlab-i-Janubi* (southern astrolabe to be employed in the southern hemisphere) contained in the Arab classics cast light on the rapid progress of astronomical instruments under the patronage of the Caliphs.[21]

In the tradition of the 'Abbasid Caliphs, the rulers of Central Asia, such as the sultans of Khwarazm, Ghazna and the Qarakhanids of Samarqand patronized scientists and men of learning, with the result that their courts also became centres of intellectual culture. The craft of constructing the astrolabe seems to have been introduced in Central Asia by the eleventh century. For example, Al-Beruni explains a flattened astrolabe, 'which served as stellar chart, on which the pole of ecliptic circles of longitude, were represented as equidistant concentric circle and the circles of latitude by equidistant radii'.[22] In this century, the planispherical astrolabe, constructed by the Spanish Arab astronomer Al-Zarqali (d. AD 1091) also found its way into other Muslim countries. Al-Zarqali successfully demonstrated the limitations of the ordinary planispherical astrolabes and showed that because of the precision of the equinoxes no ordinary astrolabe could be relied upon after the lapse of a long period of years.[23]

It is also worth-recalling that Central Asian astronomers made further advance in this field. Al-Muzaffar bin Muzaffar al-Tusi (d. AD 1213-14) constructed a linear *(khatli)* astrolabe which came to be known as *'Asa' i-Tusi* (i.e. the Staff of al-Tusi). It consisted of one single piece, viz., a rod, with a plumb line attached to its mid-point (i.e. the projection of the North Pole), a second thread fastened at its lower end, a third thread, which was freely movable.[24]

Different kinds of astrolabes seem to have become common in India after the foundation of the Sultanate in the beginning of the thirteenth century. We also find references to the astrolabes in the early Indo-Persian sources. For instance Siraji Khurasani mentions the astrolabe in one of his *qasidas* (panegyrics) composed in praise of Zia u'ddin Muhammad, son of Nizam al-Mulk Junaidi, the *wazir* of Sultan Iltutmish: 'The eye of his intellect sees through imagination the state of affairs in the space, without the help of an *ustarlab* (astrolabe)'.[25] Mention by Amir Khusrau of the astrolabe in the following couplet tends to suggest its popularity among the elite of the Delhi Sultanate. It was used by people to know the auspicious moment.

> *Ustarlab-i-Sanjabi Mauzun Qiyas,*
> *Ba-adesha gashtand S'at Shinas.*
> 'With the accurate yellowish astrolabe, the astrologers
> Buried themselves in knowing the auspicious moment'.[26]

Likewise, the *Basatin ul-Urs,* a romance brought to completion by Ikhtisan, the *dabir-i-Khas* (Minister-in-charge of the royal chancellery under Sultan Muhammad bin Tughluq) in AD 1325-6 successfully reflects the scientific and cultural ethos of the Sultanate. In this work we find references to the astrolabe, physicians, their system of treatment and *darul-shafa* (hospital), maintained with government aid. It implies that the astrolabe had become a curiosity for the elite and a favourite instrument for the scientists; with its help they determined the auspiciousness as well as the exactness of time.[27] Another scholar, and poet, Muthar of Kara who flourished during the reign of Muhammad bin Tughluq and Firuz Shah extols in a *qasida* the patronage, extended by Ainu l-Mulk Mahru to the men of talent and learning, saying, 'At times, subtleties of poetry and music are discussed, At other times, theories related to the calendar and astrolabe are taken up for discussion'.[28]

With the accession of Sultan Firuz Shah to the throne of Delhi in 1351, a new era began in the promotion of science and learning. The expansionist policy of Sultan Muhammad bin Tughlaq was abandoned and that of conservation was adopted instead. As a result, his newly-founded capital, Firuzabad (near Delhi) became the rendezvous of men of talent and art. The Sultan himself was interested in astronomy and astrology. For the purpose of observation, astrolabes of various types were constructed by his order. His patronage to the scientists and technicians made further advance possible in the construction of astronomical instruments. It is reported that with the help of these instruments the time for offering the daily five prayers, the auspiciousness of particular moments of time and the hour passed, could be exactly determined. The details, furnished to us by the contemporary writer about the magnificent astrolabe called *Ustarlab-i-Firuz Shahi*, set up on the loftiest tower of Firuzabad makes it clear that the tower was an observatory where a number of scientists remained occupied with observing the stars. This astrolabe is said to have been constructed under the direction of the Sultan himself. Before its construction, he was informed by the scientists that the astrolabe constructed in Alexandria during ancient times was *ustarlab-i-shumali* (northern astrolabe) and that it could not be used in the southern hemisphere. Thereupon, the Sultan decided to have an astrolabe made that could be both *shumali* (northern) and *janubi* (southern). Thus the astronomers, designers and engineers were ordered to construct it.[29] Its components, such as disc, the *halqah* (ring), connected with the *'urwah* (hook), *kursi* (throne), *umm* (mother or chamber) which contained *sufaf* (tablets), *safaih* (flag-stones), *'ankabut* (spider or net) and staff were exquisite and of large size.[30] This description suggests that the *Firuzshahi* astrolabe was a modified form of the *'Asa' i-Tusi* (the staff of al-Tusi), mentioned above. Shams Siraj 'Afif supplements the *Sirat-i-Firuzshahi* in this regard. He says that besides the grand astrolabe, suspended from the royal tower, Sultan Firuz Shah kept a portable astrolabe with him all the time.[31]

Since the time of Firuz Shah, the astrolabe with the staff remained in use throughout the later period. The number of experts making and using the astrolabes increased and some even gained considerable fame. For example, during the Lodi and early Mughul period. Khwajah Uways Gwaliori of Jewish origin was an authority on astronomy, geometry and astrolabes, in addition to Islamic sciences and Arabic language. The Mughul emperor Humayun patronized him as an astronomer.[32]

Similarly literary sources carry interesting information on the progress of horology. Muthar of Kara, the leading poet, associated with Firuz Shah's court, mentions in one of his poems, composed in praise of the new Capital of Firuzabad, the time-determining machine installed on the top of the royal palace. He tells us that because of it people could know the exact time for keeping the fast (during the month of *Ramadan)* and the hours of the five daily prayers, no matter whether it was a sunny or dark night during the rainy season.[33] Shams Siraj 'Afif is more fulsome in his account of this clock. He states that the rules were carefully formulated to calculate the time and an elaborate system was established. The hours of the day and the night were correctly calculated. Then the water clock (*Tas-gharyal* which literally means bowl and gong) was constructed and set up on the top of the palace. It is reported by 'Afif to have been one of the remarkable achievements of Firuz Shah's reign. He also tells us that it aroused wonder among people from the borders of Khurasan (i.e. the region now included in modern Afghanistan) to Bengal. The apparent motive behind its construction was to enhance the prestige of the Sultan, since it could be deemed as meritorious work from the point of view of religion, as its construction resolved the problem of finding proper times of prayers and beginning and end of fasts when it happened to be night time or the skies were overcast. 'Afif tells us that the gong's sound could be heard at a considerable distance after the hour had passed.[34]

It would seem that the Firuz Shahi *Tas-gharyal* was not a traditional water-clock, known to the Indians since ancient times,[35] for had it been so, it would not have aroused any wonder among the people.[36] More so, since the sounding of the gong seems to have been part of the mechanism. Though 'Afif does not describe its mechanism, the details furnished by him suggest that it was constructed on the principles of both the water clock and a sun-dial, and the clock-work machine was a single unit. The water clock was not always exact in its working. B.P. Saxena correctly points out that its errors were corrected by reference to a sundial, but also mistakenly states, 'The cup and its tub and the sundial were put on the top of the gate of Firuzabad palace'.[37] Such clocks were very popular in the Middle-Eastern countries since the twelfth century, and their construction occupied the attention of scientists and mechanics particularly because they helped determine the exact hours of prayer.[38]

Some words are in order about the progress of science and culture in the regional Sultanates that arose on the political scene in the beginning of the fifteenth century. After the death of Sultan Firuzshah in AD 1388 the dissolution of the Delhi Sultanate was paradoxically paralleled by the proliferation of its imperial culture in the regional sultanates, founded by the erstwhile governors. At the beginning of the fifteenth century a number of independent sultanates and principalities arose and their rulers vied with one another in turning their capitals into centres of learning and culture in the tradition of the Delhi sultans. Among the Bahmani Sultans of Gulbarga, Sultan Taj u'ddin Firuz Shah (AD 1397-1422) evinced keen interest in promoting natural and applied sciences. Well-versed in Euclidian geometry, dialectics, mathematics and astronomy, he invited scientists from different lands. He also undertook construction of an observatory on the Balaghat Hills near Daulatabad in 1408. Its supervision was entrusted to Mahmud Gazruni and Hakim Hasan Gilani. The observatory was still in progress when Hakim Gilani died a premature death leaving the work incomplete.[39]

The Sharqi sultans of Jaunpur were also great patrons of art, learning and science. During the reign of Sultan Ibrahim Sharqi (AD 1400-40), a fairly large sprinkling of scholars and scientists gathered at Jaunpur, the capital of the Sharqi Sultanate. One of the scholars, Shihab *hakim*, who seems to have hailed from Kirman in Iran, tells us that, besides having a *Pani-Mahal* (water-palace) with a cistern opening inside the royal garden, the sultan had constructed a clock with an automatic gong which sounded after a *ghari* (24 minutes) had elapsed. The sound of the gong was accompanied by a lotus flower studded with jewels coming out from inside a perforated box, attached to the clock, indicating that one *ghari* had passed. This clock was placed in the arch of the eastern wall of the royal palace. As for the working of the clock, Shihab *hakim* tells us that it depended upon the fire and the water in the cells inside the arch, suggesting that the clock worked through a vacuum system produced by steam. Shihab describes the practice of dividing the day and the night into sixty *gharis* (each of 24 minutes) and eight *pahrs* (watches), and how in order to avoid making fractions, the first *pahr* (watch) was taken to comprise seven *gharis*, the second one of eight, the third of seven and the fourth of eight *gharis* in the day. Likewise, the night was also divided into four *pahrs*. Thus the day and the night together still had sixty *gharis*, which unlike *pahrs* remained fixed units of time.[40]

The Lodi sultans of Delhi who revived the past glory of the Sultanate extended large hearted patronage to the men of talent and learning. During their period too, the astronomical clocks were popular among the members of the ruling elite. No doubt, the water-clock was a common time-keeping device in the whole of India. But many sophisticated nobles preferred the exquisite sundial, and employed expert astronomers and time-keepers for determining the exact hours of the day and night. Shaikh Rizq ullah Mushtaqi who served under certain Lodi nobles, mentions how, 'Daulat

Khan Lodi, the *muqta*ʻ of Lahore was a pious and law-abiding man. In the palace of his residence he had a sundial with a wooden staff fixed upon it to measure the correct time. The servants were appointed to maintain the record of the shadow and engrave it on the disc. They noted it and informed the (master) about the shadow, the changing positions, and in this way he was kept informed of the passage of time'.[41] Similarly, Miyan Sulayman Farmuli, also an important noble who resided in Agra is reported to have had the same type of sundial.[42]

The Mughul conqueror, Babur, who supplanted the rule of the Lodi dynasty, found gong-men (time-keepers) and water-clocks in use in every urban centre of some importance. Describing the division of time in India, he said:

> As in our countries what is known by the term '*kicha-qunduz*' [the day and the night in Turki] is divided into twenty-four [parts], each called a '*sa*ʻ*at*' [hour]. And, every *sa*ʻ*at* is divided into sixty [minutes] each called a *daqiqah* [minute], so that a day and night [nyethemeron] consists of 1440 minutes. The people of Hind divide a day and night into sixty parts, each called a *ghari* [hour]. Besides, they divide the day and the night into eight parts, each of four [parts], called *pahr* (watch). The *pahr* in Persian is called a *pas*. In those lands [i.e. Central Asia], the *pas-o-Pasban* had been heard but these particulars were not known there. According to this [Indian] system, in almost all the considerable cities of India a body of men, called *ghariyalis* [gongmen] is chosen and appointed. They cast a broad brass [plate] thing, perhaps as large as a tray [*tabaq*] and of about two-fingers' thickness. It is called the *ghariyalah,* and hung up in a high place. They also have a vessel perforated at the bottom like a *Jam-i-Sa*ʻ*at* [time-cup] which is filled in a *ghari* [i.e. 24 minutes]. The *ghariyalis* put the cup into water till it fills. For example, they will put the [perforated] cup into water at day-break, and when it fills the first-time, they strike the gong with their wooden hammer, when second time, twice, and so on till the end of the watch [*pahr*].[43]

It is worth noting that in the neighbouring Muslim countries the hour was measured as of sixty minutes and the day and night of twenty four hours. But, in India the Muslim rulers, perhaps out of regard for the ancient custom, did not interfere with it. The old system was retained so far as the division of time was concerned.

To conclude, the steady flow of elite emigration from the neighbouring countries in general and Central Asian lands in particular, led to the infusion of new scientific ideas and crafts. Knowledge and technical skill possessed by the immigrants obtained them the patronage of the sultans and the nobility. The munificent patronage extended by the sultans to them was a great lure, while the Mongol conquest of their homelands also drove them to India. With their influx into India, new centres of learning and culture emerged, from the north-western frontier region upto Bengal. The natural and applied sciences made further progress, owing to interaction and collaboration between the Hindu scientists and the foreign immigrants. Indepth analysis of conventional and non-conventional source material provides the progress of popular sciences, astronomy, mathematics, medicines, metallurgy, chemistry and opthomology during the Sultanate period. So far this has been unexplored territory, awaiting historical research.

Endnotes

1. 'Isami, *Futuh us-Salatin*, ed. A.S. Usha, Madras, 1948, p. 108, hereafter cited as 'Isami,
2. Cf. Iqtidar Husain Siddiqui, *Perso-Arabic Sources of Information on the Life and Conditions in the Sultanate of Delhi*, New Delhi: Munshiram Manoharlal, 1982, p. 28; *idem*, 'Relations Between Sultan Jalal al-Din Khwarazm Shah and the Turkish Sultans of North India' *Aligarh Journal of Oriental Studies;* Spring 1986, vol. 3, no. 1, pp. 55-66.
3. Isami, *Futuh us-Salatin*, pp. 114-15.
4. G.M. Wickens, 'Astronomy', *Introduction to Islamic Civilization*, ed. R.M. Savory, Cambridge: Cambridge University Press, 1976, p. 116.
5. *Tabaqat-i-Nasiri*, ed. Abdul Ha'i Habibi, Kabul. 1963, vol. 1, pp. 331-2; See also tr. Major Raverty, vol. 1, Calcutta, 1897, p. 331.
6. Amir Khusrau, *Qiran us-S'adain*, ed. Ismail Meeruti, op.cit., Institute College, Aligarh, 1918, p. 5; lines 25-6, also editor's *Introduction* in Urdu, p. 99.
7. In volume IV of the *I'jaz-i-Khusravi*, Amir Khusrau writes on different popular sciences of the day, such as *Ilm-i-maishat* (economics), prosody, grammar logic, philosophy, etc., displaying his erudite knowledge, Cf. *I'jaz-i-Khusravi*, vol. 4, Lucknow, 1876, pp. 236-318.
8. Cf. Shaikh Nur al-Haqq was the son of Shaikh Abd al-Haqq *Muhaddith of* Delhi and a contemporary of Emperor Jahangir and Shahjahan. Cf. Ismail Meeruti, *Introduction* (In Urdu), *Qiran al-Sadain*, op.cit., p. 100.

9. *Nuh Sipihr,* ed. Mohammad Wahid Mirza, Calcutta: Oxford University Press, 1950, pp. 162-3; See also 224-6, for the horoscopes drawn by him.
10. Amir Khusrau, *Aina-i-Sikandari*, ed. Muhammed Said Ahmad Farugi, Aligarh, 1917, p. 62.
11. Cf. Iqtidar Husain Siddiqui, 'The Origin and Growth of Islamicate Historiography in India: Analysis of the Thirteenth Century Indo-Persian Historians' Approach to the Foundation of Muslim Rule in South Asian Sub-continent', *Journal of Objective Studies,* New Delhi, July-October, 1989, vol. 1, nos. 1-2, pp. 65-88. See idem, *Perso-Arabic Sources on the Life and Conditions in the Sultanate of Delhi,* New Delhi; Munshiram Manoharlal 1992, pp. 2-3, 28-9, for details about 'Awfi.
12. *I'jaz-i-Khusravi,* vol. 4, tr. Iqtidar Husain Siddiqui, Illinois, USA: Islamic Thought and Science Institute, 2007, p. 188.
13. Shams Siraj 'Afif' *Tarikh-i-Firuz Shahi,* Calcutta: Bibliotheca Indica, 1891, p. 258, hereafter cited as Afif.
14. Zia u'ddin Barani, *Tarikh-i-Firuz Shahi,* Calcutta: Bibliotheca Indica, 1862, p. 112, hereafter cited as Barani.
15. Barani, 1862, pp. 362-4.
16. Anonymous, *Sirat-i-Firuz Shahi,* MS. Patna: Khuda Bakhsh Oriental Public Library, f. 153a.
17. The compiler says that he translated it from Hindvi (Sanskrit) into Persian by the order of the religious-minded Sultan, Abu al-Muzaffar Firuzshah so that people might benefit from its perusal. The rare manuscript, wrongly entitled by a later scribe as *Kitab al-Nujum,* is preserved in Sir Sulaiman Collection, Maulana Azad Library, Aligarh, ff. 1b-185b.
18. 'Awfi seems to have boarded the ship at Jeddah for Gujarat. He came to Cambay which had a sizeable number of Muslim traders who followed either Shafi'I or Hanafi school of law. The Hanafi Muslims made him their Qazi. Cf. Siddiqui, Perso-Arabic *Sources of Information on the Life and Conditions in the Sultanate of Delhi,* pp. 2-3.
19. *Jawami al-Hikayat wa-Liwami al-Riwayat,* MS. Patna: Khuda Bakhsh Oriental Public Library, Qism 4, f. 452 b; also See Siddiqui, *Perso-*

Arabic Sources of Information on the Life and Conditions in the Sultanate of Delhi, p. 37.

20. The planispherical astrolabe consists of an evenly balanced circle or disc of metal and other suspensory apparatus, comprising three parts: a triangular piece of metal called *kursi* (throne) which is attached to the body of the instrument; a handle *(urwah)* affixed to the point of the *kursi* so that it can be turned to either side in the plane of the latter, a ring (*halqah*) passing through the handle and moving freely.
21. Cf. W. Hartner, *Encyclopaedia of Islam,* Leiden: E.J. Brill, 1960, vol. 1, A.B.P. 722b. New Edition,
22. Cf. Dwight M. Donaldson, 'The Nomenclature And Common Use of the Astrolabe', *Islamic Culture,* Hyderabad, January, 1945, rpt, vol. 19, New York, 1971, pp. 49-53, also for the component parts of the astrolabe, such as disc, tablets (*safafa in Arabic),* etc.
23. Loc. cit.
24. Hartner, *Encyclopaedia of Islam,* op.cit., p. 727a.
25. Cf. Siraji Khurasani, *Diwan-i-Siraji Khurasani,* ed. Dr. Nazir Ahmad, Aligarh, 1972, *qasidah* no. 100, couplet 19, p. 304.
26. *Aina-i-Sikandari,* ed. Muhammad Said Ahmad Farooqi, Aligarh; p. 62.
27. *Bastin al-Uns*, MS, British Library, London, Add, 7717, Rieu, vol. 2, p. 753b. f.47a.
28. *Sirat-i-Firuz Shahi,* op.cit., ff. 154a-b.
29. *Diwan-i-Muthar,* ed. Abdur Razzaq, Patna: Khuda Bakhsh Oriental Public Library, 1998, p. 24.
30. Ibid., f.145a.
31. 'Afif, *Tarikh-i-Firuz Shahi,* p. 370.
32. Mulla Qati' Harawi, *Tazkira-i-Majma'a al-Shu'ara-i Jahangir Shahi,* ed. Muhammad Salim Akhtar, University of Karachi: Karachi Institute of Central and West Asian Studies, 1977, pp. 63-4.
33. 'Muthar's *Verses*, ed. Wahid Mirza, *Oriental College Magazine,* Lahore, May, 1935, p. 132.
34. Afif, *Tarikh-i-Firuz Shahi,* pp. 257-9.
35. In his article, tracing the origin of the practice of time division in India, S.R. Sarma refers to Firuz Shah's *Tas-gharyal* as the

continuation of the ancient device. He has not examined the evidence about it available in Muthar's poem and Afif's work. It was certainly not like the indigenous water-clock. 'Announcing Time - The Unique Method at Hayatnagar', *Proceedings of the Indian History Congress,* 52nd Session, New Delhi, 1991-2, pp. 427-8.

36. Afif, *Tarikh-i-Firuz Shahi,* p. 260.
37. Cf. A *Comprehensive History of India,* The Delhi Sultanate, rpt, New Delhi, 1982, vol. 5, p. 599.
38. Cf. Abdul Sattar Siddiqui, 'Construction of Clocks and Islamic Civilization', *Islamic Culture,* Hyderabad, vol. 1, 1927, pp. 245-9, for details.
39. Cf. H.K. Sherwani, *The Bahmanis of the Deccan,* Hyderabad, 1953, p. 145.
40. All this information is found in a fifteenth century *mathnavi,* composed in AD 1454-5 by Shihab *Hakim* who adopted the pen-name Shihabi. Mahmud Khan Shirani correctly identified Shihabi with Shihab Hakim, the compiler of a lexicon, referred to in another fifteenth century Persian lexicon, entitled *Sharafnamah-i-Maneri.* Since Shirani did not have access to *Ma'thir-i-Mahmud Shahi,* also compiled by Shihab *Hakim,* he falls into the error of stating that Shihab Hakim was associated with the court of the Sultan of Bengal like the compiler of the *Sharafnamah-i-Maneri* because Shihab himself states in his *Ma'sir-i-Mahmud Shahi* that he left Jaunpur, sometime after the death of Sultan Mahmud Sharqi and came to join the court of Sultan Mahmud Khalji of Malwa. His full family name was 'Ali bin Mahmud al-Kirmani Cf. *Ma'thir-i-Mahmud Shahi,* ed. and abridged by Nurul Hasan Ansari, Delhi: Indo-Persian Society, 1968, pp. 7-8.
41. Cf. *Waqiat-i-Mushtaqi,* tr. Iqtidar Husain Siddiqui, New Delhi: Northern Book Centre, 1993, p. 85.
42. Ibid., pp. 85-6.
43. I have rendered the text from Abd al-Rahim Khan-i-Khanan's Persian translation of the *Baburnamah,* but also compared it with the English translation by Mrs A.S. Beveridge, Both have minor variations. *Baburnamah,* Persian tr. Abd al-Rahim Khan-i-Khanan, Bombay, 1308H., pp.203-4; tr. Mrs A.S. Beveridge, rpt, New Delhi, 1979, vol. 2, pp. 516-17.

CHAPTER 8

The Teaching Tradition

The educational system in a civilized society during medieval times was influenced by the religion of its people and designed in the light of its teachings as well as the material needs of the society. In Islam, the basic thrust of its scripture (Quran) is man and knowledge both of religious and non-religious sciences.[1] The Quran instructs its followers to pray: 'My Lord: Increase me in knowledge.' In response to Quranic teaching, Muslims attached importance to and facilities were created, for the education of people. In the very first century of Islam, the Islamic educational system appears to have been graded. A student having completed elementary education, turned to higher levels of learning. Doubtless, the approach of Islam to education was theocentric, in the sense that God and His will were seen as the role determining norms during the early phase. Gradually interaction with the educated classes of people in the conquered countries inspired them to learn secular sciences and then make original contributions in the field through fresh research and enquiry.

In India, the Islamic educational system was introduced after the conquest of Makran, Sind and the territorial unit of Multan in the beginning of the eighth century. Education seems to have developed around learned men to whom students thronged to acquire knowledge. Even children of low-caste converts appear to have been educated by them, with the result that some who belonged to the second generation of converts turned into scholars of Islamic sciences.[2] As regards the north-western Punjab beyond the provincial unit of Multan, it began to benefit from a new educational system following its annexation by Sultan Mahmud (d. AD 1030) to his Ghaznavid Sultanate. By this time educational institutions seem to have become well-established in the Islamic world. *Bayt al-Hikmah* (House of

Wisdom) at Baghdad and the *Darul-Hikmah* in Cairo during the tenth and eleventh centuries were known as centres of higher learning and research. A great patron of learning, Sultan Mahmud founded grand madrasas which became well-established educational institutions in Ghazna and other cities of his Sultanate. Here scholars were employed to impart instruction in *tafsir* (exegesis of the Quran), *hadis* (the utterances of the prophet) and *fiqh* (Islamic jurisprudence).[3] In India also the *ulama* (religious scholars) were appointed to teach the students. Abu S'aid Gardezi writes that the Sultan ordered the construction of mosques and madrasas for catering to the educational and religious needs of people in the Indian dominions.[4]

The occupation by the Ghuzz Turks of Ghazna and the area around, in the beginning of the later half of the twelfth century, led the elite of Ghazna including the Sultan to migrate to Lahore. With their arrival Lahore became a centre of learning and culture.[5] By this time the famous syllabi laid down by Imam Ghazzali (d. AD 1111) for the *Madrasa-i-Nizamiya* at Baghdad had been adopted everywhere in the Persian-speaking lands of the Islamic world. All emphasis was laid therein on the study of *tafsir* (The exegesis of the Quran), *hadis,* (the Prophetic tradition) and *fiqh*[6]. This educational system organized by Nizam ul-Mulk Tusi and Imam Ghazzali during the heyday of the Saljuq power entailed the establishment of an education department to supervise the functioning of the madrasas. The madrasas were not simply seminaries for directing higher education but also served as training centres for teachers. The system seems to have been adopted in the neighbouring countries. Minhaj-i-Siraj's *tabaqa* (section) relating to the Ghurid rulers describes that his father held the charge of the superintendent of education and in that capacity looked after the management of *Auqaf* (endowments) and functioning of the madrasas in the entire region of Bamian.[7] The relevant evidence tends to reveal that the same system was introduced in India.

Sultan Muiz u'ddin Muhammad bin Sam who supplanted the Ghaznavid rule in the Punjab and annexed it to his Sultanate of Ghazna in AD 1186, maintained the importance of Lahore as a centre of learning and culture. Inspired by its institutions, bazaars, scholars and poets, he made it his winter capital, in addition to Ghazna, the summer capital.[8] He emulated Sultan Mahmud in patronizing the men of learning. On his assassination in AD 1206, his successors in India followed his tradition in every respect. His lieutenant, Malik Qutbuddin Aibak to whom the Sultan entrusted the *iyalat* (governorship of the territory of Kuhram and Sunam in AD 1192) took keen interest in founding madrasas in the towns under his control. The grand madrasa built by him in Delhi was named after the Sultan as *Madrasa-i-Muizi.* The references contained in the *Tabaqat-i-Nasiri* and the *Fawaid ul-Fuad* to the *Madrasa-i-Muizi* tend to show that it was an important institution and housed in a large building with an impressive lofty gate.[9]

Aibak's successors in different parts of the Sultanate also had mosques, *khanqahs* and madrasas constructed in the cities and towns. Sultan Nāsir uddin Qubācha who had declared himself the Sultan of Sind and the Punjab after the accidental death of Sultan Qutbuddin Aibak in AD 1210, founded a grand madrasa and named it *Madrasa-i-Firuzi* after Firuzkuh, the capital of the Ghurid Sultans. In AD 1227, Minhaj-i-Siraj was appointed its Principal.[10] In Bihar and Bengal, the Khalji warrior, Muhammad Bakhtiyar Khalji had mosques, *khanqahs* and madrasa built in his newly-founded headquarters of Lakhnauti.[11] After him, Sultan Ghiyas uddin 'Iwaz Khalji followed his tradition and beautified different towns with mosques, madrasas and *khanqahs.*[12] The teachers of eminence were attracted to serve the educational institutions and with their arrival, the towns of Maner and Bihar (Sharif) in the present-day state of Bihar and Lakhnauti in Bengal had madrasas for providing higher education.[13]

Delhi which had been seized by Iltutmish, the *wali* of Badaon after the death of Aibak, rapidly developed into a metropolis. Iltutmish assumed the royal title of Sultan Shams uddin Iltutmish, married the daughter of Aibak, and had Aram Shah removed from the scene in mysterious circumstances.[14] It is, however, interesting to note that Iltutmish's military weakness, in comparison with Sultan Nāsir uddin Qubācha, the senior son-in-law of Aibak, prevented him from coming to Lahore, the most important city in north India and the capital of the Indian Sultanate. In fact the political situation had forced Iltutmish to make Delhi his capital and then in due course of time, Delhi developed into a metropolis of international importance.

By the year 1228, the rival sultans of Bihar, Bengal, Sind and Multan were destroyed and the regions ruled by them annexed to the Sultanate of Delhi. Leading scholars from the conquered territories as well as from the neighbouring countries conquered by the Mongols were extended patronage and given maintenance grants. They catered to the educational needs of the expanding population of the capital. Sultan Iltutmish founded in Delhi the largest madrasa of the country and named it *Madrasa-i-Nasiria* after the deceased crown prince Nāsir uddin Mahmud. Rich endowments were made for its maintenance.[15] Moreover, Sultan Iltutmish also granted financial aid to the madrasas, established by individuals. In Multan, madrasas, maintained by Shaikh Bahauddin Zakariya and Qazi Qutbuddin Kashani respectively were important institutions that turned out scholars of distinction.[16] Besides other teachers on the staff of the respective madrasas, their founders also imparted instruction to the senior students. Both of them were widely travelled scholars and known for their erudition. Shaikh Bahauddin Zakariya is said to have paid handsome salary and allowances to the meritorious teachers.[17]

Of the Sultans of Delhi after Iltutmish, Sultan Ghiyas uddin Balban (reigned: 1266-87) appears to have taken interest in the progress of education. In each of the *thanas*, founded along the highways mosques were constructed along with madrasas for the education of the children of the armymen posted there.[18] The schools and mosques were civilizing institutions, with the result that the children of rustic and uncouth Afghan soldiers benefitted from the process of acculturation set in motion by them. In time the next generation of Afghans began to attain high positions under the Khalji and Tughlaq Sultans.

Some words are in order about individual scholars who took to the teaching profession in preference to the state service because they equated it with worship. They imparted instructions and guided the senior students in their scholarly pursuits. Mention may be made here of Maulana Raziuddin Hasan al-Saghani, the compiler of the *Hadis* Collection, *Mashariq-ul-Anwar,* Maulana Alauddin Usuli of Badaon, Maulana Kamaluddin Zahid, Maulana Shamsul-Mulk and Sayid Sharafuddin of Delhi. Maulana Raziuddin al-Saghani is reported to have started his career in the State Service as *naib-i-Mushrif* (deputy account officer) in Kol. However finding it difficult to work for the ill-behaved *Mushrif,* he relinquished his post and took to the teaching profession. He was employed by the governor of Kol to teach his son on a salary of one hundred *tankas,* perhaps per annum. Shaikh Nizam uddin Auliya told his *murids* that Maulana al-Saghani remained content with this small salary and seriously devoted himself to the study of *hadis.* He is also reported to have trained his students in *Ilm ul-Hadis* in Delhi and other cities as far as Nagaur. After some time the Maulana decided to leave for Arabia in order to visit the leading scholars there. He left India during the reign of Iltutmish. In Baghdad he was honoured by the Caliph.[19] His compilation of *ahadis, Mashariq-ul-Anwar* that contained 2253 authentic (Prophetic) traditions enjoyed wide popularity and was prescribed as a text book in the madrasas.[20] Maulana Burhanuddin Balkhi, his student and successor in Delhi also worked as a teacher with full dedication teaching both *hadis* and *fiqh.* His popularity and prestige in fact led Sultan Balban to visit him at his residence on Fridays.[21]

Maulana Alauddin Usuli lived in Badaon and also taught students, going out of his way to help poor students financially. Shaikh Nizamuddin Auliya was his student, and always spoke highly of his piety and humanism.[22] According Shaikh Nasiruddin Chirgh, the spiritual successor of Shaikh Nizamuddin Auliya, Shaikh Nizamuddin Auliya had studied *fiqh* with the Maulana in Badaon. Apparently on the completion of the study of *Qaduri* (the authoritative work on Islamic jurisprudence), the Maulana asked his student to prepare for the performance of the *dastarbandi* ceremony (the ceremony of placing a turban on the head of the scholar, declaring him an authority on the subject). Shaikh Nizamuddin is believed to have told his teacher that his widowed mother could not bear the expenses of the feast. Thereupon the Maulana himself undertook to arrange the feast. Maula Ali, a senior saint of Badaon who was an unlettered convert and the spiritual successor of Shaikh Jalaluddin Tabrizi was invited as the chief guest on the occasion. When Ali Maula began to wrap the turban, he exclaimed turning to the Maulana in his local dialect: '*Ari Maulana 'yeh bada hosi*', i.e. O! Maulana: He would be a great man'.[23]

Kamal uddin Zahid was a student of Maulana Burhan u'ddin who had trained him in *Ilm-i-hadis*. Like his teacher, Maulana Kamal uddin Zahid adopted the teaching profession and trained scholars in the religious sciences. Shaikh Nizamuddin Auliya is also said to have studied *hadis* with him. Having been impressed by the fame of his piety and scholarship, Sultan Ghiyas uddin Balban offered him the post of *Imam* to lead prayers at court but the Maulana spurned his offer, saying, 'there is nothing with us except our prayer but the Sultan wants to deprive us of it also'.[24]

Khwaja Shams ul-Mulk was one of those scholars of Delhi who relinquished his ministerial post in order to earn religious merit through the dissemination of knowledge. He was elevated to the post of the *Mustaufi-i-Mumalik* (auditor general) of the Sultanate on account of his expertise in finance. Upon his elevation to the post of *Mustaufi-i-Mumalik,* Taj Reza composed the couplet:

> 'Sadr aknun be kam Dil-i-dustan Shudi:
> Mustaufi-i-Mumalik Hindustan Shudi'.
> (O, Sadr, your friends wishes have been fulfilled in deed:
> You are now the Mustaufi-i-Mumalik [auditor general] of all India.)

Shaikh Nizamuddin Auliya also joined the circle of his students. Speaking of the Khwaja and his dedication to the cause of his students, said that if a student failed to turn up on any day or got late in attending his lecture, Shamsul-Mulk would politely ask whether any shortcoming on his part prevented the student from coming on time. Like Qazi Fakhr uddin Naqila and Maulana Burhan uddin, his friends, Shaikh Nizamuddin was also received in the balcony on the first floor of Shamsul-Mulk's house.[25]

Another teacher of eminence was Saiyid Sharaf uddin who also taught senior students at his residence in Delhi. According to Shaikh Sharaf u'ddin Yahya Maneri, Shaikh Nizamuddin Auliya and Shaikh 'Āla uddin Jyuri studied the *tafsir* and the *hadis* with him. It is reported that every time Shaikh Nizamuddin visited him, he brought a present for him. 'Once it occurred to Saiyid Sharaf uddin that very many students came daily to study with him, yet apart from him nobody else thought of this, only he used to bring some gift whenever he came to him. This thought pleased him and, in this state, he prayed for the worthy Shaikh in this manner. 'May you be greatly blessed! What you have now received comes from there'.[26] In fact, such examples of selfless service inspired students in character building.

It is also worth recalling that the madrasa and its teachers performed an important role in enhancing upward social mobility. The doors of the madrasa were thrown open to all classes, even though, there was opposition from a section of the ruling elite to the education of low-born Muslim children. Like the writers, some of the Sufis also appear to have been opposed to the admission of children from artisan class in the madrasas. For instance, the leading fourteenth century Suhrawardi Sufi, Shaikh Jalal uddin Bukhari, popularly known *Jahanian-i-Jahangasht* (globetrotter) was against the education of the children belonging to the families of artisans. His view was that they should be instructed only in the fundamentals of faith, such as prayer and fasting and not beyond, as he saw them as undeserving of higher education for it would enable them to compete with the *ashraf* (elite) and thus insult them. Further he stated that food should not be taken in the company of the cobbler, washerman, barber, etc.[27]

The brief information extracted from Ibn Battuta's *Rehla* and Barani's *Tarikh-i-Firuz Shahi* about the career of Ratan the barber, tends to suggest that low-caste Hindus could also have their children educated in Persian language and popular sciences. Ibn Battuta informs us that Ratan was skilled in calculation and the profession of a scribe. Skilled scribes were required to make copies of important books in Arabic and Persian for the libraries of the Sultan, Prince and the nobles. A certain Amir conducted Ratan in the royal presence, Sultan Muhammad bin Tughluq Shah (reigned: 1325-51) who liked his beautiful handwriting and took him in his service.[28] Ratan made rapid progress and ultimately attained the rank of a high noble as mentioned above.

Some of the Sufi *Jama'at Khanas* (hospices) also created an atmosphere conducive to the progress of learning. The thirteenth and fourteenth centuries Sufis of the Suhrawardi and the Chishti and the Firdausi *Silsilahs* (fraternities) attracted intellectuals, delivered discourses and held discussions on matters related to religion, metaphysical philosophy and poetry. Shaikh Bahauddin Zakariya Suhrawardi, his son and grandsons promoted the study of *tafsir* and *fiqh* both through their madrasa and *khanqah* in Multan.[29] Likewise, the *Jama'at Khanas* of the Chishti Sufi saints in Ajodhan and Delhi turned into a rendezvous for the scholars, poets and intellectuals. The *malfuzat* of Shaikh Nizamuddin Auliya reveal that besides the *tafsir* literature such as *tafsir-i-Kashaf*,[30] *tafsir-i-Nasiri*,[31] *tafsir-i-Usman Khairabadi*,[32] *Tafsir-i-Eijaz*,[33] and *tafsir-i-Undala*,[34] the standard *hadis* collections,[35] works on *fiqh*,[36] and Sufi classics, both in Arabic and Persian were discussed. Moreover, at the heart of it is a metaphysical debate that mixes the wisdom of Shaikh's favourite poets, metaphysical thinkers among sufi saints and his own experiences and thoughts. Thus the reader is led across a variety of subjects getting deep into the matter. Shaikh Ala uddin Jyuri the pupil of Saiyid Sharafuddin and the teacher of Shaikh Najib Uddin Firdausi combined the roles of the teacher and the Sufi *pir* (preceptor). The way he divided his weekly schedule for teaching different subjects gives insights into the syllabi and the method of teaching. Shaikh Sharaf u'ddin Yahya Maneri informs, 'One day was devoted to jurisprudence; another day was devoted to syntax, logic and polemics, another to basic principles and theology; another to Quranic exegesis and the traditions (*hadis*). In this fashion he taught a particular subject'. The Shaikh further adds: 'all the theologians, Shaikhs and religious leaders of Delhi used to go to the king. The Saiyid (Jyuri) was the only one who never went to the king. It reached the point where, on some occasions when it was announced that all the important people in the city were to be present at the royal court, all of them were – except Saiyid Ala uddin. He used to say : "*Jo ho so ho*, (i.e. whatever happens), let it happen, but I shall never go to the royal palace." That was his mind'.[37] Barani also portrays Saiyid Ala uddin Juyri as a learned teacher and one of the leading Sufis of Delhi of the fourteenth century.[38]

The *Malfuzat* collections of Shaikh Nizam uddin Auliya and Shaikh Sharaf uddin Yahya Maneri also contain interesting information about the ceremony performed in connection with the beginning of a child's education. Generally at the age of four years, a child was taught the first few Arabic letters with the recitation, 'in the name of God, the Merciful, the compassionate'. Thereafter sweets were distributed. The Shaikh also tells us, 'When I was a child, I was forced to memorize several books, such as *Masadir* (verbal nouns) and *Miftahul-Lughat* (a key to words), sections of books and even twenty sections of *Miftah-ul-Lughat*, to the measure of one volume, had to be learned by heart. They were checked by having us recite them in full.'[39]

With the expansion of Delhi owing to the exodus of emigrants from the neighbouring countries, the number of its madrasas increased to one thousand. Shihab uddin al-Umari was informed by a traveller in Damascus that one of the madrasas belonged to the Shafi's while the rest were for Hanafis.[40] Like Delhi, the provincial headquarters also expanded with an increase in educational facilities. The madrasas in the provincial cities also supplied scholars to Delhi. Ibn Battuta found a large madrasa in Sehwan which was the headquarters of the territorial unit.[41] Ibn Battuta also says about the city of Hansi, 'It is from this city (come) Kamal al-Din Sadr-i-Jahan, the grand qadi (Qazi) of India, and his brother Qutlu (q) Khan, preceptor of the Sultan, also their two brothers Nizam al-Din and Shams al-Din, who renounced the world for the service of God and Sojourned at Mecca to the time of his death.'[42] Another provincial headquarters in modern Haryana was the town of Sunam that produced leading poets and scholars of Medieval India. The thirteenth century Persian poet 'Amid Loeki' Sunami and Maulana Zia' uddin Sunami were born and educated in Sunam. Their literary works were considered by the posterity as useful and were preserved.[43]

A word may be added about the role of Maulana Zia' uddin Sunami who held the post of *Muhtasib* (public censor) since the reign of 'Ala ud'din Khalji upto that of Sultan Muhammad bin Tughlaq Shah. Barani mentions him amongst the leading *ulama* of the reign of 'Ala ud'din Khalji. Barani writes that Maulana Zia' uddin Sunami was a distinguished scholar of religious sciences, particularly in *tafsir* and fiqh and was regarded an undisputed authority. He imparted instruction to a galaxy of scholarly students of Delhi in these sciences. None could equal him in explaining the meanings of the Quranic verse, and several thousand people attended his lectures.[44] Ibn Battuta found Maulana Sunami among the courtiers of Mohammad bin Tughlaq.[45] Ibn Battuta adds when he mentions him among Sultan Muhammad bin Tughlaq's courtiers, that the Maulana Sunami incurred the displeasure of the Sultan by refusing to pull up the beard of Shaikh Shihab uddin Jam. Another contemporary, Shaikh Sharafuddin Yahya Maneri also attended his lectures during his stay in Delhi. He stated that he attended his lectures during his stay in Delhi. The Shaikh is reported to have told his disciples, 'Maulana Zia' uddin Sunami was both a renowned traditionalist and Quranic Commentator. One day I was present in his congregation. Once, somebody from the audience put down some thing on a piece of paper and passed it on to the Maulana for seeking answer. The Maulana said from the pulpit. The book provides no solution but in my view solution is this'.[46] His lectures disseminated knowledge of the religious sciences on the one hand and inspired people to be serious in their pursuit of learning. As a matter of fact the *ulama* considered teaching students a part of their religious duty.

Like the urban centres around Delhi, Bihar and Bengal in the east had centres of learning that also gained fame because of the presence of teachers of eminence. The reign of Sultan Shams uddin Firuz Shah of Bihar and Bengal (d.1322-3) is known for peace and progress in every field. It was during his reign that Sonargaon in East Bengal was developed into a centre of Islamic learning like Lakhnauti. He made Sonargaon his second capital and invited *ulama* of eminence from different parts to teach and disseminate learning in the region. Maulana Sharaf uddin Abu Tawama, a distinguished scholar of *ihadis, fiqh* and *'Ilm al-Kalam* (scholastic theology) was invited from Delhi to Sonargaon.[47] In fact Balkhi scholars, known for their authoritative knowledge of *tafsir,* also settled in Sonargaon. They are said to have handled Quranic exegesis with a particular skill.[48]

Historical information available about the madrasas founded in different cities from the later half of the fourteenth to the fifteenth century, enables us to discuss the progress that the educational system made during the period under review. Sultan Firuz Shah of Delhi (reigned: 1351-8) tried to surpass his predecessors in this field as well. He had two grand madrasas built in Delhi, in order to cater to the educational needs of Delhi, the largest city of the Sultanate. These were higher seats of learning named after the Sultan as *Madrasa-i Firuz Shahi* and after the eldest Prince as *Madrasa-i Shahzada-i buzurg* respectively. The buildings of both the madrasas are said to have surpassed the buildings of the old existing ones in beauty and grandeur.

The graphic description made by Barani of the madrasas reveals that Sultan Firuz Shah planned their construction in the midst of beautiful surroundings, each on a considerable distance from his newly-founded capital of Firuzabad (near Delhi on the bank of the Jamuna) so that the teachers and the students could devote themselves to their respective pursuits away from the hustle and bustle of the metropolis.[49] The *Madrasa-i-Firuz Shahi* was built on the southern bank of the *Hauz-i-Khass.* It had a separate hostel for students and separate apartments for Maulana Jalaluddin Rumi, the Principal.[50] Likewise, Saiyidul-a'ima Najm uddin Samaqandi, the most distinguished scholar of his time looked after the *Madrasa-i-Shahzada-i-buzurg*, built near the lofty dam of Siri. It was the only building that could compare with the *Madrasa-i-Firuz Shahi* in grandeur and beauty. The revenue from a number of villages was endowed for its upkeep and for distribution to students.[51]

Similarly, the madrasa built by the Bahmani *Wazir*, Khwaja Mahmud Gawan at Bidar in 1472, enjoyed phenomenal fame and prestige in India and Iran. It was not only housed in a magnificent building but also staffed by the teachers of distinction from both countries. The remnants of the building still show that it was the most imposing building and a unique monument in terms of architectural splendour. Designed and built under the supervision of Irani architects, its structure is an example of Irani influence, and has a striking comparison with the madrasa buildings in Iran and Central Asia. Only the lofty gates and minarets added to the structure are in the Indian style and add their own charm. The double storeyed hostel contained thirty-three suites of rooms, and approximately each one could accommodate three students. Thus one hundred and eight students could be provided with accommodation in the hostel. Mahmud Gawan not only endowed it richly but also invited well-reputed scholars from Iran and Central Asia to teach the students.[52] Firishta tells us that Mahmud Gawan possessed a rich library and donated three thousand books on different subjects to the library of his madrasa. He was particularly interested in teaching students mathematics and *tib* (medicines) besides *ulum-i-naqliya-o-'aqliya* (traditional Islamic and rationalist sciences).[53]

In the fifteenth century, the Sultans of Malwa are also credited with the construction of madrasas for the progress of learning in different towns and cities. Sultan Hoshang Shah (d.1434) had the foundation of the Jam'a 'mosque and the grand madrasa laid adjacent to each other in his capital Mandu but he died before the structures were completed. His death was followed by a civil war that brought Mahmud Khalji to the throne in 1435. The Jam'a mosque and madrasa were both completed. The building of the madrasa was lofty and named *Bam-i-Bihisht* (terrace of paradise). Shihab Hakim states that the architects were invited from Khurasan and different parts of Hindustan to prepare plans and supervise their construction. The wings of the madrasas were beautified with the use of marble of different colours and other expensive stones. Proper arrangement was made for the payment of stipend and salary to the students and their teachers who resided here.[54]

There is great debate about the liberal atmosphere created by the madrasas in the country. Since the advent of the Khaljis to power towards the close of the thirteenth century, opposition to the study of *Ilm-i-Ma'qul* (rational sciences) ended and rationalist scholars were patronized by the Sultan.[55] These scholars popularized the study of rationalist sciences. Barani writes that Sultan 'Ala ud'din Khalji consulted these scholars with regard to state problems. S'ad Mantaqi, a rationalist thinker is said to have been his counsellor.[56] There were some other rationalist thinkers also associated with the royal court. In the first unrevised version of his *Tarikh-i-Firuz Shahi*, Barani portrays them as distinguished scholars of rationalist sciences and *Ilmul-Kalam* (scholasticism). He states that Maulana 'Alim uddin, S'ad Mantaqi and Najm Intishar were leading scholars of rationalist sciences whom none could rival in scholarship. Another scholar, 'Ubaid, the poet is called by him an atheist who questioned accepted truth. Barani however, had to revise his opinion on these scholars following the death of Sultan Muhammad bin Tughlaq. The late Sultan was a follower of the rationalist thinkers and Barani as his courtier was also regarded a rationalist and underwent imprisonment for being the late Sultan's close associate. On his release, Barani compiled the *Tarikh-i-Firuz Shahi,* in order to please Firuz Shahi but in vain. But the defence of Muhammad bin Tughlaq's state policies and the praise of the rationalist scholars antagonized the reactionaries who had gained ascendancy at court. Being in a predicament Barani then revised the *Tarikh* in his own defence, condemning the rationalist thinkers.[57]

In short, the standard of education was raised, new discoveries seem to have been made in physics and astronomy. In his *I'jaz-i-Khusravi,* Amir Khusrau says that the moon is dark but shines on account of the reflected light of the sun.[58] Similarly, Sultan Muhammad bin Tughlaq adhered to the concept of linear time against that of cyclic time.[59]

A study of Barani's literary works also provides insights into the efflorescence of intellectual culture. Aware of the importance of change in time, he emphasized the need for the ruler to formulate new rules and regulations regardless of the customary law but in the light of requirements of time.[60] Similarly, the *Muqadima* (prologue) of his *Tarikh* lifts him to the rank of the philosopher of History. Therein, he considers History the third source of knowledge, after the Quran and the *hadis.* He regards history of mankind a continuous process, influenced not by historical events alone but also the ideas, thought and role of the man of strong personality. According to him the role played by the great man influences the course of history and then social transformation takes place.[61]

Our study of Sufi literature of the fourteenth century reveals that even some of the learned Sufis were influenced by rationalist thinkers. Generally Sufis are blamed by the orthodoxy for popularizing unauthentic traditions (*Zaif ahadis*). But Shaikh Nizamuddin Auliya and Shaikh Sharafuddin Yahya Maneri took a critical approach to verify the authenticity of the *hadis*. Once, while holding a discussion with his *murids*, Shaikh Sharafuddin Maneri said:

> Handling traditions is an extremely difficult task. Seven centuries have elapsed during which the traditions have come down to us. Who knows, perhaps somebody, in order to bolster his own opinion, might have said: 'The Prophet said such and such'. At this point one of those present said that a traditionalist had come to Delhi. He was saying that some of the traditions contained in the *Mishkat* and *Hidaya* were of a spurious nature. The venerable master said: 'If, in the commentary found at the beginning of each chapter of the Quran, there is a tradition saying that whoever reads the chapter will obtain such and such, then all such traditions are spurious'. Afterwards he added, 'The spurious nature of traditions can be ascertained from the effects attributed to the recital of the particular chapter: not one of them will be obtained! For example, above one chapter it is written that whoever recites this chapter will have a thousand of his needs met, yet not one is fulfilled. From this contradiction it is clear that the tradition is spurious.'[62]

To conclude, the madrasa performed an important role during medieval times, not only in the diffusion of knowledge that took place in the urban centres, but also social mobility. Thirteenth and fourteenth century writers in Persian produced significant literary works. They also inspired scholars during the subsequent period and helped maintain a literary tradition that forms part of India's intellectual heritage.

Endnotes

1. The Quran declares, 'Those who read the book (Quran) of God, who perform the prayer they are the ones who can look for a commerce that can not fail, seeing that He will pay them their full due and more so, from His beneficence'. *Surah:* 35, 29-31.
2. Cf. Nabi Bakhsh Baloch, Commentary, *Fathnama-i-Sind*, also known as *Chachnama*, (13th Century Persian translation of an Arabic work by Ali Kufi) Islamabad: Islamic University, 1983, p. 104.

3. Sultan Mahmud wanted strict adherence to orthodoxy in education. The removal by his order of the teachers belonging to the Karamiya sect is a case in point. The Karamiya sect's teachers were puritans but their opponents accused them of having faith in anthropomorphism. The Sultan was convinced against them. Cf. C.E. Bosworth, 'The Rise of Karamiyah in Khurasan', *Muslim World,* 1960, vol. 50, pp. 5-14.
4. Abu Said Gardezi, *Zain ul-Akhbar,* ed. Abdul Ha'i Habibi, Iran: Bunyad-i-Farhang-i-Iran, 1347 Shamsi, pp. 179-81.
5. Fakhr-i-Mudabbir, *Tarikh-i-Fakhruddin Mubarakshah Marvar-rudi,* ed. E. Denison Ross, London, Royal Asiatic Society, 1927, p. 19, hereafter cited as *Tarikh-i-Fakhr-i-Mudabbir.*
6. Cf. M. Umar u'ddin, *The Ethical Philosophy of al-Ghazzali,* Aligarh, Muslim University Publication House, 1962, p. 15; also Abdul Qadir b. Muhammad al-Naayam, *al-Danish fi-Tarikh al-Madaris,* 2 vols., Damascus, 1948 and 1951.
7. *Tabaqat-i-Nasiri,* ed. Abdul Ha'i Habibi, Kabul, 1963, vol. 1, p. 389.
8. Ibid., vol. 1, p. 405.
9. Ibid., vol. 1, p. 461; See also Amir Hasan Sijzi, *Fawaid ul-Fuad,* Lucknow: Nawal Kishore, 1885, p. 23.
10. Ibid., p. 420.
11. Ibid., p. 427.
12. The importance and function of the *khanqah* has been discussed in the first chapter. The translation of the term *ahl-al-Suffa* by Abdul Karim as Sufis is misleading. Cf. *Corpus of the Arabic and Persian Inscriptions of Bengal,* Asiatic Society of Bangladesh, Dhaka, op.cit., p. 18.
13. *Tabaqat-i-Nasiri,* 1963, vol. 1, p. 436.
14. Cf. Iqtidar Husain Siddiqui, *Authority and Kingship Under the Sultans of Delhi,* New Delhi: Manohar Publishers, 2006, pp. 51-2.
15. Minhaj-i-Siraj incidentally mentions that he was appointed the principal of this *madrasa* by Sultan Raziya in 1238. In 1245, he was again entrusted with its Principalship as well as the trusteeship of its endowments. *Tabaqat-i-Nasiri,* 1963, vol. 1, pp. 460-70.
16. *Fawaid ul-Fuad,* Sirajuddin & Sons, Lahore, 1966, pp. 235-6.

17. Cf. Iqtidar Husain Siddiqui, 'Pir and Murid: A Study of the Sufis of Suhrawardi Silsilah in India during the Thirteenth and Fourteenth Centuries', *The Indian Historical Review*, New Delhi: ICHR, July 1994-January 1995, vol. 21, Nov. 1-2, pp. 57-77, 61-2.
18. Afif, *Tarikh-i-Firuz Shahi,* ed. Wilayat Husain, Calcutta: Bibiotheca Indica, 1891, pp. 452-3; Isami, *Futuh us-Salatin,* ed. A.S. Usha, Madras: Madras University Islamic Series 1948, p. 164.
19. *Fawaid ul-Fuad,* Lahore, 1966, pp. 104-5.
20. Cf. *Muhammad Ishaque,* India's Contribution to the Study of Hadith Literature, Dacca: University of Dacca, 1955, p. 12, Annemarie Schimmel, *Islam in the Indian Subcontinent,* Leiden: E.J. Brill, 1980, p. 5.
21. *Fawaid ul-Fuad,* 1966, pp. 239-40; Barani, 1862, pp. 46 & 111.
22. *Fawaid ul-Fuad,* 1966, pp. 165-66 & 202.
23. Hamid Qalandar, *Khair ul-Majalis,* ed. K.A. Nizami, Aligarh, 1959, pp. 190-1.
24. *Siyar ul-Auliya,* op.cit., p. 106.
25. *Fawaid ul-Fuad,* 1966, p. 68.
26. Zain Badr Arabi, *Khwan-i-Pur N'imat,* tr. Paul Jackson, Delhi, 1986, pp. 145-6.
27. Anonymous, *Siraj ul-Hidaya* (*Malfuzat* of Shaikh Jalaluddin Bukhari, known as *Jahanian-i-Jahangasht*). ed. Qazi Sajjad Husain, New Delhi: ICHR, 1983, pp. 77-8.
28. Ibn Battuta, *Rehla,* Arabic text, Dar Sadir dar Beruit, 1963, pp. 399-400; Urdu tr. Maulvi Muhammad Husain, Islamabad, rpt, op.cit., 1983, vol. 2, p. 10; tr. H. Gibb, *Travels of Ibn Battuta,* vol. 3, Cambridge: Cambridge University Press, 1971, p. 599.
29. *Fawaid ul-Fuad,* 1966, p. 233, Barani, *Tarikh-i-Firuz Shahi*, p. 348.
30. Barani, 1862, pp. 346-7; *Fawaid-ul-Fuad,* 1966, p. 60.
31. Ibid., p. 32.
32. Ibid., p. 109.
33. Loc. cit.
34. Ibid., pp. 103 & 105.
35. Ibid., pp. 152, 165 & 239.

36. Ibid., pp. 26, 45, 75, 83 & 112, *passim.*
37. *Khan-i-Pur Ni'mat,* tr. op.cit., p. 143, See also Persian text, Patna, 132 H., p. 111.
38. Barani, *Tarikh-i-Firuz Shahi*, p. 350.
39. Zain Badr Arabi, *Maadan-al-Ma'ani, Malfuzat,* cited by Paul Jackson, *The Way of A Sufi: Sharafuddin Maneri,* Idarah-i-Adbiyat, Delhi, 1987, pp. 26 & 37.
40. Cf. Siddiqui, *Perso-Arabic Sources,* p. 116.
41. *The Travels of Ibn Battuta,* vol. 2, p. 617.
42. *The Travels of Ibn Battuta,* vol. 3, p. 617.
43. *The Diwan of Amid Loeki Sunami* has been edited and published by Nazir Ahmad while the manuscript copies of Maulana Zia' uddin Sunami are available in different libraries of the world. Cf. *Diwan,* ed. Nazir Ahmad, Lahore 1984; also Iqtidar Husain Siddiqui, *Perso-Arabic Sources of Information on the Life and Conditions in the Sultanate of* Delhi, p. 69, for the importance of 'Amid's *Diwan.*
44. *The Travels of Ibn Battuta,* vol. 3, pp. 697-8.
45. Barani, 1862, p. 356.
46. Zain Badr Arabi, *Maadan-al-Marani* (*Malfuzat*), Bihar Sharif, 1884, 2 vols., p. 117. Paul Jackson refers to the event but does not describe the Maulana's response to the query. Cf. *The Way of a Sufi: Sharafu'ddin Maneri,* Delhi, 1987, p. 57.
47. *The Way of a Sufi: Sharafuddin Maneri,* pp. 38-44.
48. Ibid., pp. 49-50.
49. Barani, 1862, pp. 562-5.
50. Ibid., pp. 565-6.
51. Barani, 1862, pp. 564-6.
52. Cf. G. Yazdani, *Bidar: Its History and Monuments,* London: Oxford University Press 1947, pp. 91-4.
53. *Tarikh-i-Firishta,* Lucknow: Nawal Kishore Press, p. 358.
54. *Ali Bin Mahmud al-Kirmani* known as Shihab Hakim. *Ma'sir-i-Mahmud Shahi,* ed. Nurul Hasan Ansari, Delhi: Indo-Persian Society 1968, pp. 23-46.

55. Cf. Iqtidar Husain Siddiqui, *Authority and Kingship under the Sultans of Delhi,* op.cit., p. 151. Idem., *Medieval India: Essays in Intellectual Thought and Culture,* ed., Manohar Publishers, 2003, pp. 86-7.
56. Barani, *Tarikh-i-Firuz Shahi*, pp. 289-99.
57. Cf. Siddiqui, *Perso-Arabic Sources of Information on the Life and Conditions in the Sultanate of Delhi,* pp. 151-163, for the difference in Barani's approach in two versions.
58. Amir khusrau, *I'jaz-i-Khusravi,* Lucknow: Nawal Kishore, vol. 2, p. 158.
59. Siddiqui, *Perso-Arabic Sources of Information on the Life and Conditions in the Sultanate* of Delhi, p. 123.
60. Zia' uddin Barani, *Fatawa-i-Jahandari,* (Persian text) ed. Afsar Salim Khan, Lahore, 1972, pp. 139-40, 218-19.
61. Iqtidar Husain Siddiqui, Barani's *Tarikh-i-Firuz Shahi*, Tajziyati Mutala (Urdu), *Qazi Abdul Wudud Commemoration volume,* New Delhi: Ghalib Institute 2000, pp. 233-7.
62. Zain Badr Arabi, *Khan-i-Pur Ni'mat,* tr., pp. 122-3.

CHAPTER 9

The Literary Tradition

Since the rise of Islam, records reveal that Muslims have sought knowledge from different sources. The Quran also encourages its followers to acquire knowledge of religious as well as secular sciences. Over time this led to the cultivation of a reading habit among the Muslim elite and books on different subjects began to be produced to cater to this need. New professions related to book production, such as of a scribe (*katib*), book-binder (*jildsāz*), paper maker (*kaghazian*), besides that of bookseller also arose. It may be recalled that though possession of books enhanced the prestige of a noble man, it was an expensive habit. Apart from the wages of the scribe, one had to spend money on purchasing the writing material that was beyond the means of an ordinary man. Since paper was not used during the early Islamic period, all writing was done with pen and ink on vellum (parchment) which was made by preparing the skins of camel, sheep and calf. The finest products, made of calf skin, were used for books and official documents. The practice of preparing the copies of the Quran with the use of pen and ink on parchment has been one of the most distinctive feature of the Islamic civilization. Parchment was a durable writing material. Its durability and also the permanency of medieval ink have enabled medieval manuscripts to survive the ravages of time.[1] Egypt was an exception with regard to the use of parchment. The Egyptians, used papyrus instead, as it was available there. Influenced by the Egyptians the Syrians also appear to have used papyrus as the first century Hijra document discovered in Egypt shows.[2] The craft of paper making was introduced in the ninth century A.D.

Paper was made out of rag and cotton fibre. A very good quality of paper was also made out of silk rag. Lahore and Multan seem to have had expert *Kaghziyan* (paper-makers) since the eleventh century. The eleventh and twelfth centuries scholars and poets of Ghaznavid Lahore left behind their works.[3] In the beginning of the thirteenth century, Sadid uddin Muhammad 'Awfi utilized paper in the preparation of his *Lubab ul-Albab*, his *Tazkira* cum-anthology of Persian poets,[4] including those poets who flourished in Lahore during the Ghaznavid period. Likewise, the *farman* and official documents issued by the rulers were written on paper and utilized by the contemporary and later writers in the compilation of their histories.[5] On the emergence of the Sultanate, the scholars of Lahore and Delhi wrote books on paper that they dedicated to the early sultans in the hope of getting rewarded.[6]

It is worth noting that the use of paper in India remained prevalent only in the region under the Muslim rule while outside it there seems to have been resistance to the change. Even in the fifteenth century, the Hindu elite in South India did not adopt paper. Abdur Razzaq Samarqandi, the Central Asian envoy to the court of Vijaynagar writes, 'The people of Bijaynagar have two kinds of writing, one upon a leaf of the coconut which is two yards long and two yards broad, on which they scratch with an iron stylus. These characters present no colour, and endure but for a little while. In the second kind they blacken a white surface, on which they write with a soft stone cut into the shape of a pen, so that the characters are white on a black surface and are durable'.[7] On the contrary, the locality of the *kaghziyan* paper manufacturers could be found in every city under the sultanate. Amir Khusrau describes their lane in these words, 'The lane was very narrow and the walls very high. In the location of the paper manufacturers the houses were (frail as if) of paper'.[8]

The foundation of the Sultanate and the educated Muslims' love for books gave a boost to the book trade and also promoted a library culture[9] long after the decline of Buddhist power and influence. Evidence contained in medieval sources of information about libraries, material used in writing and people engaged in the craft of book-making provides us with insights into the proliferation of a literary culture in India during the Delhi Sultanate period. Libraries were built both by the members of the ruling elite and scholars, and every town and city had libraries owned by individual scholars, These were open to students and young scholars who could not afford to buy books.

Central to a literary tradition was the use of paper, which was, as already mentioned, less expensive and easier to write on than parchment. Yet all classes could not afford paper and it seems probable that the paper-makers had developed the art of washing written paper clean for reuse. Zia'uddin

Barani provides us with interesting information about this while mentioning the standard histories written in India during the thirteenth century. According to him, unlike the popular standard works, the substandard, books of history, written by unknown writers often found no buyers. 'Thus,... unknown and careless narrators who had no regards for facts, their writings could not attract the attention of knowledgeable people. Their works remained lying unsold in booksellers' shops. These works were ultimately made over to the *Kaghziyan* (paper-makers), so that they could be washed clean.'[10] This practice seems to have continued throughout the medieval period. Mian Zain uddin, the governor of the *sarkar* of Badaon under Sultan Sikandar Lodi (reigned:1488-1517) is also reported to have had the written documents washed clean, in case they were not needed any longer.[11]

The relevant evidence available in the *Malfuzat* of Shaikh Nizamuddin Auliya gives some idea about the price of paper during the Shaikh's life time. One day, Shaikh Nizamuddin Auliya told his disciples that Shaikh Najib uddin Mutawakkil desired to have a copy of Sadid uddin Muhammad 'Awfi's *Jawami 'ul-Hikayat wa-Livami 'ul-Riwayat* made for his personal collection. But he could neither purchase paper nor did he have enough money to pay the scribe his wages. One day, the scribe Hamid visited him. The Shaikh told Hamid what he desired, but his means did not allow him to fulfil this. Hamid is believed to have asked, 'What have you got at the moment? The Shaikh replied: 'I have got only one dirham'. Hamid got the dirham and went to buy a few sheets of paper. He started the work. After some time the Shaikh (*Mutawakkil*) received good *futuh* (unasked for gift) that could suffice for buying paper, ink and engaging the scribe.[12]

The interest evinced by the Sultan, his nobles and social elite in the sale and purchase of books, written on religious as well as secular themes led a large number of the educated people to take to the scribe's profession. People adopted it either as a means of livelihood or for earning religious merit because they considered dissemination of learning by making books available at a low price a part of divine worship. Expert calligraphers were employed by the Sultan and nobles to work in their libraries and paid high wages. The scribes worked for booksellers also. Once Shaikh Nasir uddin Chiragh-i-Delhi said in this regard, 'Maulana Fakhruddin Marvazi, the *murid* of Shaikh Nizamuddin (Auliya) inscribed books (for earning his livelihood). He asked the customer to fix the price of the book himself. If the latter fixed one *Shashgani* (i.e. six annas), he would charge only four *jitals*. He would refuse to accept more than four *jitals*. If any person desired to pay twelve *jitals* or more out of respect, he refused to accept more than four *jitals.* When he was too old to carry on his work, Qazi Hamid Uddin, the *Malik ul-Tujjar* who was elevated to the position of the chief *qazi* and *sadr,* submitted to Sultan 'Ala ud'din Khalji that the pious man who earned his keep by inscribing the books was unable to carry on his work, owing to old age and, therefore, he should be granted maintenance allowance. The Sultan made the grant of one *tanka* daily for the Maulana. But the Maulana refused to accept any grant of more than one *Shashgani.* At last, the Maulana was persuaded to accept the grant of two *Shashganis*'.[13]

Some words are also in order about the progress of the book trade. The reading material was in high demand and the booksellers employed scribes to produce books on popular subjects to earn money. The discussion of spurious *malfuzat* in the *khanqahs* of Shaikh Nizam uddin (Auliya) and Shaikh Nasir uddin Chiragh of Delhi tends to reveal that both the booksellers and scribes were involved in such forgery. The *malfuzat* of the leading Sufi saints were prepared and their compilation was attributed to Shaikh Muinuddin Chishti, Shaikh Qutbuddin Bakhtiyar Kaki, Shaikh Farid uddin Ganj-i-Shakar and Shaikh Nizamuddin Auliya. When Shaikh Nizamuddin was asked about their genuineness, he called them forged ones.[14] After Shaikh Nizamuddin, the query was made by some vistor to Shaikh Nasir uddin Chiragh-i-Delhi regarding the authenticity of the *malfuz* of Shaikh Osman Harooni. The Shaikh replied, 'I have also looked up the manuscript but the utterances are not authentic, the content in it is not worthy of the Shaikhs' conversation'. Further, he quoted Shaikh Nizam uddin's (his *pir*) remark, 'His Holiness, Shaikh Nizamuddin said: "I have not authored any book, neither Shaikh ul-Islam Farid uddin nor Shaikh ul-Islam Qutbuddin, (Kaki) nor any one of the *Khwajgan-i-Chisht* (plural of the Khwaja) has written any work."'[15] Having critically examined all the fabricated *malfuz* literature, Mohammad Habib comments, 'A careful examination of all relevant circumstances leaves me no alternative but to conclude that this very large mass of forged mystic literature was purposely "uttered" by the booksellers of Delhi and the provincial capitals for the purpose of "honest trade". And by "honest trade" I mean that the booksellers were not concerned with anything except the sale of the books they had got written for payment. They had no ulterior motives'.[16]

It is true that before Saiyid Muhammad Gesudaraz, no Chishti Sufi is said to have left behind any literary work, yet they always inspired their disciples to acquire knowledge both of religious and non-religious popular sciences. Every great Chishti Sufi appears to have possessed his own personal collection. Shaikh Farid uddin Ganj-i-Shakar used to bring out books to explain difficult passages to his *murids* and other visitors. He explained to Shaikh Nizamuddin the chapters of Imam Ghazzali's *Ihya ul-Ulumid-din* and Shaikh Shihabuddin Suhrawardi's *Awariful-Marif.* The poet, Shams Dabir also studied the *lawih*, written by Qazi Hamid uddin Nagauri under his guidance.[17] The spiritual successor of Shaikh Nizamuddin, Shaikh Nasir uddin Chiragh-i-Delhi possessed a *Kitab Khana* and would bring the book when he had to explain any subtle point to the visitor.[18]

Mention should be made of the nobles and scholars who maintained libraries and patronized the writers. 'Ainu l-Mulk 'Ashari, the *wazir* of Sultan Nāsir uddin Qubacha helped financially the scholars who migrated from the neighbouring countries in search of fortune and settled in Uchh and Multan. Of the works dedicated by these scholars to him, Ali Kufi's *Fathnama-i-bilad-i-Sind-o-Hind,* better known as *Chachnama*[19] and Sadid uddin Muhammad 'Awfi's celebrated *Lubab ul-Albab*[20] are extant. Like Ainul-Mulk Ashari, Sultan Shams uddin Iltutmish's *wazir* Nizam ul-Mulk Junaidi was the patron of scholars and poets. Sadid uddin 'Awfi who had joined his service after the destruction of Nāsir uddin Qubacha tells us that he held the combined charge of *wizarat* and *sadarat* under Iltutmish. As *sadar* he made maintenance grants to the men of learning. 'Awfi writes, 'Though there is dearth of patrons of the men of talent and learning, yet all those who turn to the exalted Court of the *Sadr* and *Wazir* are done favour. The *Wazir's* glance having the brightness of the sun turns the stone into a pearl. Since his elevation to *Wizarat,* talent and skill have been saved and rewarded'.[21] Likewise, another emigrant, Majd uddin Abul M'ali Muaiyid bin Muhammad Jajarmi who translated Imam Ghazzali's *Ihya ul-ulum id-din* from Arabic into Persian at the instance of Nizam ul-Mulk Junaidi states that the *Wazir* spared time to study books and hold discussions with the learned on literary problems. Further, he says that the *Wazir* was fond of books and spent huge amount of money on purchasing them.[22] Minhaj-i-Siraj incidentally refers to his collection of books in his notice of Malik Tajuddin Sanjar Qutluq. Praising the noble man for his excellent conduct, he tells us that in 1237 when he was to leave Gwalior for Delhi, the Malik helped him by providing him with his camel to carry two boxes full of books.[23]

Amir Khusrau who served as court poet under different Sultans since the close of the thirteenth century appears to have possessed a rich library as the references to innumerable books bearing on different subjects in his epistles contained in his *I'jaz-i-Khusravi* demonstrate.[24] He was not only a voracious reader but also a prolific writer. Barani tells us that the books written by Amir Khusrau were in such a large number that they formed by themselves a separate library.[24]

A word may be added about the import and export of books between the Sultanate of Delhi and the foreign countries. If Rashid uddin Fazlullah's letters contain references to the commercial goods including herbs and books imported from India to Iran, the evidence of the supply by foreign traders of books to India is not wanting.[25] Sultan Muhammad bin Tughluq is reported to have encouraged foreigners to supply books on philosophy and science. Shihab uddin al-Umari was informed by a trader who had visited the Sultan's court in Delhi, 'A learned man came (to the Sultan) from Persia and presented him books on philosophy including Ibn-i-Sina's *Shifa*. By chance, when he presented himself with the books at court, it happened that a bundle of precious gems was brought to the Sultan, he took a handful of the gems and gave them to the foreigner in reward. The gems were worth twenty thousand *mithqul* of gold. Besides, the Sultan gave him other gifts afterwards'.[26]

With the annexation of south Indian territories under the first Tughluq Sultans, the Delhi court culture spread southwards. Many educated officers, posted in the cities of the Deccan went there with their book collections. Hajib Khairat Dehlevi who was in the service of Shams uddin Muhammad, the provincial *Sadr* of the Khitta-i-Ustadabad (present-day Gogi in Telangana) compiled a standard Persian lexicon *Dastur-al-Afazil* at his masters instance and found no difficulty in utilizing Persian classics in its preparation. He found all the works in the libraries there. He states, 'I borrowed the *diwans* (collections of verses) of great poets who were famous for their mastery over sciences and studied them from the beginning to the end'. His references to the dictionaries of different languages that he consulted, such as Tazi (Arabic), Turki, Mughli (Mongol language), Pehlavi (ancient Persian), Afghani, Jahud (Hebrew) and the dialects spoken in the Hejaz (present-day Saudi Arabia) and Transoxiana reflects on the richness of personal collections of the Indian scholars.[27] Consequently, the lexicon, *Dastur al-Afazil* came to be regarded as one of the most standard dictionary in the subsequent period.

Upon the dissolution of the Sultanate of Delhi caused by Amir Timur's invasion in 1398, the new regional sultanates and principalities arose in different parts of north India. The founders of the regional sultanates and principalities studded their newly founded capitals or old ones, with magnificent buildings and institutions of public utility so that they could take the place of Delhi as centres of culture. The Delhi Sultan's court provided a cultural reference point. Odd bits of information gleaned from literary works demonstrate how rich the libraries built by the local rulers were.

Mention may be made here of the grand library built up by the Faruqi rulers of Khandesh in Burhanpur. Faizi, the *Malik us-shu'ra* of Emperor Akbar's court was amazed when he visited this library as it contained rare Arabic and Persian classics, besides important works written by Indian scholars since the beginning of the Sultanate period. The best copy of Amir Khusrau's *masnavi, Tughluq nama* was available in this library during Faizi's time.[28] Likewise, the princes and the nobles of the Bahmani kingdom also appear to have maintained grand libraries. The case of the Bahmani *Wazir*, Khwaja Jahan Mahmud Gawan may be cited. He is reported to have collected thousands of books for his library. Upon his murder, though his property was pillaged, seventy thousand books were still found lying in the library.[29]

Incidentally, Shaikh Rizq ullah Mushtaqi also provides hints about the libraries possessed both by the scholars of average means and the educated grandees, occupying key positions in the Delhi Sultanate under the Lodi Sultans as well as provincial kingdoms. Describing the close and cordial ties between Mian Zain uddin (the governor of Badaon) and his servants he makes allusions to the library owned by his own father, Shaikh S'ad ullah, certainly an *alim* of small means. He tells us that on the dismissal of Mian Zain uddin by Sultan Ibrahim Lodi (reigned: AD 1517-26) many of Mian Zain uddin's servants, officers as well as soldiers, stayed with him. Shaikh Rizq ullah's father being an old associate of the dismissed governor stayed with him. When Shaikh Sad ullah was short of money, his relatives and friends advised him to seek employment with some other noble as he no longer was able to support him financially. The Shaikh did not accept their advice because he did not think it becoming of him to part company with his old benefactor in the days of adversity. He said for their satisfaction, 'I have got a residential building that I would dispose of for the sustenance of my family. In addition to it, I have a *Kutab Khana* (library), the sale proceeds of which would suffice for long. I have no worry so long as these belongings last. All these were acquired during my association with him (Mia Zain uddin)'.[30]

Shaikh Rukn uddin Chishti's testimony to this fact is of immense significance. Mentioning Babur's invasion of the Punjab in 1523-4, Shaikh Rukn uddin says that the invaders did not even spare the libraries in the towns of the Punjab, and all of them were plundered along with the residential houses.[31] Babur himself describes the library of Ghazi Khan Lodi, son of Daulat Khan Lodi in the town of Milvat.[32] In this library, the invader found a large collection of books relating to different subjects. Babur states, 'I went into Ghazi Khan's books room, some of the precious things found in it, I gave to Humayun; some were sent to Kamran (in Qandhar). There were many books of learned contents, but not so many valuable ones as had at first appeared'.[33]

In the final analysis it may be recalled that the maintenance of libraries by the elite was thought to be a part of the intellectual culture and learning across the subcontinent of India. No doubt, libraries helped in the diffusion of knowledge and promoting an intellectual culture. The old collections left by the scholars and nobles of pre-Mughal India inspired the later generations to maintain libraries during the Mughal period and even afterwards. The library culture also led to the progress of the craft of paper making in the country on the one hand and provided job opportunities to people in the urban centres. The scribes, bookbinders and those who dealt in the trade of books also benefitted from it.

Endnotes

1. The oldest copies of the Quran written on parchment are found in different libraries of the world. Two beautiful copies of the Quran the writing of which are ascribed to Ali, the fourth caliph, are available in India, one in Maulana Azad Library, Aligarh, and the other one in Raza Library, Rampur (UP).
2. Cf. Clifford Edmund Bosworth, *The Later Ghaznavids: Splendour and Decay,* New Delhi: Munshiram Manoharlal, 1992, p. 128; See also Hamilton Gibb, *Studies on the Civilization of Islam,* ed. Stanford J. Shaw and William R. PolK., London: Routledge and Kegan Paul Limited, 1962, p. 115.
3. The earliest extant Persian works written in Lahore are the *diwans* of Abul Faraj Runi and Mas 'ud S 'ad Salman, and Shaikh Ali Hujwiri's *Kashful-Mahjube,* the first ever written treatise on *Tasawwuf* in Persian prose, Abul Faraj Runi, *Diwan,* Tehran, AD 1925; Mas'ud S'ad Salman, *Diwan,* Tehran, 1879; Shaikh Ali Hinwiri, *Kashful-Mahjub,* tr. R.A. Nicholson, rpt, Lahore: Taj Company, 1982.
4. Sadid uddin Muhammad 'Awfi, *Lubab ul-Albab,* ed. E.C. Browns, Muhammad Qazwini and Said Nafisi, Tehran, 1341 Shamsi,

pp. 188-91 & 205; also see Clifford Edmund Bosworth, *The Later Ghaznavids: Splendour and Decay,* op.cit., pp. 127-8, for details.

5. Hasan Nizami, *Taj-ul-Ma'asir,* MS. British Library, London no. Add. 7623.

6. Fakhr-i-Mudabbir dedicated his *Shajra-i-Ansab* to Sultan Qutbuddin Aibak, the founder of the Sultanate in India. E. Denison Ross separated its *Muqadima* and published its critical edition under the wrong title '*Tarikh-i-Fikhr uddin Mubarak Shah Marvar-rudi.* Fakhr-i-Mudabbir has been confused with his namesake, Fakhruddin Mubarak Shah Marvar-rudi, the author of *Bahr ul-Ansab.* They were contemporaries. Cf. Iqtidar Husain Siddiqui, *Authority and Kingship Under the Sultans of Delhi,* New Delhi: Manohar Publishers 2006, p. 45.

7. Cf. Nazir Ahmad, 'Abdur Razzaq Samarqand's Account of Life and Culture in South India 15th Century', *Islamic Heritage in South Asia,* ed. N. Ahmad and Iqtidar Husain Siddiqui, Publication Scheme, Jaipur, 1998, vol. 1, p. 158.

8. *I'jaz-i-Khusravi* tr. Iqtidar Husain Siddiqui, Illinois, USA: Islamic Thought and Science Institute, 2007, vol. 4, p. 322.

9. The Tibetan monk Dharmaswamin, who visited Nalanda during Sultan Shamsuddin Iltutmish's reign (1210-36) studied Buddhist literature in Nalanda's Library. The evidence contained in his travelogue corrects the historiographic error that Nalanda was destroyed by the Muslim invaders. Nalanda continued to flourish till the fourteenth century. A later Tibetan pilgrim Taranath states that 'years after the establishment of Turkish rule in Bihar, the Tirthankars who had a quarrel with the Buddhists during a religious sermon burnt Buddhist temples, religious places and Ratanodadhi, one of the three buildings of the Nalanda University Library'. Cf. Biography of Dharmaswamin, tr. George Roerich, Patna: K.P. Jayswal Research Institute, 1959, pp. 73, 90-1; Taranath as cited by Hasan Nishat, *The Comprehensive History of Bihar,* ed. Syed Hasan Askari, Patna: K.P. Jayaswal Institute, 1983, vol. 2, Part 1, p. 40.

10. *Tarikh-i-Firuz Shahi,* Calcutta, 1862, p. 14.

11. Shaikh Rizq ullah Mushtaqi, *Waqi'at-i-Mushtaqi,* tr. Iqtidar Husain Siddiqui, New Delhi: ICHR, 1993, p. 76.

12. Hasan Sijzi, *Fawaid ul-Fuad*, Lahore: Malik Siraj uddin & Sons, 1966, pp. 45-6.
13. Hamid Qalandar, *Khair ul-Majalis*, ed. K.A. Nizami, Aligarh: Aligarh University Publication, 1959, p. 88.
14. *Fuwaid ul-Fuad*, 1966, op.cit., p.76.
15. Hamid Qalandar, *Khair ul-Majalis*, ed. K.A. Nizami, Aligarh, 1959, p. 52.
16. Mohammad Habib, 'Chishti Mystics Records of the Sultanate Period', *Medieval India Quarterly*, (Aligarh) vol. 1, no. 2, October 1950, p. 39.
17. *Fuwaid ul-Fuad*, 1966, pp. 127-8 & 228.
18. Qalandar, *Khair ul-Majalis*, op.cit., p. 85.
19. Cf. Ali Kufi, *Chachnama*, ed. Nabi Bakhsh Baloch, Islamabad: Islamic University, 1983, p. 6.
20. *Lubab ul-Albab*, ed. E.C. Browne and Mirza Muhammad Qasvini, London, 1906.
21. Iqtidar Husain Siddiqui, *Perso-Arabic Sources of Information on the Life and Conditions in the Sultanate of Delhi*, New Delhi: Munshiram Manoharlal 1992, p. 36, for translation of *Jawami ul-Hikayat wa Livami ul-Riwayat.*
22. Ibid., p. 49.
23. Minhaj-i-Siraj, *Tabaqat-i-Nasiri*, vol. 2, ed. Abdul Hai Habibi, Kabul, 1963-4, p. 26.
24. Iqtidar Husain Siddiqui, 'Amir Khusrau: A Political and Social Thinker', *Indo-Iranica*, Kolkata, March and July 2007, vol. 60, nos. 1-2, pp. 1-12, for details.
25. Cf. K.A. Nizami, *Studies in Medieval Indian History and Culture*, Allahabad: Kitab Mahal, op.cit., 1966, p. 6-7.
26. See *Masalik ul-Absar fi, Mamalik ul-amsar* in *Perso-Arabic Sources of Information on the Life and Conditions in the Sultanate of Delhi*, op.cit., p. 125.
27. Hajib Khairat Dehlavi, *Dastur ul-Afazil*, ed. Nazir Ahmad, Bunyad-i-Farhang-i-Iran, Tehran, Series no. 168, pp. 56-7; also *Perso-Arabic Sources of Information on the Life and Conditions in the Sultanate of Delhi* , pp. 78-86, for detail.

28. Abul Faiz Faizi, *Insha-i-Faizi,* ed. A.D. Arshad, Lahore: Majlis-i-Taraqi-i-Adab, n.d., p. 296.
29. *Waqi'at-i-Mushtaqi,* tr., p. 242.
30. Ibid., tr., p. 76.
31. *Lataif-i-Quddusi,* p. 64.
32. The town of Milvat is situated in the Salt Range, in 32'° 42 in Jhelum district (Pakistan).
33. *Baburnama,* tr. Mrs A. Beveridge, rpt, New Delhi, 1975, ii/460.

CHAPTER 10

Syncretic Tradition: Translation of Arabic and Sanskrit Classics into Persian

The Ghurian conquest of north India during the last decades of the twelfth century coincided with the emergence of a Persian-speaking intelligentsia in Khurasan (i.e. present-day Afghanistan) and the neighbouring lands. The conquerors of India who hailed from Ghazna and the area around spoke Persian. Malik Qutbuddin Aibak, the lieutenant of Sultan Muiz u'ddin Muhammad bin Sam became an independent Sultan after the assassination of the latter in 1206. The adoption by the new Sultan of Persian as the official language contributed to its growth. In the beginning, the dearth of Arabic-knowing Muslims led the early sultans and the members of the ruling elite to get the Arabic classics on religion and statecraft translated into Persian for the benefit of Persian-speaking immigrants from Khurasan and Central Asia. In time, Sanskrit classics related to Hindu religious philosophy and sciences were also taken up for translation. Such translation brought many advanced ideas and concepts into Persian. So far the Persian language had served as a vehicle for expression in poetry but with the translation of Arabic and Sanskrit treatises it grew into a language both of science and religious philosophy.

Several works from different branches of learning have survived the ravages of time. Besides the translation of Arabic and Sanskrit classics, works on Persian lexicography, fiction (i.e. *dastan* writing in Persian prose), Sufi *Malfuzat* (collection of utterances) and historiography are of outstanding merit as well as trendsetting in Persian literature. In history writing, the works compiled by the Indo-Persian writers are very important in that they have not been equalled, much less excelled by their counterparts in contemporary Iran and Central Asia. Moreover, the Indo-Persian writers invented new genres and styles while producing literature in Persian prose.

It is also worth pointing out that the translation of Sanskrit classics helped the establishment of a symbiotic relationship between the followers of Islam and Hinduism. It brought them culturally closer to each other, paved the way for interaction and also provided creative initiative.

The Persian translation of the Arabic work, *Fath-i-Bilad-i-Hind-wa-Fath-i-Sind,* better known as *Chachnama,*[1] relating to the early history of Sind and its Arab conquest under Muhammad bin Qasim al-Saqafi is a signtificant work. Its translator was Ali bin Hamid bin Abu Bakr Kufi, who completed his translation in 1216. Unlike an Arabic writer of the classical period, the translator seems to have taken to a literary style, investing the historical content of the original Arabic text with romantic stories in a truly pre-Islamic Persian tradition in order to adorn it. The stories incorporated in the translation were either invented by Ali Kufi or based on what he might have heard of the advent of Chach Brahman to power in Sind. The stories read like modern fiction, free from the supernatural element but full of suspense. Since the Indo-Persion writers were inspired by Indian fiction and they introduced a new genre in Persian prose, I summarize here the story of the love affair between Chach Brahman and the queen of Rai Sahasi, the King of Sind.

> The king Sahasi was sterile and under the control of his wife, Sunhindeo. One day the king summoned to the palace the *hajib,* Ram to draft an urgent letter in reply to a letter received from one of his vassal chiefs. Ram was not available in the *Diwan-i-Insha* (Chancellery) So his *naib* (deputy) came instead. At that time the king was with his Queen in the inner Chamber. He asked the queen to move behind the curtain as a stranger was to be called inside. She said that there was nothing wrong if she remained in the presence of a Brahman known for his good conduct. As usual, the king gave in and Chach was conducted inside. He was handsome and youthful, and the queen was captivated by his charming personality and desired intimacy with him. In the beginning Chach did not respond as he thought it sinful, his elder brother and father having become monks. But the queen's persistence and coquetry had their effect on Chach. He fell into her trap and began to visit her. After some time, the king fell ill, suffering from a serious disease. When his condition deteriorated and all hope was lost queen and Chach conspired to invite the relatives of the king so as to have them arrested and eliminated. Following the death of the king, Chach married the queen and occupied the throne. She gave birth to three children, including Dahir.[2]

Similarly, the story relating to the treachery committed by Dahir's two daughters against Muhammad bin Qasim, the conqueror of Sind and Multan is fiction and a later day concoction.[3] The tradition of fiction writing was thus laid down by Ali Kufi and followed by the Indo-Persian writers during the subsequent period. Some of the history writers followed this tradition, interpolating romantic tales along with historical content. This literature awaits the attention of the scholars of Persian literature and medieval Indian culture.

The Arabic text of the *Chachnama* seems to have been compiled during the ninth century on the basis of Arab histories and local traditions of Sind. Much information contained in the translation about the socio-political conditions in Sind and South-Western Punjab on the eve of Arab conquest is of immense importance. Because *Chachnama* corroborates the account of the Chinese traveller Hieun Tsang who had visited Sind earlier and described the unfavorable conditions in which the Buddhists lived there, the Buddhist chiefs had no hesitation in transferring their allegiance to the foreign invader.[4] For the guidance of the Sultan Nāsir-ud-Din Qubācha and the members of the ruling elite, the translator is careful enough not to omit those details which bring into greater relief the need for a Muslim ruler not to interfere with the social system of the Hindus in India. For example, Muhammad bin Qasim is said to have sanctioned the privileges of high castes and the degradation of the low ones. The Brahmans were given full religious freedom and appointed to important positions in the administration of Sind whereas the Jats were kept as degraded as they were under Dahir.[5] The Sultans of Delhi seem to have followed the same policy during their rule.

Likewise, the translator's introduction to the work is important in so much as it yields information about the achievements of Qubācha and his *wazir*, the emergence of some cities into centres of learning and culture and the state policy towards scholars and men of talent. Both the Sultan and his *wazir*, Ain-ul-Mulk al-Ash'ari were great patrons of learning and the learned; everyone of them who stood in need of support from the state wrote something either in Sultan Qubācha's praise or dedicated it to his *wazir* and then achieved his end. For instance, Ali Kufi who had incurred royal displeasure, sometime before 1216, decided, to do something in order to regain his lost position.[6] In Bhakkar he got hold of a historical work in Arabic (Hejazi dialect) in the possession of the local Qazi Ismail bin Ali al-Saqafi, the descendant of Muhammad bin Qasim. Ali Kufi rendered it into Persian, dedicated it to the Sultan's *wazir*, Hussain bin Ali Bakr bin Muhamad al-Ash'ari, entitled *Ain-ul-Mulk (al-Ash'ari)*.[7]

Besides praise for the reigning Sultan and his *wazir*, the introduction also mentions the cities of Uchh and Bhakkar that had already emerged as centres of culture and learning in Sind. Ali Kufi is the only contemporary writer who informs us that Uchh was the capital of Sultan Nāsir-ud-Din Qubācha. He mentions the metropolitan city Uchh along with the prefix

'*Hazrat*', used for the royal capital in Central Asia.[8] The town of Bhakkar (former Mansura, founded on a rock in the Indus) is said to have had a large number of the descendants of the early Arab settlers. All of them maintained the traditions of religious learning.[9] The text also contains a number of Hindi and Persian terms that got currency during the Sultanate period, such as *takur* (for *thakur), deodar* (the cedar tree), *mati* (mud), *Jogni* (female Hindu recluse), *rai* (ruler), *rangan* (land chiefs).[10]

It is also worth mentioning that there is a great deal of touching up of the original Arabic text by Al-Kufi, reflecting the political traditions in Sind vis-à-vis the relations between the Sultan and the hereditary chiefs. Al-Kufi's purpose in alluding to *rais, thakurs* and *rangans* was to apprise Sultan Nāsir-ud-Din Qubācha (foreigner by birth) of the need to foster cordial relations with the local potentates for they constituted an important element in Indian polity. He implies that a victorious ruler should regard his victory over the chiefs as a prelude to a settlement and not to their annihilation.

Like Qubācha and his *wazir*, Sultan Ilututmish and his *wazir*, Nizam-ul-Mulk Junaidi also encouraged emigrant scholars to render Arabic classics into Persian. In Delhi the first important Arabic work to be translated was al-Beruni's famous book on *tib* (Greek System of medicines), i.e. *Kitab-ul-Saidna*. The translator Abu Bakr bin Ali bin Usman al-Kasani (Kasan being in Central Asia) seems to have arrived in India, sometime in the beginning of the reign of Sultan Shams-ud-Din Iltutmish (1211-36).[11] The translator tell us that he was driven away from his ancestral place by the hot wind of calamity (i.e. unstable political conditions, caused by Mongol invasion in the first decades of the thirteenth century). In India he was attracted by the generosity of the reigning 'King Sultan-i Muazzam, Shahinshah al Azam, the lord of Arabia and Ajam, the shadow of God on the living beings, Shams-ul-Dunya wad-Din Abul Fath Iltutmish and settled down in *Hazrat-i Delhi*. He writes:

> I decided to study the conditions and found the metropolis rich in wealth and full of people of learning and talent; in fact it had turned into a centre of culture. Everyone of them who had been attracted by the Sultan's generosity was constrained to come here. The *ashraf* (social elite) from Khurasan and Mavraulnahr (Transoxiana) who were driven away by the vicissitude of circumstances in their own lands got refuge under the patronage of the Sultan. Everyone of them is full of praise for the Sultan for his generosity and love for justice.[12]

Describing the qualities of the reigning Sultan, (Shams-ud-Din Iltutmish), al-Kasani tells us that one of the signs of his (Iltutmish's) royalty was that the late Sultan Qutb-ud-Din Aibak perceived at the very first glance the superb intelligence, modesty, faithfulness, perseverance and undaunted courage possessed by the fortunate *Majlis-i ali.*[13] Thereafter, the Sultan favoured him with high positions ad utilized his services in meeting difficult situations from time to time. Another sign of divine mercy on him was that everyone who harboured ill-will towards him was doomed to failure.[14] Al-Kasani says:

> During the one and half a year. I have spent in this Hazrat (i.e. metropolitan Delhi) several persons rose in revolt against this just and pious monarch, but all of them disappeared from the scene,[15] with the result that the fear and grandeur of his royalty got hold of the hearts of the *raiyat* (commoners), Turks and Tajiks (Taziks in the text), noble-born and low-born people alike. All of them became subservient to him. Then peace prevailed and people were saved from confusion and tyranny. The country prospered, owing to the establishment of law and justice. Likewise, the *rais* (chiefs) of Hindustan acquiesced and the grandeur of the realm increased through their co-operation.

Concluding his introductory part, al-Kasani, showers praises on the Crown Prince Nasir-ud-Din Mahmud (d.1230), who is said to have been endowed with excellent qualities of the head and heart and many scholars and men of letters basked in the sunshine of his patronage. Al-Kasani, also mentions how he was anxious to get something to present at the royal court as *khidmati.*[16] It came to his mind that he should compile a book, the *debacha* (opening part) of which should be devoted to the life and achievements of the reigning, *Shahinshah* (emperor). He thought that the best offering at the royal court was an account of the blessings of his auspicious reign, so that the coming generations might know of it. 'After much deliberation' says he, 'I decided to translate Abu Rayhan's (al-Beruni) *Kitab-ul-Saidna* from Arabic into Persian for the benefit of people'.[17]

As for the text, al-Kasani did not simply translate the Arabic terms into Persian but also added much fresh material, regarding the location and particulars of certain minerals as well as the views of the authorities on their nature. All this is not found in the Arabic text. Likewise, the use of Hindi equivalents along with Persian terms for certain medicines is indicative of the fact that the process of cultural fusion had started in the Sultanate of Delhi since its very beginning. The references to Kashmiri fruits, particularly apple, tends to point to the existing inland trade between the Hindu kingdom of Himalaya and the Sultanate.[18]

The translation of Imam Ghazzali's famous work on religious sciences *Ihya-ul-Ulum-id-Din* from Arabic into Persian by an emigrant scholar Majd-ud-Din Abul Ma 'ali Muaiyid bin Muhammad Jajarmi also deserves to be mentioned. The work in Arabic commanded immense prestige as it had countered the influence of the teachings of rationalist philosophers and revived the interest of the educated Muslims in the traditional Islamic sciences in the Islamic countries. In view of its importance and the need of the emerging Persian-knowing intelligentsia in India, Nizam ul-Mulk Junadi, the *wazir* of Sultan Iltutmish, asked Jajarmi to take up its translation for the diffusion of Islamic learning in the Sultanate. The translator writes in the introduction to his translation that he was engaged in teaching and instructing people in religious sciences for quite some time in Lahore. His classes were attended even by scholars. It is also implicit in the *muqadima* (introduction) that in certain branches he had acquired good knowledge and impressed the elite in Lahore. As a result, the number of his pupils increased. By the year 1223 his lectures had gained such popularity that the cream of all classes of people from the *imams* (scholars who led prayer) and *Shaikhs* (saints) down to the traders and others had begun to attend them. This led a section of people to spread calumnies against him. Though the doctors of Hanafi law tried to protect him, he was ultimately forced to leave Lahore for Delhi, which he reached towards the end of 1223.

Jajarmi does not explain the nature of charges levelled against him. His popularity could not be a sufficient reason for his exile form Lahore. It may, however, be inferred that he was perhaps secretly in alliance with the Delhi court against Nāsir-ud-Din Qubācha as Lahore was a bone of contention between Nāsir-ud-din Qubācha and Iltutmish, on the one hand and exposed to Mongol raids on the other. Nāsir-ud-Din Qubācha had already failed to defend it against both Taj-ud-Din Yildoz in 1210 and Sultan Jalal-ud-din Khwarazm Shah in 1221-2.[19] However, he reached Delhi which he calls '*Hazrat-i Delhi*' towards the close of the year 1223 and 'got shelter under the protection of the 'Sultan of Sultans, Shams-ud-Din wal-Din' (Iltutmish). According to him the Sultan bestowed royal favour upon him. After the Sultan, he praises his patron, Nizam-ul-Mulk Junaidi for his benevolence and munificence to scholars. He mentions all the titles held by the *wazir* as Muaiyid-ul-Mulk, Malik-ul-Wuzra, Asif-ul-Asr, Abul Maʿali Muhammad bin Fakhr-ul-Mulk Sharaf Abi Sʿad al-Junaidi. Further, he says that the *Majlis-i ʿali* asked him to render *Ihya-ul-Ulum* into Persian so that people might benefit from it.[20] The *wazir* granted him financial assistance and also assured him of royal favours in return for the work.

Again, Jajarmi tells us about Sultan Iltutmish's liberal policy towards the immigrants from foreign lands, and how he treated the refugees with consideration in general and men of learning in particular. As for the *wazir's* devotion to learning, he spared much time to studying books and held discussions with the learned on scholarly matters. He was also fond of purchasing books and spent huge amounts of money on them, and also gave financial assistance to men of piety. He did not care for money, for he knew its transitory nature. For him spiritual pleasure was preferable to worldly things.

In rendering the Arabic text into Persian, Jajarmi employed a specific method so as to be as close to the original as possible. Thus, the verses from the Quran, the traditions of the Prophet (*hadis*), the sayings of the companions of the Prophet are given in the original Arabic, along with their Persian translation and explanation for the benefit of general readers. As for the style employed by the translator in the text, it is largely free from metaphors, affectation and poetical artifices but the introduction to the work is marked by floridity at places.

Majd-ul Mulk Jajarmi's translation soon gained popularity as it was considered a yeoman service to the cause of learning. At places he made his own additions, for instance where Imam Ghazzali quotes ruling from the Shafi'ite sources with regard to legal problems, Jajarmi replaces them by those of the Hanafite school. It reveals the indifference, if not hostility of the Hanafite *ulama* towards the Shafi'ite school of law.[21] For all these reasons, Jajarmi's translation became a standard work to be taught in the colleges at higher levels. Both Amir Khusrau and Barani pay tribute to Jajarmi for his scholarly translation.

Amir Khusrau's assessment of the value of Jajarmi's translations deserves to be referred to. Discussing the problems, connected with prose styles, Khusrau refers to Jajarmi along with other leading writers. Of the six writers, mentioned by Khusrau only two are those who had adopted India as their country. They are Shaikh Ali Hujwiri, the author of *Kashf ul-Mahijub* and Majd ul-Mulk Jajarmi, the translator of *Ihya ul-Ulum-id-Din.* If Hujwiri invented the simple style of the Sufis, the latter style came to be known as that of the doctors of law, characterized by flow and gentleness in expression.[22] Barani also includes it in the list of the classics of Arabic and Persian that were discussed in the Jama'at Khana of Shaikh Nizam-ud-Din Auliya and says that it was a good seller like the *Awarif-ul-arif,* the *Kashf-ul-Mahjub,* the *Risala-i Qushairi* (of Abul Qasim Abdul Karim Qushairi), the *Lawaih and the Lawami of* Qazi Hamid ud-Din Nagauri and *Fawaid-ul-Fuad*[23] (of Amir Hasan Sijzi).

The last Arabic work, undertaken for translation towards the close of Iltutmish's reign was *al-Sirr al-Maktum*', the authorship of which is ascribed to Imam Fakhruddin Razi (d. AD 1210). As Imam Razi was an orthodox 'Asharite scholar, its authorship is open to doubt because it deals with occult science and beliefs of the Sabeans of Hassan (a town in Mesopotamia), which are at variance with the teaching of Quran. It is also doubtful that Sultan Iltutmish showed interest in its translation because Islamic orthodoxy was in complete control of religious affairs of the Sultanate. The *ulama* suppressed all innovations and practices, even those not in clash with the Quranic teaching. Even the Sufis were not allowed to hold *sama* (music) gatherings in their *khanqahs* during his reign. The situation changed with the advent of the Khaljis to power in 1290. The Khalji Sultans not only allowed scholars of '*Ilm-al-Ma'qul* (rationalist sciences) full freedom but also employed them as their courtiers.[24] Probably the work was written in Arabic by some little known person and the bookseller ascribed its authorship to Imam Razi, in order to enhance its sale. As regards its Persian translation, it might have been done during the fourteenth century and the anonymous translator mentioned Iltutmish and his son and immediate successor Sultan Rukn uddin Firuz Shah as his patrons at the instance of some bookseller. As discussed in the preceding chapter, the scribes were highly educated people and booksellers engaged them to write books or translate books from Arabic into Persian on popular themes. The authorship of the books written by the scribes was ascribed to important persons of the past. It may also be added that occult science and practices, astrology and much other material found contained in *al-Sirr al-Maktum* must have had a great deal of appeal to the ruling elite during the fourteenth century. The extant copies of the Persian translation of the work are in Indian *Nastaliq* hand of the sixteenth century. One of the manuscript copy was made for Emperor Akbar.[25]

Likewise, the translation of *Awarif-ul-Maarif* by Qasim Daud Khatib, sometime between the years 1243-5 is also an important contribution to early Persian literature, made in India during the thirteenth century. This work produced by the Suhrawardi Sufi Saint, Shaikh Shihab-ud-din Suhrawardi (d. AD 1234) had gained worldwide popularity just after its publication. The leading Chishti, Suhrawardi and Firdausi Sufi saints in India during the thirteenth century studied and explained it to their *murids*[26] (disciples) and also tried to live according to it. In the beginning of the Delhi Sultanate no other work seems to have made so much impact on the life of Sufis as the *Awarif-ul-Arif*. In fact, according to the historian Mohammad Habib, the India of early Sufis was 'exclusively in the sphere of the *Awarif*, which is a textbook of mystic but not of Mulla-orthodoxy,'[27] In an attempt to make the work useful for the Muslim elite not at home in Arabic, the Sultan of Multan and Sind, Taj-ud-Din Abu Bakr (d.1244-5) asked one of his scholarly servants, Qasim Daud Khatib[28] to render it from Arabic into Persian so that it could benefit a larger number of people.

In the introduction to his translation, Qasim Daud Khatib tells us that the *Badshah-i 'azam,* the great Tajul-Haque wad-Din Abu Bakr, son of Kabir Izz-ud-Dunyya wad-Din, supporter of Islam and Muslims, the warrior of Iran and Turan Mangbarni,[29] Aiyaz Kabir Khani said to him, 'the *Awarif-ul-Maarif* compiled by Shaikh-ul-Mashaikh Shihab-ud-din al-Suhrawardi that contains the traditions and sayings (of the Prophet and saintly people) be rendered from Arabic into Persian, the sweetest of the tongues. It will serve the purpose as many people would be able to study it and live to its contents. Because most of the educated people were not conversant with Arabic and, therefore, they could not benefit from the Arabic text.' Further, the translator tells us that his *Pir* (religious preceptor), Shaikh-ul-Islam Baha-ud-Din Zakariya[30] also encouraged him to take up the work. With the Shaikh's blessing the work was completed sometime before the death of Sultan Taj-ud-din Abu Bakr in 1245 as the references to him in the introduction suggest.[31] The Shaikh also appears to have assisted the disciple to explain the spiritual subtleties in the Arabic text.[32] Thus, it was the earliest translation made within about ten or eleven years of Shaikh Shihab-ud-din Suhrawardi's passing away.

Undoubtedly, the translator was learned in the Sufi tradition. His work shows that he also possessed profound knowledge of Islamic theological sciences. The explanations of theological and mystic problems bear testimony to his erudition in religious sciences. The text is also interspersed with verses composed by Qasim Daud Khatib but they may be set aside as mere versification devoid of any literary charm worth considering. But it is an important contribution to early Persian prose literature in so far as its straightforward but idiomatic style is concerned. His style is effective and not hackneyed. This single fact according to Nazir Ahmad, 'may reasonably assign it an honourable position in the realm of important Persian works.'[33]

The Arabs appear to have shown an interest in Indian sciences and learning, at least, since the Abbasid period. But the distinguished Muslim scholar scientist who really made Sanskrit works popular in the Islamic world through his translation and further research was Abu Rayhan al-Beruni (d. AD 1046). The annexation of the Punjab by Sultan Mahmud of Ghazna (reigned: AD 998-1030) to his Empire paved the way for interaction between the Hindu and Muslim scholars and scientists in Central Asian lands. Seized with a passion for learning, Abu Rayhan al-Beruni acquired firsthand knowledge of Indian sciences and culture. He learnt the Sanskrit language from Brahman teachers and improved his understanding through interaction with them. Having acquired competence in Sanskrit, he translated Sanskrit treatises on astrology and mathematics into the Arabic language that was the *lingua franca* of the Islamic world. Though most of the works translated by al-Beruni from Sanskrit into Arabic on astrology are not extant, one of them entitled *Ghurat al-Zijat* is available in the Pir Muhammad Shah Dargah Library in Ahmadabad. It is a rare manuscript copy of the translation of original *Karna Tilak* which is untraceable. It records observation of solar and lunar eclipses.[34] This translation was brought to completion before al-Beruni started his famous work on India, *Kitab al-Hind fi-Tahqiq Milal Hind.* The tradition laid by al-Beruni was followed by other scholars during the Delhi Sultanate period. However, these Sultanate scholars wrote in Persian and belonged to different classes.

Of the Muslim religious elite, the Sufis, particularly the Chishtis got interested in the science of yoga and adopted yogic exercise of breath-control (*Pas-i-anfas*). It was found helpful in meditation and complete absorption could be achieved in *zikr* (litany) with its performance. The work *Amrit Kund,* dealing with yoga exercises and philosophy was the first treatise translated from Sanskrit into Persian for this purpose. It was titled '*Hauz al-Hayat*'.[35]

The translation of *Amrit Kund* enjoyed popularity among the Sufis through out the Delhi Sultanate period. The fifteenth and sixteenth century Chishti Sufis, Shaikh Abdul Haque of Radauli[36] and Shaikh Abdul Quddus Gangohi taught *Hauz ul-Hayat* and trained their *murids* in performing the exercise of breath-control. To them the attainment of the state of complete absorption through meditation was the real worship and a means of having communion with God. Shaikh Abdul Quddus Gangohi (d. 1536) is reported to have said, 'One night I was in *namaz-i-makus*[37] when the *Sultan-i-zikr* manifested itself and put to flight my external existence, a state of obliteration *(mahviyat)* then came to pass and there was no consciousness apart from my consciousness of myself. In that state I had to pass beyond this consciousness of myself and reach the annihilation of annihilation (*fana al-fana*). By God's grace this came to pass and the world of eternity (*baqa*) was revealed. When I descended from this state, a man appeared from the unseen *(az ghayb)* and said, "Blessed be it, at this time you were united with God (*wasil bi-haqq*)!" He then Vanished'.[38]

It may also be added that this *Hauz al-Hayat* remained popular even after the sixteenth century famous Shatari Sufi, Shaikh Muhammad Ghaus Gwaliori had translated *Amrit Kund* second time in a popular literary Persian prose. Muhammad Ghaus Gwaliori's translation, entitled *Bahrul-Hayat,* could not replace the *Hauz al-Hayat* as seventeenth century Mulla Shaida's reference to the older work suggests. Describing the philosophy and practices of the yogis of Gorakhnath sect in his journal, '*Sair-i-Kashmir*' during the reign of Shah Jahan, Mulla Shaida calls the Gorakhnath yogis the guides of the Muslim Sufis in practising breath-control exercises. He also mentions *Hauz al-Hayat,* dealing with the practice.[39]

Undoubtedly, the Sufis learnt and practiced yoga for spiritual development, yet many Hindus and Muslims did not consider it only a spiritual science but also a physical one that could be helpful in keeping one healthy and lengthening his lifespan. The relevant evidence, contained in the *Waqi'at-i-Mushtaqi* reveals that youthful people joined the company of yogis in order to learn the secret of building a vigorous body for the enjoyment of health and sex.[40]

As regards the translation of Sanskrit works on astrology, texts related to the planets and their movement held great attraction for the Muslim scientists. It is true that the *ulama* (clerics) opposed the study of astrology and thought it at variance with the Quranic teaching, but the intellectuals disagreed with them. The statement by Shams Siraj Afif in the defence of astronomy and astrology is worth quoting because it sheds light on the popularity of astrology among the ruling elite. Afif writes, 'Astronomy is one of the fourteen sciences known to the scholars. But its study has been forbidden by the Prophet (of Islam). The *ulama* (orthodox scholars) also disapprove of it. It is, however, permissible to know the rules, concerning the shadow of the sun and that in a particular month in what degree of what sign of the zodiac the sun would be, the hours of the short night and the long night and when it (the night) turned into the day'.[41]

A word about the popularity of astrology among the Muslim ruling elite may be added. Unlike the *ulama* the social elite both in Central Asia and India patronized the astrologers. The Muslim astronomers practised astrology and prepared astrological tables and horoscopes, in order to earn their livelihood. Zia'uddin Barani not only informs us about the famous astronomers of Delhi during the thirteenth and fourteenth centuries, but also provides us clues about the interaction and cooperation between the Hindu and Muslim astronomers. According to Barani, there was considerable observation and experiment. The sultans patronized the men of talent and promoted the cause of different sciences, natural as well as applied. The science of astronomy and astrology became so popular among the elite of Delhi that none of its quarters was found without an astronomer. The astronomers and astrologers got gifts and rewards both in cash and kind from the Sultan, the grandees and other important persons of the city. Many of them even got villages and stipends from Sultan 'Ala ud'din Khalji. Further, many Hindu and Muslim astronomes were held in great favour, owing to their fame. According to Barani, 'The elite of Delhi could not start any work or undertake any project without consulting the astronomer. Even the wives of Sultan 'Ala ud'din Khalji patronized them'.[42] All this tends to suggest that astrology had become linked with astronomy and had the making of a shared interest for the Hindu and Muslim elite of India.

The official history of Sultan Firaz Shah's reign, *Sirat-i-Firuz Shahi* (compiled in AD 1370) also provides us with interesting information about the Sultan's interest in astronomy and astrology. According to it, royal inquisitiveness promoted research into the particulars of astronomy and a number of treatises were composed in consequence. The ancient Sanskrit works on astrology were translated into Persian and the *Dalail-i-Firuzshahi* was compiled on their basis. It dealt with the systems of rainfall, eclipses, conjunction of stars and the impact the stars had on the earth and its inhabitants.[43] This work has in fact survived. It was compiled by Abdul Aziz Shams Thanesari and it is significant in sofar as it casts light on Sultan Firuz Shah's belief that the heavenly bodies influenced the earth and its inhabitants.[44]

Likewise, the interaction between the experts of *Tib* (traditional Muslim system of medicines) and Ayurveda (Hindu system) went a long way to enrich each system. The discovery of the rare manuscript copy of *Majmu'a-Ziya'i,* written by Masud Rashid Zanji Umar Ghaznavi in AD 1329 contains a list of works, including Sanskrit ones that were utilized in its preparation. This is an important work, produced in the field of medicines and pharamacy. (Its rare copy is available in the Library of Jamia-i-Hamdard, New Delhi).

However, the most important work is the *Ma'dan ul-Shafe* alias *Tib-i-Sikandar Shahi,* compiled by Masnad-i-ali Mian Bhua, the *wazir* of Sultan Sikandar Lodi (reigned: 1489-1517). It is based on the translation of Sanskrit literature on medicine. The study of the book, *Ma'dan ul-Shafa-i-Sikandarshahi* shows that Mian Bhua did not like rhymed prose or the use of metaphorical language. He preferred a lucid and straightforward style to the ornate one. This style was popular during the Afghan period as the works of Shaikh Jamali Kambo and Shaikh Abdul Quddus Gaugohi in prose show. Mian Bhua however failed to realize the importance of literary elegance.

In the preface of the *Ma'adan al-Shafa,* having praised God and the Prophet, Mian Bhua draws upon the good qualities of the reigning Sultan, Sikandar Shah (Lodi). He states that due to the just government of the Sultan, despondency had disappeared and peace and prosperity prevailed everywhere, education and learning made progress due to his patronage. The learned men produced books and wrote *Fathnamas* about his victories. The praise of the Sultan is in both prose and verse.[45] Further he writes that after much deliberation he sought royal permission for undertaking the compilation of the *Ma'dan al-shafa.* He submitted to the Sultan that the purpose of human life is to rightfully earn livelihood and follow the law of *Sharia* (canon law). The fulfilment of this life mission depends on the maintenance of good health and treatment of illness through *ilm-i-tibb* (science of medicines). It has also been established that the Greek medicines do not suit the temperament of the Indians and the diseases of the patients are not cured as names of the medicines are of Greek origin or written in Persian and their nature unknown. They are not easily available in the country either. It was therefore, necessary that attention be paid to the literature produced by Indian experts and the Indian system of medicines found agreeable to the Indian climate be practised. The request was acceded to through the royal *farman.*[46]

For the compilation of this work, many Sanskrit classics, such as *Sasrat, Ja Deokarat, Ras Ratnako, Suangdhar, Chintama,* etc. were utilized, as their list given in the introduction of the translation shows. The terms and the names of the medicines, plants and herbs were translated into Persian and, if the equivalent of any term was not found in the Persian language, it was written with its original name in the Persian script with necessary explanation.

Besides, Mian Bhua seems to have patronized scholars to take important Sanskrit books and translate them into Persian for the benefit of the Persian reading intelligentsia. Sultan Sikandar Lodi happened to be a connoisseur of music and appreciated both Indian and Irani music. Umar bin Yahya al-Kabuli who was in the service of Mian Bhua was encouraged to compile the *Lahjat-e-Sikandar Shahi* a voluminous work on classical Indian music, entirely based on Sanskrit classics.[47]

For the preparation of the *Lahjat-i-Sikandar Shahi,* Umar al-Kabuli depended largely on the old Sanskrit works to which he refers in the preface.

The preface is important as it casts light on the cultivated taste and passion of Mian Bhua for the knowledge of different sciences and arts. Though Umar al-Kabuli seems to have been fond of writing in an elegant style with rhetorical artifices and figures of speech, he had to write the *Lahjat-i-Sikandar Shahi* in a simple style agreeable to his patron, Mian Bhua. I quote in translation some portion of the preface shedding light on the compiler's style as well as Mian Bhua's love for learning:

> When by the nature of the sun of the firmament of royalty and the pearl scattering moon of the chieftainship the melancholic pen attained perfection in swift speed that it could adorn the face of beauty of the bride of the language of some of the Hindi [Sanskrit] books which were on the subject of music, with the brocade of Persian and could decorate it with the ornaments of metaphors in a style agreeable to Bandagi Masnad-i-ali-o-Mansab-i-Mu'ali and could complete a book on the art of melody and music and on the principles of harp and flute and could arrange a spring of *Bihisht* [paradise] by a description of the heaven like assembly, it sat at work. But that swift charger ran so fast it fell down. As I had struck a blow against its head, it could not disobey me and [consequently] got itself prepared to serve me and with its double tongues it effected a translation of *Sangit Ratnakar, Nirit Sangarah, U'd Bharat, Sudhanidhi, Sangit Samassiya, Sangit Kalpataro*, Sangit *Satang etc.*, into *dari* [i.e. Persian] and it caused the bridles of melodies to come out from behind the curtain of nonentity on the stage of page in the presence of men of excellence of the time-and having strung the beautiful and attractive melodies in the thread of Persian style it left a valuable present.[48]

It may also be stated that in reaction against Mughal Emperor Akbar's religious policy, the historians of his age portray Sultan Sikandar Lodi as an ideal Muslim king who acted under the influence of the orthodox *ulama*. That the sultan was prejudiced against the non-Muslims is contradicted by what we find in the earlier sources, including the works translated from Sanskrit into Persian during Sultan Sikandar Lodi's reign. The Sultan sipped wine, shaved his beard and had works translated from Sanskrit into Persian during his reign, this gives us insight into the complex social phenomena of the Lodi period. In fact, the Delhi Sultanate culture had attained by now its complete form, exercised its shaping influence on the society of the country and given rise to a culture of shared Indo-Islamic values. The Persian translation of the Sanskrit classics enabled the Hindu and Muslim scientists to integrate the experience and knowledge of the past with their own new discoveries, particularly in astronomy and medicines.

Likewise, mention should also be made of *dastan* writing in Persian prose in pre-Mughal India because this tradition began under the influence of Sanskrit *kathas* (fiction). Inspired by indigenous tradition, the Indo-

Persian writers prepared adaptations of Indian romances. Ikhtisan, the *dabir-i-Khas* (minister-in-charge of the royal chancery) of Sultan Muhammad bin Tughluq (reigned: AD 1324-51) was a pioneer in this field. He made an adaptation of Indian tales in ornate Persian prose, interspersed with Arabic and Persian verses. Ikhtisan writes that his friends related tales from Indian books to him during his prolonged illness. Fascinated by the contents of some stories, Ikhtisan decided to restate them in his literary style. He completed his collection of tales in 1325-6, and in each tale the characters (heros and heroines) were given Persian Muslim dress.[49] This tradition laid by Ikhtisan was followed by other writers subsequently.[50] Ikhtisan's contemporary, Zia Nakhshabi (d.1350) also translated Indian folktales into Persian both in verse and prose. His *Tutinama* (tales of a parrot) is the famous translation of the Sanskrit tale of a parrot telling narratives of love and romance. Nakshabi writes that an elderly person came to him with a book and told him that the fifty-two tales described therein were translations from Hindi (i.e. Sanskrit) in an archaic and bombastic style, and should be rewritten lucidly, not lacking literary charm. Nakshabi acceded to his request.[51] It should be added that the original Sanskrit work contains seventy tales.[52]

To conclude, it may be stated that the early Persian translations of Arabic and Sanskrit classics have historical and intellectual dimensions. They not only helped the development of Persian prose into an effective vehicle for expression of religious and philosophical ideas but also provide us with insights into the state of Muslim culture, and interaction between the Hindu and Muslim scholars. Immigrants from Muslim countries from as far as Gharnata in Spain, came with new scientific instruments, such as the astrolabe and magnetic compass that attracted the Indian astrologers as well. The physicians synthesized the *tib* with Ayurvedic system, rendering it more effective. Moreover, such translation and symbiosis inspired foreigners who also evinced interest in this type of literary work creating new genres that enriched the Indo-Persian literature.

Endnotes

1. Ali bin Hamid, al-Kufi, *Fathnama-i-Sind,* popularly known as *Chachnama,* ed. N.A. Baloch, Islamabad, 1983 hereafter cited *Chachnama.*
2. *Chachnama,* 1983, pp. 10-20.

3. Ibid., pp. 187-90.
4. The Buddhists in lower Sind are reported to have extended co-operation to the Arabs against Dahir. See ibid., pp. 90-2.
5. Cf. Y. Friedmann, 'The Origin and Significance of *Chachnama*', *Islam in Asia*, ed. Y. Friedmann, Jerusalem, 1984, pp. 31-2.
6. *Chachnama*, 1983, p. 5.
7. Ibid., p. 6.
8. Ibid., pp. 5-6. As Delhi was made the capital by Iltutmish, the scholars writing books there mentioned the city as *Hazrat-i Delhi* long before any saint was buried there as will be discussed later.
9. Ibid., p. 6.
10. Ibid., pp. 81, 86, 88, 90.
11. *Kitab-ul-Saidna,* Persian tr. ed. by M. Sotudeh and Iraj Afshar, Bunyad-i-Farhang-i-Iran, 1352 Shamsi, pp. 11-12.
12. Ibid., pp. 13-14.
13. The prefix *Majlis-i 'ali* or *Masnad-i-'ali* were was used in the sense of exalted lordship. During the Delhi Sultanate period the *wazir* was addressed as *Majlis-i ali* (also exalted lordship was used for the high grandees and army generals). Both the expressions remained in usage till the fall of the Lodi dynasty. Cf. I.H. Siddiqui, 'Composition of the Nobility Under the Lodis', *Medieval India: A Miscellany,* Aligarh, 1977, vol. 4, pp. 10-30.
14. *Kitab-ul-Saidna,* op.cit., p.15.
15. Incidentally Minhaj-i-Siraj al Juzjani states in the account of Malik Saif-ud-Din Aibak that the latter was directed by Sultan Iltutmish to kill the undesirable nobles and seize their property for the state. The Malik being a God fearing noble detested the job assigned to him. Al-Kasani also implies indirectly that the rivals of the Sultan were eliminated in different ways, for poison as well as the assassins dagger were resorted to throughout the Sultanate period. Cf. *Tabaqat-i-Nasiri,* tr. Raverty, vol. 2, pp. 729-30.
16. *Kitab-ul-Saidna,* Persian tr. op.cit., pp. 15-17. The term *khidmati* means the offering that a visitor presented to the Sultan. See Siddiqui, *Perso-Arabic Sources of Information on the Life and Conditions in the Sultanate of Delhi,* p. 29, f.n. 62.
17. *Kitab-ul-Saidna,* ibid.,

18. Ibid., pp. 92 & 180.
19. Sultan Jalal-ud-din Khwarazm Shah entered India after his defeat by Chinggis Khan on the Indus in 1221. In India he defeated both the armies of Qubācha and Iltutmish. But Qubacha had to suffer more at his hands than Iltutmish, for Punjab and Sind were the scene of his military operations. The Mongols who entered India to pursue Khwarazm Shah, also plundered the territory of Qubācha twice, with the result that Qubācha's prestige suffered and his military strength weakened. Cf. I.H. Siddiqui, 'Relations between Khwarazm Shah and the Turkish Rulers of North India,' read at the Calicut Session of the All India History Congress, 1976 and published in *Aligarh Journal of Oriental Studies,* Aligarh, Spring, 1986, vol. 3, no. 1, pp. 55-66.
20. *Tarjuma Ihya-ul-Ulum-id-Din,* MS, British Library, No. Or. 8194, ff. 1a-2b.
21. Translation (only a part) MS. British Museum, Or. 8194, f. 3a.
22. Amir Khusrau, *I'jaz-i-Khusravi,* vol. 1, Lucknow: Nawal Kishore Press, 1865-7, pp. 56-7.
23. Barani, *Tarik-i-Firuz Shahi,* 1862, p. 346.
24. Cf. Iqtidar Husain Siddiqui, 'Muslim Intellectual Life in India', *Medieval India: Essays in Intellectual Thought and Culture,* ed., New Delhi: Manohar Publishers, 2003, vol. 1, pp. 84-6.
25. Cf. Ziva Vessel, The Persian Translation of Fakhr al-Din Raz *al-Sirr al-Maktum* (The Occult Secret) for Iltutmish, translation from French into English by Sanjay Subramanyan, *Confluence of Culture,* ed. Françoise Delvoye, New Delhi: Manohar, 1995, pp. 14-22.
26. *Fawaid ul-Fuad,* Lahore, 1966, pp. 26-7.
27. Mohammad Habib, Chisti Mystics Records of the Sultanate Period, *Medieval India Quarterly,* Aligarh, 1950, vol. 1, no. 2, October 1950, pp. 1-42.
28. *Tarjuma-i-Awarif-ul-M'arif,* MS, University Collection, Maulana Azad Library, Aligarh, no. 320, ff. 4a-b.
29. Minhaj-i-Siraj al-Juzjani mentions him among the leading slave nobles of Sultan Iltutmish. After the accession of Sultan Muiz u'ddin Bahram Shah to the throne in 1240, he assumed independence of the Centre, in Multan. He also, seized the the unit of Uchh and, upper Sind region and successfully defended his possessions against

the Mongol invaders from across the borders. He and his son, Sultan Taj-ud-din Abu Bakr are also reported to have defeated the Qarlugh Turks several times. Cf. I.H. Siddiqui, 'The Qarlugh Kingdom in the North-Western India during the Thirteen Century', *Islamic Culture,* Hyderabad, vol. 54, no. 21, April 1980, p. 79; See also Siddiqui, 'The Pir and Murid: A Study of the Sufis of Suhrawardy Silsilah in India during the Thirteenth and Fourteenth Centuries', *The Indian Historical Review,* New Delhi, vol. 21, nos. 1-2, July 1994 and January 1995, pp. 57-77, for different approach.

30. Shaikh Baha-ud-din Zakariya of Multan was the *Khalifa* (spiritual successor) of Shaikh Shihab-ud-Din Suhrawardi. On his return from Baghdad, Shaikh Zakariya settled down in Multan and preached the teachings and popularized the practices of his *silsilah* (order) in the Punjab and Sind. He died in 1267 and was buried in Multan. Cf. K.A. Nizami, 'The Suhrawardi Silsilah and its Influence on Medieval Indian Politics,' *Medieval India Quarterly,* Aligarh, July-October, 1957, vol. 3, nos. 1-2, pp. 109-49.
31. Cf. *Tarjuma-i-Awarif-ul-M'arif,* ff. 4 a-b.
32. Ibid., f. 5a.
33. Cf. Nazir Ahmad, 'The Earliest Persian Translation of *Awarif-ul-Maarif,' Indo-Iranica,* Calcutta, September-December, 1972, vol. 25, nos. 3-4, p. 38.
34. Iqtidar Husain Siddiqui, 'Abu Raihan Al-Beruni; His Life and Works', in I.H. Siddiqui, ed., *Medieval India: Essays in Intellectual Thought and Culture,* New Delhi: Manohar Publishers, 2003, vol. 1, pp. 17-24, for details.
35. The introduction appended to the translation tells us of how after the conquest of Bengal by Muhammad Bakhtyar Khalji, a Brahman became curious about Islam and decided to interact with the Muslims in Lakhnauti. In Lakhnauti he established contact with the Muslims and became acquainted with their ways and the teaching of Islam. Impressed by Islam, he embraced it. The Sufis amongst his new friends enquired from him about Hindu spiritual philosophy and exercises that Hindus performed for expanding their cosmic consciousness. Thus Sufis decided to have *Amrit Kund,* the Sanskrit treatise on Yoga philosophy translated into Persian with his help. Though the original *Amrit Kund* seems to have been lost, its Persian

translation has survived the ravages of time. The rare copy of its manuscript is available in the Library of Anjuman-i-Taraqi-i-Urdu, Karachi. See the earliest Persian work on Hindu Philosophy and Religion, *Islamic Heritage in South Asian Subcontinent,* ed. N.A. Ahmad and Iqtidar H. Siddiqui, Jaipur Publication Scheme, 1998, vol. 1, pp. 1-18.

36. Cf. Simon Digby, 'Abdal-Quddus Gangohi (AD 1456-1537): The Personality and Attitudes of a Medieval Indian Sufi', *Medieval India; a Miscellany,* Department of History, Muslim University, Aligarh vol.3, 1975, pp. 4-6, for Shaikh Abdul Haque Radaulvi.
37. The devotion performed upside down while hanging suspended by a rope tied to the heels., Ibid., p. 20.
38. Ibid., pp. 21-2.
39. Mulla Shaida, *Sair-i-Kashmir* in *Maj ma'ul-Afkar* (a collection of documents, letters and other writings from the pen of eminent prose writers, made by some unknown writer), ed. Iqtidar Husain Siddiqui, Patna: Khuda Bakhsh Oriental Public Library, 1993, p. 57.
40. Shaikh Rizq ullah Mushtaqi, *Waqi'at-i-Mushtaqi,* tr. Iqtidar Husain Siddiqui, New Delhi: Indian Council of Historical Research, 1993, pp. 257-9.
41. *Tarikh-i-Firuz Shahi,* Calcutta: Bibliotheca Indica, 1891, p. 258, hereafter cited as Afif.
42. Barani, *Tarikh-i-Firuz Shahi,* pp. 363-4.
43. Anomymous, *Sirat-i-Firuz Shahi,* rare MS, Patna: Khuda Baksh Oriental Public Library, f. 153a.
44. The translator says that he translated it from Hindvi (i.e. Sanskrit) into Persian by the order of the religious minded Sultan, Abul-Muzaffar Firuz Shah so that people might benefit from its perusal. The rare manuscript copy, wrongly entitled by a later scribe as *Kitab al-Nujum,* is preserved in Sir Sulaiman collection, Maulana Azad Library, Aligarh. Ff. 185b.
45. *M'adan al-Shafa-i- Sikandar Shahi*, Lucknow: Nawal Kishore Press, pp. 2-3.
46. Ibid., p. 8.
47. Cf. *Lahjat-e-Sikandar Shahi,* ed. Shahab Sarmadee, New Delhi: Indian Council of Historical Research, 1999, pp. 13-14.

48. Ibid., pp. 14-15.
49. Cf. Siddiqui, *Perso-Arabic Sources of Information on the Life and Conditions in the Sultanate of Delhi,* See pp. 90-101 for details.
50. Of the early works on fiction in Persian language, produced in India, besides *Baratin al-urs* only *Tutinama* translated by Zia Nakhshabi (d.1350) a contemporary of Ikhtisan is extant. As for the fifteenth century *Jami'al-Hikayat* and *Dastan-i-Amir Hamza* (both anonymous) are mentioned by Abdul Qadir Badaoni in his account of Emperor Akbar's reign. That they were read to the Emperor. The manuscript copies of the *Dastan-i-Amir Hamza* are found in different libraries but that of the *Jami'al Hikayat* are rare. The only known copy is available in the Institute of the Peoples of Asia, Leningrad. Its microfilm is available in the department of History's research library, Aligarh Muslim University.
51. *Tutinama,* MS, Sriram Collection, Library, Banaras: Banaras Hindu University, f. 2b.
52. In the narrative, a lady asks the parrot a series of questions. The parrot answers each question, illustrating his answer with a story and prevents her from having love affairs with other people during the absence of her husband. *Tutinama,* tr. Muhammad Simsar, *Tales of a Parrot,* by Ziya u'd-Din Nakhshabi, Cleveland Museum of Art, 1978, pp. 100-1.

CHAPTER 11

The City of Kalpi

The fifteenth century is a period of great cultural significance in the history of north India but little work has been done on it. Many aspects of the Indo-Muslim culture during the subsequent centuries, particularly the background of the rise of religious trends, both revivalist and syncretic, would remain obscure unless a detailed and indepth study is made of life and culture in the fifteenth century. Towards the close of the fourteenth century, the Delhi Sultanate disintegrated giving rise to centrifugal tendencies. The legacy of its cultural and political system, however, remained. Gradually, certain *muqtas* and *zamindars* managed to seize neighbouring territories, established peace and order there and thus carved out independent kingdoms and principalities for themselves. The hagiographic literature and the chronicles produced in these kingdoms, provide interesting information not only about the proliferation of Indo-Muslim culture that developed in Delhi, but also shed considerable light on the activities of the Sufi saints and *ulama* (religious divines) who had migrated from Delhi to different cities on the eve of Timur's invasion in AD 1398. These also provide insights into the social life of the new urban centres founded by the regional sultans.

The kingdoms and principalities being smaller in area were more manageable and the respective rulers took keen interest in the development of different areas under their rule. In an attempt to augment their resources and surpass the neighbouring rulers in power and grandeur of their courts, these rulers tended to create conditions conducive to peace and prosperity in their territories. The rise of principalities and regional kingdoms is thus marked both by the growth of population and by urbanization. New cities and towns were founded and adorned with beautiful buildings, madrasas, mosques, palaces and gardens. Some of these newly founded cities not only succeeded in rapidly developing the economic functions of a true city but also met with Barani's definition of the *misr-i jami*[1] (the perfect city). Their rise helped the growth of Muslim population on the one hand and the spread of an Indo-Muslim culture on the other. In this context, the history of the rise of the principalities of Kalpi, Nagaur and Khandesh calls for an indepth study for their social and economic significance. Available sources reveal how with urbanization a pastoral economy or barter system was replaced by a monetized one.

It should also be pointed out that most founders of regional kingdoms and principalities represented the culture and traditions of the Delhi court, which had been the resort of *ulama, Mashaikh* (sufi saints), artists and men of culture for two centuries. The courts organized by them were a replica of the Delhi Sultan's court. Moreover, they patterned their administrative system on the model of the Delhi Sultanate. In the beginning, scholars, poets, artists and craftsmen, who contributed to the growth and glory of their cities, generally came from Delhi, and through them the Delhi culture permeated far and wide. Afterwards, the generous patronage extended by the rulers to men of learning, religion and arts attracted foreign emigrants to their cities. They came from different Muslim countries and were able to make their own contribution to the Indo-Muslim culture of northern India.

The towns and cities which the regional rulers chose or founded as their military and administrative headquarters developed into centres of such a syncretic culture, and played an important role in sustaining not only the Islamic institutions and the traditional Indian arts and crafts but also the arts and crafts that had developed in Delhi under the influence of foreign immigrants during the thirteenth and fourteenth centuries. The references contained in miscellaneous contemporary sources to the immigrants from Delhi and the area around it, seeking asylum in places of safety, help us analyse demographic, social and economic processes.

This chapter attempts first to describe the transformation of Kalpi into a centre of Islamic learning and culture, its population and social structure, and then to discuss the cultural and political influence that Kalpi exercised on the satellite towns and villages included in the principality. Further, the problem of social relations that the rulers of Kalpi faced, and the efforts made by the members of the military and religious elite to bring about co-existence of different communities and social groups in society have been analyzed. The political developments that affected socio-economic life in Kalpi have also been discussed.

Kalpi, though reduced to the size of a small and unimportant village in the fourteenth century,[2] was a place of great antiquity. Till the close of the fourteenth century it formed part of a nucleus of classical Hindu culture which Islamic institutions and Muslim culture had not been able to penetrate. It, however, underwent socio-economic change and began to grow into a city when Malikzadah Mahmud, son of *Majlis-i ali*[3] Azam Humayun Firuz Khan Turk[4] (the *Wazir-i Mumalik* under Sultan Tughluq Shah (AD 1388-98), who had been driven away by Rai Sabir of Etawah and Rai Adhran of Bhogaon[5] from the *shiqq* of Firuzpur,[6] made it the headquarters of his army in AD 1390.[7] Shortly afterwards he was joined by many other nobles who also had been forced to vacate their forts and *iqtas,* such as Tughluqpur (former Akhal), Phapoond, Chandwar, Shamsabad, Patiali, etc. because of the threat posed by the Chauhan chiefs of the region.[8] All of them came to Kalpi with their followers with the result that it rapidly developed into a city of great importance. Being resourceful, they built beautiful houses for their residence with mosques and madrasas adjacent to them. Gardens were also laid down all around the city. The *Tarikh-i-Muhammadi,* though very brief, sheds some light on the rapid expansion of Kalpi into a city. According to it, Azam Humayun Mahmud Khan bin Firuz Khan Turk, whom Sultan Muhammad Shah II (son of Firuz Shah) had honoured with the title of *Khan* and the grant of the *Iqta* of Mahoba in addition to the *Iqta* of Kalpi in 1393 took pains to develop his seat of government as a centre of culture.[9] He demarcated a fairly large area adjacent to the village of Kalpi, encircled it with strong and lofty walls and then diverted much of his resources towards the building of a massive palace fortress.[10] A number of mosques and other buildings of public utility were erected. On the completion of the *hisar*[11] (fortification), he named his city Muhammadabad after the Prophet of Islam. Along with the city, the suburb of Kalpi was also developed.[12] Mahmud Khan welcomed all those scholars, *Sayyids,* artisans, etc. who fled from Delhi and other disturbed areas to escape from Timur's army and sought asylum in Muhammadabad in 1398. As a result of this influx, Muhammadabad became *Shahr-i Muazzam* (great city). It expanded and then the suburbs including old Kalpi formed its part, with the result that it became famous as Muhammadabad alias Kalpi.[13]

In fact, the exodus of people caused by Timur's invasion of Delhi considerably added to the population of towns in the Sharqi dominions, Kalpi principality and the Malwa region. The refugees went as far as Gujarat. The contemporary writers of Gujarat and Kalpi refer only to refugees belonging to the class of *Akabir, Ashraf* and *Umara-i Namdar,* i.e. the members of the religious/military elite,[14] but, as Sharaf uddin Yazdi tells us, often the entire population evacuated towns or cities on the approach of Timur's army.[15] We may, however, assume that the greater part of the caravans of refugees consisted of noblemen, traders, craftsmen and workers. The evidence available in Sufi literature shows that the larger portion of Delhi's population had already left for safety before Timur reached the vicinity of Delhi.[16]

The cities of Jaunpur, Mandu and Kalpi, being comparatively close to Delhi, received the largest number of immigrants. With their arrival, Kalpi began to develop as a centre of Muslim culture and Islamic learning and started humming with economic activity. This influx considerably enhanced the military strength of Kalpi's ruler who seized territories from the neighbouring Muslim *Muqta's* and Rajput *zamindars* and declared his independence. He assumed the title of Sultan Nāsir uddin Mahmud Shah.[17] With his declaration of independence, Kalpi, his capital, was addressed as *Hazrat-i Muhammadabad*.[18]

I attempt here to form an idea about the size of the population of Kalpi in the fifteenth century. Authentic information about the size of the city's population is lacking. I apply the method suggested by Zia'uddin Barani in his *Tarikh-i Firuz Shahi* to arrive at a rough estimate. Barani has quoted Sultan Balban as having said that army generals commanding twelve thousand *sawars* were required for the effective control of a newly-conquered vilayet. Considering the families and dependants of the *sawars* and the officers, such as *karkuns* (account clerks), domestic servants and footmen, the total number would be around one hundred thousand persons. Barani approves of the figure.[19] If we accept it, the average number of dependants of one military man comes to more than eight persons. We should exclude the footmen from this class of people, as there is no evidence of their actual strength in Kalpi, and reduce the number of dependants for each *sawar* to four in order to be more reasonable in working out a tentative figure.

According to Shihab uddin al-Umari, a *Khan* in India, commanded ten thousand *sawars*,[20] a *Malik* one thousand, and an *Amir* one hundred. Al-Umari's statement about the contingents of the *Malik* and the *Amir* is corroborated by circumstantial evidence contained in other sources, yet the actual number of the *sawars* commanded by a *Khan* does not seem to have been more than five thousand in the fifteenth century.[21] Another point to note is that the high nobles who lived at the court in Kalpi kept only a part of their army contingents at the centre, and a large number of their army followers stayed in their respective *iqtas*.[22] Putting bits of evidence together, it seems that at that time there were eight *Khans* and one *Malik* residing in Kalpi, commanding 50,000 *sawars.* But they seem to have stationed 50 per cent of their army in their respective *iqtas*. Therefore, the number of *sawars* under the nobles staying in Kalpi was in no way higher than 25,000. The Sultan also seems to have had a personal force of equal size in which slaves accounted for the major part.[23] Thus, the cavalry stationed in Kalpi seems to have consisted of 50,000 *sawars,* and about two hundred thousand persons dependent on them. Besides, there were other servants employed by the Sultan and the nobles in different capacities. Apart from the large number of domestic servants, the Sultan had a number of petty officials, such as clerks and spies, officially designated as *karkuns* and *munhiyan* respectively. They were part of the royal establishment.[24] The army camp of the Sultan, which was a mobile version of his capital, also required the services of a large number of non military men. Sultan Mahmud Shah and his son and successor, Sultan Qadir Shah, frequently led plundering expeditions into the neighbouring area and also made conquests. A large number of people were employed to level the ground, pitch *sarapardah* (royal enclosure) and tents. Moreover, the conquests and successful raids on enemy territories caused a flow of wealth and slaves into Kalpi.[25]

Likewise, the *karkhanahs* maintained by the Sultan and high nobles absorbed a large number of skilled artisans and workers. The interesting pieces of information available in the *Tarikh-i-Muhammadi* reveal that the local court gave impetus to the weaving industry in Kalpi. The Sultan is reported to have conferred upon his nobles, *zamindars, ulama* (religious scholars) and other distinguished residents of the city the robes of honour of different types, some of *zarbaft* (cloth woven with silk and gold threads mixed).[26] For this purpose, the Sultan had a *Khil'at-Khanah* (big wardrobe) and Ismail Khan was incharge of this department.[27] The nobles followed this tradition of their master in their *iqtas;* they also honoured their officers and *zamindars* with *khilats* and other rewards.[28] This might have encouraged the Muslim weavers to settle down in Kalpi in considerable number, making Kalpi a famous market for textile goods.[29] Other important industries that seem to have been established at this time were those of sugar and boat-building. The sugar manufactured in Kalpi was of extreme whiteness and excellent quality. Since the Jamuna from Kalpi onward was navigable, large boats and small ships were built for military purposes.[30] The copper mine that continued operating till Akbar's reign might have provided job opportunities to local people.[31] Similarly the expansion of the city and the building activity provided work to masons and labourers. The use of chiselled stones in the buildings of the period indicates the presence of stone-cutters. Stone seems to have been brought from the quarries in the *iqtas* of Jathra and Erachh as both extended upto the Vindhyachal range. The monuments constructed in Kalpi afford clear evidence of the fusion of Muslim and Hindu styles, throwing light on the cultural side of the town.[32]

References contained in different sources point to the presence of traders in Kalpi in good number. Actually, the court-generated trade was always an attraction to the merchants and traders. We in fact find Kalpi traders supplying food grains and other essentials even outside the boundaries of their principality.[33] Here, mention may be made of the liquor-sellers and musicians who seem to have prospered because their product was much in demand as many nobles had cultivated a taste for alcoholic drinks, as will be shown later.

As regards social life and cultural activities in Kalpi, contemporary sources show that by the death of Sultan Mahmud Turk in AD 1412, Kalpi had already turned into a city of light and shade. With the passage of time, alongside the *ulama,* scholars and Sufi saints, the number of those who were fond of pleasure and fine arts increased considerably. The princes and nobles spent lavishly on food, perfumes and on maintaining musicians and dancers in their service. Some of them even patronized poets and artists which led to the progress of literature and the arts, such as classical Indian music and dance. The banquets hosted by the princes and nobles in the pleasure gardens and at their residence were attended by musicians, dancing girls and poets where poets often recited their panegyrical poems[34] in praise of their patrons while the dancers gave performances for the entertainment of the guests assembled there.[35] *Akhara,* a group dance in which a troupe of dancing girls decked in embroidered silk and adorned with jewels performed with lighted earthen lamps on their palms, held a profound fascination for aristocrats.[36] In short, aristocratic aesthetic standards set in metropolitan Delhi provided a cultural frame for Kalpi.

Another important group of people, who also contributed to the process of urbanization in Kalpi, was that of the *ulama* and Sufis. Muhammad Bihamad Khani glows with pride when he describes their arrival in Kalpi and would have us believe that owing to their presence the village of Kalpi and the densely forested area around it, which happened to be the stronghold of non-Muslims, totally unfamiliar with Islamic culture, were soon transformed into an Islamic centre. It does not occur to him, however, that most of the *Sayyids* and *ulama* were worldly people. They took part in court politics and were often found hanging around the court of the Sultan or of a noble in the hope of material benefit;[37] genuine spirituality was the concern of only a few. Nevertheless, their association with the court was valued by the Sultan. The *ulama* and Sufi held great influence over the soldiers and the masses, and the patronage extended to them and the interest shown by the Sultan in their well-being increases his popularity. It is true that many scholars and Sufis played an important role in disseminating learning and making Kalpi a seat of culture. A few scholars and leading Sufis who had settled down in Kalpi enhanced the prestige of Kalpi in medieval times. They also catered to the religious needs of the people.

The Sufi saints who settled in Kalpi chiefly belonged to the Chishti and Suhrawardi *silsilahs* (orders). Afterwards, the *Zahidi, Shattari* and *Madari* saints were also attracted by Kalpi's fame. Everyone of them tried to turn Kalpi into a centre of their *silsilah.* I discuss here the *ulama* and then the Sufis who belonged to different *silsilahs.*

The most famous scholar here was Bandagi *Malik al-Ulama'* wa al-Fuzala' Mawlana Humam Ahmad Thanesari, celebrated for his mastery over both prose and verse. He was the *Dabir-i-Khass* under Sultan Firuz Shah and is said to have drafted most of the letters on behalf of the Sultan to Amir Timur, the ruler of Central Asia. Muhammad Bihamad Khani writes that he left Delhi after the invasion of Timur and settled 'in this auspicious city'. Sultan Mahmud Shah Turk provided him with the comforts and necessities of life. Many people including Ahmad Khan, the brother of Sultan Mahmud Shah Turk, became his disciples. On his death, Ahmad Khan constructed a grand mausoleum on his grave the lofty dome of which filled visitors with wonder.[38] Another famous scholar, Mawlana Shams uddin, known as Nahwi, who had no rival in learning and sophistication, also sought asylum in Kalpi. On his death he was buried outside the fortification of the city and a tomb was erected over his grave.[39] According to the author of the *Tarikh-i Muhammadi,* the city of Muhammadabad (alias Kalpi) rose in dignity and gained wide fame on account of the shrines of these two pious scholars.[40]

Likewise, Bandagi Shaikhzadah 'Ali, Mawlana Muhammad Thanesari who had got the title of *Malik al-Ulama'* in *Hazrat-i Dihli,* and Mawlana Ashraf Sami, all recognized as leading scholars of their age, joined the court of the Sultan and received royal favours.[41] Mawlana Ashraf Sami was also a *Khalifah* of Shaikh Nasir'uddin Chiragh of Delhi.[42]

The hagiographic sources add to the information available in the *Tarikh-i Muhammadi* about the early Sufi saints of Kalpi. Their inclusion by Shaikh 'Abd al-Haqq Muhaddis Dihlawi in his biographical work is indicative of the fact that they were eminent Sufi scholars of their age. Among them Mawlana Ahmad Thanesari, son of Mawlana Muhammad Thanesari settled in Kalpi along with his family and followers in the beginning of the fifteenth century. A disciple of Shaikh Nasir' uddin Chiragh of Delhi, he had also acquired wide fame for his mastery over different Islamic sciences including Hanafite *fiqh* (jurisprudence). He imparted instruction in Islamic jurisprudence and popularized the teachings of the Chishti *silsilah* by accepting *murids*.[43]

A few distinguished disciples and *khalifahs* of Sayyid Muhammad Gesudiraz (the *khalifah* of Shaikh Nasir' uddin Chiragh) also settled in Kalpi. For example, Shaikh 'Ala uddin Quraishi and Shaikh Abu al-Fath Ala'i Quraishi were two leading Chishti saints who settled in Kalpi, sometime after the invasion of Timur. The former hailed from Gwalior. He generally lived in seclusion, spending his time in prayer.[44] The latter lived in the midst of the people, wrote a number of treatises on Sufism and taught his disciples esoteric as well as exoteric sciences.[45] After his death, his rich disciples built a grand tomb over his grave in 1450. This tomb is built of stone and brick in lime and covered over with lime plaster, with a bulbous lofty dome raised on an octagonal drum. The inscription on the southern doorway calls him *Za'ir al-Haramayan,* one who paid visit to the *harams* (holy places) in Mecca and Medina.[46]

An important Suhrawardi saint who was also a profound scholar and won followers among various sections of people in Kalpi was Shaikh Siraj Sokhtah. First he committed the Qur'an to memory, and then studied other popular sciences of his time. For his deep learning, he was included among the distinguished pupils of Mawlana Nahwi like Qazi Shihab al-Din Dawlatabadi. It was due to his learning that Shaikh Jalal uddin Bukhari, popularly known as *Jahaniyan-i-Jahangasht,* selected him as one of his *khalifahs.* After his arrival in Kalpi, he became one of the most respectable Sufis of the city. Sultan Qadir Shah, son and successor of Sultan Mahmud Shah (AD1411-32), held him in high esteem.[47]

Another Suhrawardi saint of eminence was Shaikh Yusuf Buda Erachhi. He was also the disciple of *Makhdum-i Jahaniyan-i Jahangasht.* A distinguished scholar of Arabic, known for his mastery over Islamic doctrinal and Sufi texts, high literary ability and a refined sensibility for poetry, Erachhi had become one of the most popular and respected Sufis of north India. He is credited with having written a number of books. His translation of Imam Ghazali's *Minhaj al-Abidin* in *masnawi* form, consisting of two thousand five hundred and twenty verses and entitled *Fatuhat-i Ahmad,* was as popular as his *diwan* (the collection of poems). Like the Chishti Sufis, he was also fond of *sama* (audition party) and considered it a means of spiritual development. In 1430 he attended a *sama* party in which he passed into an ecstatic state and remained in it for several days and then passed away in Erachh. It should at the same time be pointed out that the biographical notices contained in the *Tarikh-i-Muhammadi* tend to show that the Shaikh was never negligent of social obligations incumbent upon a Sufi of his eminence. He took his duty of instructing his *murids* (disciples) seriously and maintained the traditions of his *silsilah.*[48] Mahmud Khan (son of Mughith Khan), later Sultan 'Ala uddin Mahmud Shah Khalji of Malwa, had a mausoleum constructed over his grave.[49]

As regards the Zahidi *silsilah,* Baha' uddin Ganj-i Rawan introduced it in Kalpi during the reign of Sultan Qadir Shah. Both the members of the ruling elite and the commoners had faith in him. Ghawasi Shattari informs us that the Sultan and his officers offered him cash, villages and gardens but he never accepted any gift from them. Nevertheless, he fed a large number of people daily and for this reason was called by the people *Ganj-i Rawan* (ever flowing reservoir). He occupied an unclaimed tract of land on the bank of the Jamuna towards the end of his life and carried on cultivation there. He also built a house and planted a garden. The spiritual qualities, possessed by him to an impressive degree, helped his successors to keep their *silsilah* alive after him.[50]

Similarly, the founder of the Madari *silsilah* in India, Shaikh Badi uddin, popularly known as Shah Madar, came to Kalpi during the reign of Qadir Shah. He was a Syrian Sufi of Jewish origin. On his conversion to Islam, he was enrolled among the disciples of Shaikh Tayfur Shami. He acquired mastery over Ibn Arabi's metaphysical doctrine, known as *al-wujud,* in addition to his knowledge of Jewish and Christian mystical practices. However, the paucity of authentic information about him makes it somewhat difficult to attempt a detailed study of his life and teachings. Some seventeenth century writers, such as 'Abd al-Rahman Chishti, the author of *Mirat-i-Madariyah* and the compiler of *Dabistan al-mazahib,* have confused historical traditions with fiction and incorporated in their works all that they found floating down the stream of time. In fact, they wrote their works when the followers of the Madari *silsilah* had begun to indulge in all sorts of vices in complete disregard of the teachings of the great Shaikh. The odd bits pieced from different standard works reveal that he was respected and generally held by orthodox Sufis to be in the first rank of the Indian Muslim

Sufis. He commanded great respect among people for his religiosity and piety and was never opposed to the observance of Muslim rituals. For instance, a contemporary inscription found in a step-well in Chanderi, dated 1436, mentions the builder of the well, Taghi, the learned *wazir* at the court of Malwa, along with his *pir*, Shah Madar. The latter has been mentioned as 'the great, pious and religious-minded saint.'[51] Likewise, the references to Shah Madar contained in the *malfuzat* of the fifteenth-century Sufi saints tend to show that the leading Chishti saints held him in high esteem. The sixteenth century historian Badaoni also incorporates a few anecdotes in his *Najat ur-Rashid*, showing that he also had no doubts about Shah Madar being a pious Sufi.[52]

In Kalpi, Shah Madar got in touch with the Hindu yogis and is believed to have discussed Yogic philosophy with them. The testimony of Shaikh Abd al-Haqq Muhaddis of Delhi is significant in this regard. According to him, Shah Madar was very fond of the company of the yogis and discussed with them problems relating to Hindu mysticism.[53] The association of the Sufis with the yogis was not objectionable during the fifteenth century. Some of the leading Chishti saints also adopted certain yogic practices. For instance, Shaikh Abd al-Haqq of Radauli and Abd al-Quddus Gangohi regularly practised controlling of breath, burying themselves alive or offering devotions while hanging head down suspended by a rope tied to the heels.[54]

A few words may be added about Shah Madar's departure from Kalpi to the Sharqi Kingdom of Jaunpur. It is said that he refused to receive Qadir Shah of Kalpi who was desirous of calling on him. Feeling insulted, the Sultan asked Shah Madar to leave his territory. Thereupon Shah Madar went to Jaunpur and finally settled down in Makanpur,[55] (a small town now included in the district of Kanpur). One of his disciples and successors, Qazi Mazhar, however, stayed in Kalpi. Ghawasi Shattari states that Qazi Mazhar was an '*Alim* and a devout Sufi, sincerely devoted to the cause of religion.[56]

Another scholarly Sufi who flourished in Kalpi during the fifteenth and sixteenth centuries was Shaikh Burhan Ansari. Devoted to religion and piety, he preferred a life of abject poverty to that of comfort. He spent his time either in offering prayers in his cell or imparting knowledge of religious lore. In his daily public lectures, he explained the significance of the Qur'anic verses. Mulla Abdul Qadir Badaoni visited him in Kalpi and found him more than a hundred years old.[57] People considered him a Mahdawi but Ghawsi Shattari states that this charge was not borne out by facts. Shaikh Burhan Ansari composed verses in Hindwi, as well as in Persian. His *diwan*, entitled *Firaqnamah,* was available in the seventeenth century. Praising it, Ghawsi Shattari says that every line of the *diwan* is full of pathos and marked by an intensity of feeling.[58]

The entire area within the boundaries of the principality formed the hinterland of the city of Kalpi. The *iqtas* and *parganas,* mentioned by the medieval writers, help identify its frontiers. For example, the *pargana* of Chaurasi,[59] that lay on the boundary of the *Khittah-i-Qilah-i Qanauj* (later included in the modern district of Farukhabad UP), the *pargana* of Baladar,[60] Sugandpur,[61] Adampur[62] (in Etawah), Kakura,[63] Chachawali,[64] and Dirapur[65] included in the *iqta* of Shahpur[66] (now in Kanpur district of UP) constituted its northern frontier. These *parganas* comprised parts of the modern districts of Farukhabad, Ettah and Etawah, and shared borders with the Sharqi territorial units of Qanauj, Kara and Manikpur,[67] and with the *zamindari* of the Chauhan ruler, Rai Sabir of Etawah.[68] The eastern *iqta* of Mahoba extended over the area upto the boundaries of the regions under the rule of the Rais of Kalinjar and Bath Ghora.[69] The southern frontier was bound by the *iqtas* of Jathra and Bhander that comprised the area upto the boundary of the Malwa territory of Chanderi.[70] The western frontier was bound by the *iqta* of Erachh (in Jhansi district of UP) that included the entire area running parallel to the region of the principalities of Gwalior and Bayana.[71]

Besides the aforesaid border *iqta's* and *parganas,* there were old and newly-carved out *parganas,* lying inside the frontiers of the principality. Undoubtedly, the information available in our sources is very inadequate; only the military conquests and expeditions, rebellions and their suppression by the Sultan find a detailed description. Despite this, there is enough evidence of the construction of fortresses, *hisars* and bazaars in the old and newly-founded towns. For example, the first place captured by the ruler of Kalpi was the small locality of Khandaut[72] that belonged to the *zamindari* of Rai Bahraj, the *zamindar* of Hamirpur. The Sultan fortified Khandaut, built a palace-fortress and named it Mahmudabad after his own name. The author of the *Tarikh-i Muhammadi* informs us that due to the interest taken by the Sultan in its development, Mahmudabad emerged as a centre of Islam.[73] Likewise, references contained in our sources to the *pargana* of Chhaparghatta (twenty miles from Kalpi) town of Ratha[74] and the town of Chakni[75] tend to reveal that these were fortified and economically developed during this period. Equally important was the tendency among the *muqia's* to increase the income of their *iqtas* by clearing jungles, founding villages and establishing *thanas*[76] (military outposts) for the protection of the roads and villages. The *thanas* had the full potential to develop into towns. In fact, many of them became flourishing towns in the sixteenth century.[77]

Mention may be made here of the revenue accruing to the ruler of Kalpi from the dense forests that existed on its western and eastern borders. The availability of timber gave rise to the boat-building industry in Kalpi. Moreover, herds of wild elephants in the forests attracted the elephant-catchers who settled along Kalpi's border villages, numbering thirty to forty. They paid tax directly on every catch to the royal exchequer. The elephants caught were sold in the neighbouring cities. Babur says that the value and price of an elephant were judged on the basis of its height and size and the larger it was, the higher was its price.[78]

The network of roads built by the rulers for linking different towns and *parganas* with one another and with capital, and connecting Kalpi with the neighbouring kingdoms, changed the socio-economic set-up in the region. Evidence available in the *Ma'sir-i Mahmud Shahi* sheds light on this. The towns of Mahoba and Shahpur are reported to have become centres of trade, and of Islamic learning and culture owing to the presence of scholars and craftsmen. We also learn that necessary steps were taken for safeguarding the roads against highwaymen.[79] Gradually, an increase in the population, and rural and urban development took place.

The limited resources of the principality, surrounded by the kingdoms of Delhi, Jaunpur and Malwa, led the Sultan to take interest in the extension of cultivation, as it was the main source of income to the State. As a result, the forests were cleared and villages were founded. These measures seem to have considerably increased the financial resources of the State. For example, the *pargana* of Chaurasi that had long lain desolate became prosperous within a short time due to efforts made by the officers that its revenue was doubled and began to yield one lakh *tanka*.[80] Likewise, Jathra, a small town without a fort in the fourteenth century, developed into a beautiful city. It was assigned by the Sultan to Nizam Khan, his second brother, as maintenance-*iqta* and was held by Nizam Khan's descendants for generations. *Majlis-i ali* Nizam Khan and his descendants beautified it with buildings and planted gardens and orchards outside the city walls.[81] Moreover, epigraphical evidence shows that in Jathra certain arts and crafts also developed. In any case, Jathra became famous for wine manufacturing and for its musicians. The *khammars* (liquor sellers and manufacturers) and *kalawants* (musicians), i.e. grew very rich, acquiring aristocratic habits. They spent money on the construction of buildings of public utility and had inscriptions in Persian fixed on them in imitation of the members of the ruling elite.[82] The wine industry led to the extension of grape cultivation all around Jathra. We can also assume, on the basis of this information, that socio-economic development benefited all social classes.

The *iqta* and city of Erachh also merit discussion for their economic development during the period under review. The town of Erachh had been the headquarters of an *iqta* since the fourteenth century. It had one of the strongest forts of north India and was occupied by the *ashraf*, i.e. the elite.[83] Erachh developed from a town into a city after its annexation by Sultan Mahmud Shah. The Sultan gave it to his brother, Khan-i-Azam Junayd Khan, the *wazir*, in *iqta*. The *wazir* and, later, his sons made all possible efforts to raise it to the size and importance of Kalpi itself. They made generous land-grants to scholars and *mashaikh*, invited artisans from different places and gave them all the facilities for their permanent settlement. They expanded the town by building new quarters and bazaars. For its defence, an outer fortification was raised in addition to the inner walls.[84] The Jami Mosque constructed by the *wazir*, Junayd Khan, in Erachh in AD 1408 bears testimony to the building activity there. The inscription points to the considerable increase in the population of the town, which rendered the old mosque insufficient for Friday congregations. The *qadi* of Erachh, Zia uddin, therefore, persuaded the *wali* to construct a new and more spacious mosque.[85] The tombs built over the graves of Khwajah Ikhtiyar uddin Umar Erachhi[86] (d. AD 1406) and Shaikh Yusuf Buda[87] (d. AD 1430) are worth mentioning. The tomb over the grave of the former was built by the ruler of Kalpi. The tomb of Shaikh Yusuf Buda was built by Sultan Mahmud Khalji of Malwa who happened to be one of his disciples. According to both Muhammad Bihamad Khani and Shaikh 'Abd al-Haqq Dihalwi, its lofty dome had no match in height and beauty in the neighbouring territories.

The evidence; accessible to us in the historical and hagiographical sources, about social relations between the members of different communities and social groups, though scanty, remains interesting. It points to a spirit of mutual understanding and cooperation among the people. In fact, two centuries of co-existence seems to have brought Hindus and Muslims together, narrowing down their social and cultural differences. Both, the Sufis and the yogis stood for pulling down of social barriers between various culture-groups.[88] As in other cities and towns in the early period, the Sufis and the yogis lived in peace and amity in Kalpi, discussed spiritual matters to one another's benefit and initiated trends of social importance that shaped the cultural pattern of society and influenced people's attitudes towards life and humanity. In short, the impression created by the hagiographic and historical literature is that the fifteenth century in north India was marked by the revival of Islamic orthodoxy on one hand and the rise of syncretic trends and the popularity of eclecticism on the other.[89] The fourth ruler of Kalpi, Nasir Shah bin Qādir Shah, is reported by medieval writers to have abandoned the path of orthodoxy and adopted heretical practices. This implies that he was deeply influenced by the syncretic movements and thought of the day. He was severely resisted and condemned by the orthodox Muslims in Kalpi.[90]

It may be pointed out that the details furnished by Muhammad Bihamad Khani about the religious policy of his patrons, the Sultans of Kalpi, fail to provide a true picture of the age. He would have us believe that in every village and town the Muslim conquest was followed by the suppression of Hindu practices and the introduction of the Islamic customs instead.[91] This is not corroborated by the circumstantial evidence available even in his own *tarikh*, wherein the rulers seem to have re-ordered their relations with the Hindu *zamindars* who had deep-rooted local control of land and peasants.[92] The latter acquiesced to the Sultan's authority when he left them untouched, with complete autonomy in the area of their *zamindaris*. There is no dearth of information to show that these *zamindars* were invited to social functions held at the royal court and honoured with precious gifts and robes. In return, they rendered military service at the time of need, paid *khidmati* along with annual *kharaj*.[93] Information is also available about the intertribal conflict and feuds that were common among the Rajput chiefs in this region. People suffered much from this internecine strife. The case of Ra'i Sabir of Etawah is a case in point. He was hostile to the Raja of Bhogaon, also a Rajput chief, belonging to the Bhaduriya branch of the Chauhan tribe. The latter had succeeded in building up a tiny principality that embraced portions of Mainpuri, Farrukhabad and Etah districts. For his destruction, Ra'i Sabir Chauhan accepted allegiance to Qādir Shah of Kalpi and persuaded him to invade Bhogaon. The joint armies of Etawah and Kalpi are reported to have done great damage to the Rai of Bhogaon by ravaging most of his principality in 1413. The author of *Tarikh-i-Muhammadi* informs us had Sultan Ibrahim Sharqi not marched against Kalpi, they would have completely destroyed Bhogaon.[94] In this way the rise of regional powers led to the establishment of peace, as the chiefs accepted the overlordship of someone among the sultans who could protect them against other rulers.

As regards the increase in Muslim population in the region, low-caste conversions at least to some extent, combined with the process of urbanization, were responsible for it. In the towns and cities, the *khanqahs* of the Sufi saints attracted Muslims and Hindus alike who visited with different personal problems, psychological as well as economic, and sought their blessings. Impressed by their piety and spiritual qualities many individual Hindus adopted the Islamic faith and then became devout Muslims under their influence.[95] The slaves purchased by the Muslim aristocrats added to the number of Muslims in urban centres as the slave boys and girls were brought up like Muslims.[96] Even the *ulama* possessed both male and female slaves. However, the sultans and nobles never appear to have taken interest in the conversion of unwilling non-Muslims to Islam.

Rural-urban relations are also discussed here as these cast light on the concern that Muslim rulers had for the economic development of the countryside. We have definite evidence revealing the close ties established by the members of the ruling elite with the rural people in the area. A contemporary historian, who was himself a part of the ruling class, emphasizes over and over again the fact that the sultans took pains in promoting the general good, and people owed allegiance to the dynasty out of gratefulness for the good done to them by the rulers.[97] Likewise, the *muqtas* whose *iqtas* were seldom transferred came into direct contact with the peasants and encouraged them to extend the area of cultivation by clearing forests and ploughing fallow land. Most probably the small size of the territory and its limited resources forced the ruling class to adopt this policy.

The close ties, existing between the urban centres and the villages, are also discernible in the details about the decoration and illumination of the city carried out by the citizens for welcoming the Sultan, or an army general on his successful return from a military campaign, or for celebrating the births and marriages of princes. Such occasions provided people with an opportunity for general rejoicing in the city and the *haveli* (suburb).[98] But there is no direct evidence to show the reaction of people living in remote villages. A few anecdotes in the *Waqi'at-i Mushtaqi* show that village women usually came out of their villages, singing songs to welcome the army from their side. The generals used to distribute money to them.[99]

Nevertheless, there was a great deal of scorn among the urbanites for the rustics. 'Isami calls the latter impure demons, unworthy of taking the place of the former in any walk of life. Comparing the two he goes to the extent of calling people of the city nightingales and those of villages no better than owls.[100] The evidence available in the *Tarikh-i-Mubarak Shahi* shows that in the city people made fun of the villagers for their simplicity or lack of urbanity.[101] The same attitude can be seen in the anecdotes narrated by Shaikh Rizq Allah Mushtaqi, wherein a villager can easily be made out from others on account of his rusticity.[102] Sadly, the townsfolk seem not to have realized that most of their urban amenities depended on the supply of produce from the countryside and the grandeur of their cities was sustained, to a large extent, by the revenue levied on agriculture.

A significant role was played by the land grant holders and the primary *zamindars,* who acted as intermediaries between the urban-based State and the peasantry. As I have dealt with this problem at length elsewhere,[103] I do not go into details here, however, it needs to be stressed that the distinct practice of the land grant holders from the fourteenth century onwards was to develop on their land a series of gardens and orchards with beautiful villas inside.[104] This urban culture penetrated the countryside. At the same time it may be stated that it was not at all a one-way traffic. The aristocratic customs of the landed gentry seem to have influenced the urbanized nobility of the Sultanate period as well.[105] People bowed low before the noble as villagers humbled themselves before the Chaudhri (big land chief). Similarly, medieval urban crafts, such as weaving and boat-building in Kalpi, also had a rural base.

Finally, something may be said about the period during which the principality enjoyed absolute independence. It continued to exist as a buffer to the Sultanates of Delhi, Jaunpur and Malwa till 1442. During this period it survived two invasions by Sultan Ibrahim Sharqi of Jaunpur. At the time of the first Sharqi invasion in 1413 Sultan Hoshang Shah came to Kalpi's rescue.[106] In 1432-3, when the second invasion took place after the death of Qādir Shah, both Sultan Mubarak Shah of Delhi and Hoshang Shah marched from their respective capitals against Sultan Ibrahim Sharqi. As a result, Kalpi was saved and Jalal Khan (son of Qadir Shah) remained unaffected.[107] The course of later events suggests that the aim of the Sharqi Sultan was limited; instead of a full conquest he wanted the ruler of Kalpi to pay allegiance to him. But his rivals wanted Kalpi to exist as a buffer State between them.

In the year 1442 the situation took an unfavourable turn against the ruling dynasty. By this time, Sultan Mahmud Sharqi had already won over the Kalpi nobility and the *ashraf* to his side through a bribe. Assured of their support, he sent his envoy to the court of Sultan Mahmud Khalji of Malwa with precious gifts and 29 elephants as an offering. The Sharqi envoy, having presented the gifts, conveyed the verbal message of his master, that Nasir Khan-i Jahan, son of Qadir Shah (the fourth ruler of Kalpi), had abandoned the path of Islamic orthodoxy and was harming the interests of Muslims and Islam. He had given Muslim girls to Hindus for being trained as dancers and musicians, and he should either be corrected through punishment by the Malwa court or the Jaunpur Sultan be permitted to set him right. The gifts had the desired effect on the Malwa Sultan. The latter gave permission to the Sharqi Sultan to punish the ruler of Kalpi for his misconduct.[108]

On the occupation of Kalpi and its dependencies by Sharqi, Nasir Khan approached the Malwa courts, pleading not guilty and saying that Sultan Mahmud Sharqi had arrested Muslims, and had confiscated their property as that of the infidels in *Dar al-Harb* (non-Muslim territory), and that his allies were Hindus, such as the Rais of Bath Ghora and Bhakesar.[109] Sultan Mahmud Khalji (AD 1436-69) wrote a letter to the Sharqi Sultan asking him to restore the territory of Kalpi to Nasir Khan as it was his ancestral possession and as he had repented for his past lapses and had reformed himself. Since the letter did not evoke a favourable response, the Malwa Sultan marched towards Kalpi. In a series of battles, Malwa had the upper hand. Realizing his military weakness, Sultan Mahmud Sharqi agreed to restore Kalpi to Nasir Khan, and the conflict came to an end.[110]

Subsequently, Nasir Khan of Kalpi became a vassal of the Sharqi Sultan in order to avoid further conflict, for all his old supporters had already accepted allegiance to the latter. Kalpi thus became a part of the Sharqi Sultanate. The copper coins issued from the mint of Kalpi mention the name of Nasir Khan along with the dates of issuance from AD 1439 to 1443.[111] In the year 1479, Sultan Bahlul Lodi, having driven away Sultan Husain Sharqi from Jaunpur, occupied Kalpi along with other territories. He entrusted the charge of Kalpi to his grandson, Azam Humayun Lodi. During the Lodi regime, none of the scions of the Kalpi dynasty, except the Jathra branch, appears to have held any important position. Khan-a Azam Tatar Khan, son of *Masnad-i-ali* Isma'il Khan of Jathra is mentioned in the list of the nobles of Sultan Sikandar Lodi (1489-1517).[112] Tatar Khan's son, Muhammad Khan of Jathra, was one of the nobles of both Sultan Ibrahim Lodi and Babur. His son, Bayazid Khan of Jathra, was favoured by Humayun with precious gifts in 1533.[113] According to Shaikh Rizq Allah Mushtaqi, no Mughal noble could rival Muhammad Khan of Jathra in culture and sophistication.[114] This points to the fact that Jathra continued to flourish as a centre of culture and learning till the first half of the sixteenth century.

During the Lodi period, the territory of Kalpi was held by one of the Lodi princes. The city continued to flourish and successive *muqta's* were known for their extravagance and generous patronage of scholars and artists.

One of the princes, Jalal Khan Lodi, known as Jighat, loved pomp and show. Besides other aristocratic paraphernalia, he had a large number of women, including dancing girls, whose maintenance involved huge expenditure. Hundreds of rupees were spent on buying flowers for the harem.[115] Building activities also continued during this time.[116] The revenue of Kalpi, excluding that of the *iqta* of Jathra, amounted to 42,855,950 *tankas.*[117] The Lodi *muqta* of Kalpi maintained 12,000 *sawars*, an equal number of footmen and many war-elephants.[118]

In conclusion it may by stressed that the dissolution of the Sultanate of Delhi at the beginning of the fifteenth century was paradoxically paralleled by the growth of an Indo-Muslim culture, socio-economic growth and the emergence of new centres of Islamic learning in different regions that were ruled in the past by the Delhi Sultans through governors called *walis* or *muqta*'s. The metropolitan cities founded by the regional sultans had, like religion and philosophy, intellectual and historical dimensions. In each regional Sultanate, small as well as large, socio-economic progress and a growth in the Muslim population resulted partly from the process of urbanization and partly because of the Muslim socio-political system. The social role of the Sufis in particular and of the ruling elite in general was largely positive. At least in the lives and practices of genuine Sufis and representative *ulama*, Islamic concepts of egalitarianism and universal brotherhood found expression. Also the contribution made by these men to the progress and growth of Indo-Persian literature was great. Some of the best Persian *ghazals* were composed and sung in the *khanqahs* of Sufis. Further, I would like to point out that for an indepth study of the history and culture of the Mughal Empire, it is imperative to examine the social and economic developments in the regional Sultanates during the fifteenth century; indeed the basic material for the social life and culture of the Mughal Empire was prepared there.

Endnotes

1. According to Zia'uddin Barani, a city that contained, in addition to its vast population and bazaars, a large number of scholars, scientists, artists, traders, craftsmen and artisans skilled in their respective professions and crafts deserved to be called *misr-i-jami'.* In his days Delhi had acquired the status of a perfect city. He glows with pride when he refers to Delhi's scholars, scientists, craftsmen, etc. who

had gained worldwide fame for their mastery over different sciences, crafts, etc. See *Tarikh-i-Firuz Shahi,* ed., Sir Sayyid Ahmad Khan Calcutta: Bibliotheca India, 1862, pp. 352-3, 355, 469 & 474.

2. Kalpi is the headquarters of a *tahsil* of the same name in the district of Jalaun, Uttar Pradesh site 26' 8' N. 79'45'E on the Jamuna river, 22 miles away from the district headquarters.
3. *Majlis-i-'ali* and *Masnad-i-ali* (exalted lordship) were the honorific titles used as prefix to the names or main titles of the high grandees during the Sultanate period. For instance, the *wazir* in the thirteenth and fourteenth centuries was addressed as *Majalis-i-ali.* Majd al-Din Abu al-Maali Muayyid bin Muhamamd Jajarmi, who translated Ghazali's *Ihya Ulum-id-din* in Persian in 1220-1 at the instance of Nizam al-Mulk Junaydi, calls his patron *Majlis-i-ali* Nizam al-Mulk. The *Insha-i-Mahru* also contains Sultan Firuz Shah's (1351-82) *farman,* relating to the appointment of Khan-i-Jahan Maqbul as *wazir.* In this *farman,* Khan-i-Jahan Maqbul has been mentioned with all his titles including those of *Majalis-i-ali* and *Azam Humayun.* See Jarjamji's Persian translation, MS, British Museum, London, Or. 8194, f.3a; See also Ayn al-Mulk 'Abd Allah bin Mahru, *Insha-i-Mahru,* ed. Shaikh Abdur Rashid, Research Society of Pakistan, Lahore, 1965, letter no. 2, p. 9; Muhammad Bihamad Khani, *Tarikh-i-Muhammadi,* MS., British Museum London, Or. 137, ff.419b, 430a & 442a-b. Similarly, *Masnad-i-ali* and *Majlis-i ali* have also been used with titles of Malwa high nobles in the official histories of Malwa (Ali bin Mahmud al-Kirmani, known as Shihab Hakim, *Ma'asir-i-Mahmud Shahi,* MS, British Museum, London, Or. 11,140 f.38b; Anonymous, *Tarikh-i-Nasir Shahi,* MS, British Museum, London, Or. 1803, f.14a). Hajji Dabir gives clues to their connotation. Explaining these titles he states that it was the custom in his country to entitle the King's deputy (*Naib-i Mutlaq*) as *Masnad-i-ali* and the *wazir* as *Majlis-i ali* (Zafar al-Walih (ed.) London, 1921, vol. 2, p. 613).
4. Both Muhammad Bihamad Khani and Yahya Sirhindi regard the founder of Kalpi dynasty as of Turkish origin. Contrary to them, Shihab Hakim calls Mahmud 'Mughal' not Turk. Since the Mughals were looked down upon after Timur's invasion, the rulers of Kalpi must have liked to call themselves 'Turk' instead of 'Mughal'. Yahya b. Ahmad Sirhindi, *Tarikh-i-Mubarak Shahi,* ed. M. Hidayat Husain,

Calcutta: Bibliotheca Indica, 1931, p. 134; *Maasir-i Mahmud Shahi,* abridged and ed. Nurul Hasan Ansari, Delhi: Indo-Persian Society, 1968, p. 59.

5. It is the headquarters of a *tahsil* in the district of Mainpuri, site 27° 16 N 79° 11 E.

6. Its former name was Kanar. Sultan Firuz Shah built a fort and having named it Firuzpur, made it the headquarters of the *shiqq* of the same name (Shiqq-i-Firuzpar). It is now a deserted place, about two miles off Jagmanpur. Sit 26° 25' N.79° 16E and is still known as Kanar Khera. (Cf. *District Gazetteer,* Jalaun 1921, vol. 25, 170).

7. *Tarikh-i Muhammadi,*, f. 419b.

8. Ibid., ff. 418b-419a-b.

9. Ibid., ff. 429b-430a; Yahya Sirhindi says that the combined *Iqtas* were called *Shiqq-i Kalpi wa-Mahboba,* See *Tarikh-i Mubarak Shahi,* p.168.

10. *Tarikh-i-Muhammadi,* ff. 419b, 439a-b, 437a, 439a-b.

11. Ibid., 419b,450a-451a, for the description of *hisar* (fortification).

12. Ibid., f. 438b.

13. Ibid., f. 443a.

14. Anonymous, *Tarikh-i Gujarat,* MS, British Museum, London, Or. 1819, f. 27b; *Tarikh-i Muhammadi,* f. 442b.

15. *Zafarnamah,* ed. Muhammad Allahabad, Calcutta, 1888, vol. 2, pp. 77-8.

16. Mahmud Sufi Iriji, '*Tuhfat al-Majalis, the Malfuzat* of a 15th century saint, Shaikh Ahmad Maghribi', quoted by K.A. Nizami, *Medieval India-A Miscellany* Aligarh, 1975, Vol. 3, p. 246.

17. *Tarikh-i Muhammadi,* f. 416a.

18. Ibid., ff. 439a-b, 442b. It is wrongly held by modern scholars that Delhi was called *Hazrat-i Dihli* on account of the tombs of many leading Sufi saints there. In fact, the permanent headquarters of a Sultan was known as *Hazrat.* For instance, Delhi came to be known as *Hazrat-i Dihli* in 1210 when Iltutmish made it the capital of his Sultanate, much before any famous Sufi saint was buried there. The writers who compiled works on different subjects under the patronage of Nizam al-Mulk Junaydi refer to Delhi as *Hazrat-i Dihli.* (Cf. Persian translation of *Ikya' Ulum id-Din,* f. 3b., *Kitab al-Saidna,* ed. M. Sotudeh and I. Afshar, Tehran: Bunyad-i-Farhang-i-Iran, 1352

Shamsi, p. 13. Muhammad Bihamad Khani refers to Mandu also as *Hazrat-i Shadiabad,* See, Tarikh-i Muhammadi, f. 428a.)

19. Barani, 1862, pp. 51-2.
20. Shihab uddin al-umari, *Masalik al-Absar,* Chapters on India. *A Fourteenth Century Arab Account of India under Sultan Muhammad bin Tughluq,* tr. Iqtidar Husain Siddiqui, International Book Traders, Aligarh, 1971, p. 38.
21. Cf. Iqtidar Husain Siddiqui, *Some Aspects of Afghan Despotism in India,* Aligarh, 1969, p. 14.
22. *Tarikh-i Muhammadi,* f. 468a.
23. Some of the royal slaves were raised to the rank of *Malik* and assigned *iqtas* independent of the nobles. For instance, *Malik* Durraj is reported to have been one of those slaves whom Sultan Mahmud Turk raised to high positions in his personal army. He was assigned the charge of the *Iqta'* of Shahpur (*Tarikh-i Muhammadi,* f. 444b). The nobles also assigned important positions to their slaves in their armies and i*qtas.* (Ibid., f. 468a.).
24. The spies were posted in the city of Kalpi as well as in neighbouring areas under the occupation of rival rulers. They supplied information to the Sultan about political developments inside the principality and outside. (Ibid., ff. 439a, 449b.).
25. The Sultan of Kalpi led a number of expeditions for conquest and plunder from time to time. Their victims were both the Hindu chiefs and the Muslim *muqta's*, holding towns and *parganas* in the neighbouring area. They fought a number of battles against the *Rais* of Etawah, Bath Ghora and Gwalior, but the latter survived on account of their strength and resources. The *muqta's* and petty *zamindars* were destroyed or made vassals. This state of affairs lasted till the period of turmoil continued. By the year AD 1415 a balance of power was established between the regional sultans in north India. The *zamindars* could remain safe by paying allegiance to one or the other Sultan as the situation demanded of them. The Sayyid Sultans of Delhi and the Sultan of Malwa took interest in the survival of Kalpi as a buffer state between them and the Sultan of Jaunpur. see *Tarikh-i Muhammadi,* ff, 443b, 444a, 445b, 476b; *Tarikh-i Mubarak Shahi,* 1931, op.cit., pp. 207-9, 234; *Maathir-i Mahmud Shahi,* pp. 52-4 for interest shown by the sultans of both Delhi and Malwa in the survival of Kalpi.

26. *Tarikhi-i Muhammadi,* f. 439a, 449b.
27. Ibid., f. 446b.
28. Ibid., ff. 444a, 449b, 454a & 461a.
29. Cf. *Epigraphia Indica, Arabic Persian Supplement* (EI), ed. Z.A. Desai, Calcutta: 1953-4, p. 39.
30. The industry of boat-building continued to flourish in the sixteenth century also. See *Baburnamah,* tr. Mrs. Beveridge, vol. 2, rpt, Delhi, 1970, pp. 598-684.
31. Irfan Habib, *An Atlas of the Mughal Empire,* New Delhi: Oxford University Press, 1982, pp. 8A, 26+80+.
32. *Tarikh-i-Muhammadi,* f. 437a, See also Y.K. Bukhari, 'Some Inscriptions from Kalpi and Jathra', '*Epigraphia Indica, Arabic and Persian Supplement,* 1953-4, p. 39.
33. *Maathir-i Mahmud Shahi,* p. 37.
34. *Tarikh-i Muhammadi,* ff. 446b, 447a.
35. Ibid., 465b; See *Maathir-i-Mahmud Shahi,* p. 49, where Nasir Khan, son of Qādir Shah, is reported to have forced the Muslim girls to get trained in dance and learn the art of music; also Rizq ullah Mushtaqi *Waqi'at-i Mushtaqi* eds, Iqtidar Hussain Siddiqui and Wigarul Hasan Siddiqui, Rampur: Raza Library, 2003 p. 88, for the popularity of *Akhara* among the nobles.
36. See Sikandar b. Muhammad alias Manjhu, *Mirat-i Sikandari,* ed. Satish Chand Misra, M.S, Baroda: University Publication, 1961, p. 288, for the description of *Akhara.*
37. *Tarikh-i Muhammadi,* ff. 441b, 451ab.
38. Ibid., ff. 442b-443a.
39. Ibid., f. 443a.
40. Ibid., f. 442b. The authors of *Akhbar al-Akhyar* and *Gulzar-i Abrar* say, perhaps on the basis of later traditions, that they were the *khalifahs* of Shaikh Nasir' uddin Chiragh. But their statements are not supported by the contemporary source, *Tarikh-i Muhammadi.* As Mawlana Humam Ahmad held the government post in Delhi, he was not fit for *khilafah.* Shaikh Nizam' uddin Auliya' and Shaikh Nasir' uddin considered association with the royal court injurious to spiritual life. They did not confer *khilafat* on those who held any post at the royal court. But Shaikh Abdul Latif accepts their

statements. See Cf. 'A Study of the Muslim Saints of Kalpi', *Indian History Congress, Proceedings of the 28th Session*, 1972, pp. 337-8.

41. *Tarikh-i Muhammadi,* f. 443a.
42. Ibid., ff. 161ab.
43. *Akhbar al-Akhyar,* ed. Shaikh Zafar Ali, Delhi: Ahmadi Press, n.d. p. 166.
44. Ibid., pp. 183, 188.
45. Ibid.
46. Cf. *Epigraphia Indica, Arabic and Persian Supplement*, (EI), 1953-4, pp. 35-36.
47. *Akhbar al-Akhiyar,* p. 188.
48. *Tarikh-i Muhammadi,* ff. 169b-173b.
49. Ibid., ff. 174,173b; *Akhbar al-Akhyar,* p. 178, Erachh is included in the district of Jhansi in Uttar Pradesh.
50. Muhammad Ghausi Shattari, *Gulzar-i Abrar,* ed. Muhammad Zaki, Patna: Khuda Bakhsh Oriental Public Library, 1996, p. 127.
51. Cf. *Epigraphia Indica, Arabic and Persian Supplement*, ed. Z.A. Desai, (EI) 1966, p. 68.
52. Abdul Qadir Badaoni, *Najat ur-Rashid,* op.cit., ed. Syed Moin ul-Haque, Lahore, 1972, op.cit., p. 173.
53. *Akhbar al-Akhiyar,* op.cit., p. 188.
54. Cf. Simon Digby, 'Abdul Quddus Gangohi: The Personality and Attitudes of a Medieval Indian Sufi', *Medieval India- A Miscellany,* Aligarh 1975, vol. 3 pp. 36-9.
55. *Akhbar al-Akhiyar,* p.188.
56. *Gulzar-i Abrar,* Urdu tr., p.77.
57. *Muntakhab al-Tawarikh,* vol. 3, Bibliotheca Indica, Calcutta, 1869, pp. 6-7.
58. *Gulzar-i Abrar,* Urdu, tr. 305.
59. Muhammad Bihamad Khani says that his father was assigned the charge of the *pargana* of Chaurasi in 1393-4. After his posting, he cleasned it of the contumacious elements and also seized several villages that were included in the territorial unit of the Fort of Qanaj. *Tarikh-i Muhammadi,* f. 467a).

60. *Baburnamah,* vol. 2, 1970, pp. 649-50, for the *parganas* including the *sarkar* of Kalpi in the beginning of the sixteenth century. Neither the Lodis nor Babur made any alteration in the size of the unit as will be shown later.

61. Ibid.

62. Ibid.

63. Ibid.

64. Ibid.

65. Ibid.

66. The *iqta* of Shahpur was held by *Malik* Durraj, one of the chief slaves of Sultan Mahmud Shah of Kalpi.

67. The towns of Jajmau and Kanpur formed part of the administrative unit of Kara and Manikpur. It shows that the region of the modern district of Kanpur was included in the *shiqqs* of both Kara and Kalpi. Cf. Iqtidar A. Siddiqui, 'Evolution of the Vilayet, the Shiqq, and the Sarkar', *Medieval India Quarterly,* 1963, Aligarh, vol. 5, p. 29 (fn5).

68. The relations between the Sultan of Kalpi and the Chauhan ruler of Etawah, Rai Sabir, were strained in the beginning. There remained a constant conflict of arms between them and they fought a number of battles for the control of border *parganas.* On Sultan Mahmud Shah's death, Rai Sabir reached a compromise with Qādir Shah (son of Sultan Mahmud Turk) in 1413. Since then they remained allies and lent military support to each other when ever need arose. *Tarikh-i Muhammadi,* ff. 443b, 44a & 448a b).

69. Mahoba was the headquarters of one of the important *iqtas* in the principality of Kalpi. As it was exposed to raids by the chief of Bath Ghora, a rival, Sultan Mahmud Shah constructed a very lofty, impregnable fort with a strong *hisar* (walls) all around. On its completion he posted there Muzaffar Khan bin Mukarram Khan with a strong force. *Tarikh-i Muhammadi,* f. 439a.)

70. Jathra lies in 25° 1' N and 79° 6E, in the Tikamagarh district, MP. Bhander is the headquarters of a *pargana* in the Bhind district, MP. site 25° 44' N. 78° 45' E.

71. The *iqta* of Erachh was one of the most important units in the principality. Formerly, the *iqta* of Erachh was held by Malik Sulayman. Sultan Mahmud Shah of Kalpi seized it with the help of

Dilawar Khan of Malwa in the beginning of the fifteenth century. He first brought it under *Khalisah* but then assigned it to his brother Khan-i Azam Junayd Khan, the *wazir* of Kalpi. It comprised the entire area of the modern district of Jhansi and a portion of Gwalior district. *Tarikh-i Muhammadi,* ff. 440ab, 442a).

72. Khandaut is still in the district of Hamirpur, UP.

73. *Tarikh-i Muhammadi,* f. 438a.

74. It is a *tahsil* headquarters in the district of Hamirpur, U.P. sit. 25° 36' N., 79° 34° fifty miles south-west of Hamirpur. It was held by Malik Ibrahim Razi one of the trusted nobles of the sultan.

75. *Ma'athir-i Mahmud Shahi,* p. 60.

76. Muhammad Bihamad Khani enlightens us on this point when he describes his own achievements in his Tarikh. He says that Bihamad Khan, the deputy of the *wazir,* built a strong fort along with *hisar* at the village of Koeth in the *iqta* of Erachh in 1430. He also established *thanas* and assigned their charge to officers designated as *thanahdars* for its protection against the decoits. *Tarikh-i Muhammadi,,* ff. 474a-b.

77. Emperor Akbar divided the vast sarkar of Kalpi into two *sarkars, sarkar* of Kalpi and *sarkar* of Erachh. See Abul Fazl, *Ain-i Akbari,* tr. Colonel H.S. Jarrett, 1978, vol. 2, pp. 195, 198-9. New rpt.

78. *Baburnamah,* vol. 2, op.cit., p. 488.

79. *Maathir-i Mahmud Shahi,* p. 49.

80. *Tarikh-i-Muhammadi,* f. 467a.

81. Ibid., f. 465.b.

82. Two Persian inscriptions have been found fixed on two stepped-wells. One assigns the construction of the big well to Bhola Maharaj Khammar (a liquor-seller) who resided in Jathra. It is dated 24 February AD 1436. The other records the construction of the stepped-well by Shyam Kunwar Kalawant (musician) in AD 1500-1. The first was completed in the days of Khan-i A'zam, Ismail Khan, son of Nizam Khan. According to the second inscription, the chief of Jathra was Khan-i A'zam Tatar Khan, son of Muhammad, the latter being the grandson of Nizam Khan. (Cf. *Epigraphia Indica, Arabic and Persian Supplement,* 1953-4, pp. 39-41.)

83. *Tarikh-i Muhammadi,* f. 442a.

84. Ibid., ff. 472a, 474a-b.

85. Cf. *Annual Report on Indian Epigraphy,* 1963-4, No. 367, Appendix D.

86. He was the *murid* (disciple) and *khalifah* (spiritual vicegerent) of Shaikh Nasir' uddin Chiragh of Delhi. (*Tarikh-i Muhammadi,* f. 162a.)

87. He was the *murid* and pupil of Khwajah Ikhtiyar al-Din 'Umar. Later on, he became the *khalifah* of Shaikh Raju Qattal of the Suhrawardi order. A distinguished scholar, he left a number of books including a *diwan.* (*Tarikh-i Muhammadi,* ff. 165-170a; *Akhbar al-Akhyar,* p. 178.)

88. The doors of *khanqahs* of the Muslim Sufis were thrown open to all people irrespective of creed. Hindus and Muslims visited the Sufis for their blessings. The information contained in the collections of the sayings (*malfuzat)*of the Sufis reflects the humanism and catholicity of views that shaped their attitude towards people regardless of religion. (Cf. Iqtidar H. Siddiqui, *Modern Writings on Islam and Muslims in India,* Aligarh, 1972, pp. 21-4.)

    Ibn Battuta furnishes interesting details about the popularity of the yogis among the Muslims from the King down to the beggar. He says, 'Many Mussalmans follow them [yogis] in order to take lessons from them.' See *The Rehla,* tr. Mahdi Husain Baroda, 1953, p. 166.

89. *Akhbar al-Akhyar,* pp. 188-9.

90. Muhammad Qasim Firishtah, *Ta'rikh-i Firishtah,* Lucknow: Nawal Kishore edition, vol. 3, p. 247.

91. *Tarikh-i Muhammadi,* f. 437a, 438a, 438b.

92. Here, cases of Ra'i Bhairaj of Hamirpur *pargana,* Bhilam, the *muqaddam* of Sinehal, Ra'i Kalyan of Samoni (all holding *zamindaris)* in the region between the Kalpi's *iqta* of Mahoba and the territory of Bath Ghora (modern Rewa) may be referred to. They resisted the expansion of Sultan Mahmud's rule in the beginning and then became his trusted vassals after they had failed to achieve success. (*Tarikh-i Muhammadi,* ff. 438, 439a-b.)

93. Ibid., ff. 444a. The term *khidmati* was synonymous with Persian *peshkash* that in Mughal times a noble or chief had to offer to the Mughal Emperor. Muhammad Bihamad Khani is not the only writer of the pre-Mughal period to use it. Zia' uddin Barani and Yahya Sirhindi also use it in the same sense (Barani, pp. 577-8; *Ta'rikh-i*

Mubarak Shahi, p. 184). Shihab Hakim also uses *khidmati* in the sense of offering. (*Ma'asir-i Mahmud Shahi,* p. 52.)

94. *Tarikh-i Muhammadi,* ff. 449 v45a.
95. *Akhbar al-Akhyar,* pp. 209-255; *Lata'if-i Quddusi,* Mujtaba'i Press, Delhi, pp. 57-8.
96. *Waqi'at-i Mushtaqi,* tr. p. 74.
97. *Tarikh-i Muhammadi,* ff. 442b.
98. Ibid., ff. 465b-466a.
99. *Waqi'at-i Mushtaqi,* tr. p. 102.
100. Isami, *Futuh us-Salatin,* ed. Usha, A.S. Madras: Madras University Islamic Series No. 9, 1948, p. 450.
101. *Tarikh-i Mubarak Shahi,* p. 95.
102. *Waqi'at-i Mushtaqi,* (Persian Text), pp. 54-5.
103. See Iqtidar H. Siddiqui, *History of Sher Shah Sur,* Aligarh, 1971, where I have analyzed the nature of land grants during the Sultanate period.
104. Ibid.
105. Referring to the Mongol prisoners, 'Isami says, 'They belittled themselves before every soldier of the royal army in the same way, as people belittle themselves before the Hindu Chaudhri.' See 'Isami, *Futuh us-Salatin* op.cit., p. 321.
106. Sultan Ibrahim Sharqi is reported to have appeared before the gates of Kalpi with his entire army, elephants and war machines, *manjaniqs* and catapults. He struggled for more than two months but failed to capture the city. In fact, the army of Kalpi enabled Qādir Shah to defend him successfully. Being disappointed, Sultan Ibrahim Sharqi made peace with Kalpi and left for Jaunpur. *(Tarikh-i Mubarak Shahi,* p. 180; *Tarikh-i Muhammadi,* ff. 451a-b.)
107. *Tarikh-i Muhammadi,* ff. 457a-b, 458a-b 459a; *Tarikh-i Mubarak Shahi,* pp. 207-9 & 234.
108. *Ma'athir-i Mahmud Shahi,* pp. 49, 52, 54, 59.
109. Ibid., pp. 59-60; also Firishtah op.cit., pp. 247-8.
110. Nizam' uddin Ahmad, *Tabaqat-i Akbari,* ed. B. Day, Bibliotheca Indica, Calcutta, 1927, vol. 1, p. 315.
111. Cf. Stan Goron and J.P. Goenka, *The Coins of the Indian Sultanates,* New Delhi: Munshiram Manohar Lal, 2001, pp. 349-50.

112. *Tabaqat-i-Akbari,* vol. 1, op.cit., p. 315.
113. Khwanda Mir, 1927, p. 315.
114. *Waqi'at-i-Mushtaqi,* (Persian Text), op.cit., p. 111.
115. Ibid., p. 82.
116. *Epigraphia Indica, Arabic and Persian Supplement,* 1953-4, pp. 36-8.
117. *Baburnama,* vol. 2, 1970, op.cit., p. 521.
118. *Tabaqat-i Akbari,* vol. 1, p. 521; Nimatullah, Harevi, *Tarikh-i Khan-i Jahani,* vol. 1, op.cit., Dacca: Asiatic Society of Pakistan, vol. 203, 1960, p. 203.

APPENDIX A

War-Horse and Its Trade

With the exception of a small tribe of Turks inhabitating the territory of Kaikan (present-day Kalat in Balochistan, Pakistan) good war-horses in the Indian subcontinent were not bred. The Turks developed horse-breeding centres and reared horses of the Tatar breed for their personal use. The Kaikanian steed was considered by Caliph Muawiyah a choice possession after he had received a few as his share in the booty captured by his governor of Iran.[1] Since the larger part of Makran was a barren desert, the cultivation of crops or rearing of animals was possible only in a small area, where water was available from streams or rivulets as rainfall was insufficient. This region could not be a source of the supply of war-horses to the Sultan's army during the Ghaznavid or the Delhi Sultanate period.

The supply of war-horse by the merchants continued unchecked during the early decades of the thirteenth century. After the Mongol conquest of Central Asia and Khurasan, Mongol rulers seem to have banned the supply of Tatar horses to India on account of hostility between them and the Sultans of Delhi. This provided the Afghans inhabiting the tribal region between the Delhi Sultanate and the Mongol Empire with an opportunity to smuggle Tatar horses from beyond the frontier and sell them in India. The Afghans also seem to have reared war-horses through cross-breeding with the Tatar horse as they were sometimes sold in Delhi as imported ones during the reign of Sultan 'Ala ud'din Khalji.[2]

It is worth pointing out that Barani's reference to the Tatar horse, presented by Prince Muhammad Khan, the governor of Multan and Sind to Sultan Balban, his father as part of *khidmati* (annual offering at court) suggests that the Afghans smuggled Central Asian horses in large number. Sultan Balban is said to have remarked that the horses sent by his son from

Multan were enough to meet the need of the central army.[3] Moreover, the Indians in Punjab also developed horse-breeding centres in Punjab and reared war-horses through cross-breeding with the foreign horse. Balban found the horse from Siwalik hills and the areas of Jatwans, Khokars and Mandahar comparable to the war-horse from beyond the north-western frontier (called *Mulk-i-bale*, i.e. highland).[4]

By the time of Sultan Muhammad bin Tughluq, the merchants had again started to supply horses from Central Asia to India in large number. Ibn Battuta states about the horse supply from the region of Qipchaq: 'the region around Azaq abounds in horses as sheep in our land (Morocco). The main source of livelihood of the local people is horse-trade alone. Each merchant has one or two hundred horses or more or less. The merchant employs a drover for every fifty horses who looks after their pasturage, like sheep (in Morocco). These horses are brought to India for sale. On their arrival in Sind, they are fed with forage, because the grass in Sind does not suit them, many horses either die or are stolen. They are taxed (on the border of Sind) seven silver dinars (*tankas*) a horse. On their arrival in Multan, the headquarters of Sind (Province) the tax is realized a second time. Formerly, the merchants had to pay as duty a quarter of what they imported, but the (reigning) Sultan Muhammad (bin Tughluq) abolished this practice and ordered that the Muslim merchants would pay only *zakat* (2 ½ per cent) and *ushr* (one-tenth) would be realized from the non-Muslim merchants. The merchants earn handsome profit, in-spite of the payment of duty, for even a horse of inferior quality (from abroad) is sold for one hundred silver *tankas* and, at times, it fetches two hundred *tankas*. A good horse is sold for five hundred dinars or more'. Further Ibn Battuta says that the Tatar horses were used in warfare, while for racing, the Indians bought Arab horses imported by sea from the Persian gulf countries. They were very expensive, their price ranged from one thousand to four thousand silver tankas.[5] Certainly the possession by a rich man of an Arab horse was a status symbol. Generally, the Sultan purchased the Arab horses and distributed them among his high nobles by way of favour. The information contained in the *Masalik ul-Absar* with regard to the distribution of horses by Sultan Muhammad bin Tughluq is worth quoting, 'Every year the Sultan distributes ten thousand branded Arabian horses, ... As regards the horses of Turkish or cross-breed, the Sultan distributes them by herds without any account. Despite the fact that there is a large number of horses in the Empire a large number is brought from foreign lands, the Sultan imports them from every country because he is very generous in distributing them as presents. He spends a large sum of money on purchasing them. As there is large demand of horses on account of the existence of a large army and the large hearted distribution by the Sultan, their prices are quite high, the merchants earn good profit. Among the merchants of Bahrain who supply horses to the Sultan, Ali bin Mansur al-'Uqili told me that people of India have got a knack to distinguish the horses of good breed. As they find the mark in a horse known to them, they would purchase it at any price'.[6]

Lastly, it may be stated that the horse of foreign breed was the main import item that cost the state exchequer heavy expenditure. Next to the horse was the import of slaves from countries as far as Ethopia in Africa, China, Turkistan in the East and eastern Europe in the West.[7] As regards the luxury goods, including Chinese silk brought by the merchants from foreign countries, their use was confined to the aristocracy and, therefore, their import seems to have been limited. Compared to the import items, the export items from India were several times in excess and constituted the source of wealth to the State exchequer and prosperity to the Indian artisans and cultivators.

Endnotes

1. Cf. Ali bin Hamid al-Kufi, *Fathnama-i-Sind*, known as *Chachnama*, ed. N.B. Baloch, Islamabad: Islamic University, 1983, p. 56.
2. Cf. Simon Digby, *War-Horse and Elephant in the Delhi Sultanate*, Karachi, Oxford University Press, 1971, p. 28. See also Zia'uddin Barani, *Tarikh-i-Firuz Shahi*, Saiyid Ahamd Khan, Calcutta: Bibliotheca Indica, 1862, pp. 144-5.
3. Simon Digby's statement, 'Barani, in the speech of Sultan Balban, seems to imply that Tatari horses also arrived by sea from the Persian Gulf. This may indicate that some of the drovers took a more southerly route through Persia', does not seem to be correct. As a matter of fact he has analysed Balban's speech along with Ibn Battuta's statement about the arrival of horses by sea from Iran and Arabian lands to South India during the fourteenth century. The situation was different at the time of Ibn Battuta's arrival owing to the establishment of friendly relations between the Sultanate of Delhi and Tarmashirin of Central Asia. The supply of horses from Central

Asia to north India was always by land route. Cf. Digby, Ibid., p. 36; Barani, Ibid., p. 53.

4. Barani, p. 53.
5. Ibn Battuta, *Ajaib-ul-Asfar,* Urdu tr. Maulana Ataur Rahman, Delhi: Rahmani Press, vol. 1, p. 483.
6. I. H, Siddiqui, *Perso-Arabic Sources of Information on the Life and Conditions in the Sultanate of Delhi,* New Delhi: Munshiram Manoharlal, 1992, p. 119.
7. Ibid., pp. 117-22.

APPENDIX B

The Currency of the Delhi Sultanate

The introduction by the early sultans of gold and silver *tankas* (*tanka-i-nuqra* and *tanka-i-tila*) bears testimony to the economic development and progress of trade but the contemporary sources of information reveal that the medium of transaction generally was *jital,* the token copper coin till the end of the thirteenth century. For example, Minhaj-i-Siraj tells us in the biographical details of Iltutmish that when the slave merchant, Chust Qaba brought Iltutmish and another Turkish slave to Ghazna for sale, Sultan Muiz u'ddin Muhammad bin Sam decided to buy them for one thousand dinars (probably silver coins). The merchant did not agree to sell them at that price. Annoyed by his refusal, the Sultan issued the *farman* that no person would buy them in Ghazna. Thereupon, the merchant left for Bukhara. After three or four years the merchant brought them to Ghazna again. Since the *farman* was not withdrawn, none could buy them. After one year Malik Qutb u'ddin Aibak visited Ghazna (1197-8). He decided to buy them and sought royal permission for that purpose. The Sultan told him about the farman and also advised him to take them to India and buy them there. In Delhi Qutb uddin Aibak bought both of the slaves for one lac *jitals.*[1] The prices of the slaves bought by Sultan Iltutmish are also mentioned in *jitals.*[2] The salary and allowances paid by the state exchequer to the nobles were also fixed in *jitals.*[3] Minhaj-i-Siraj states that on the completion of the *Tabaqat-i-Nasiri,* in AD 1260, he presented its copy at court, Sultan Nāsir uddin Mahmud (reigned: AD 1246 to 1265-6) rewarded him with a piece of *Sanjab* (costly fur), besides the grant of one village and ten thousand *jitals* every year. On the same day, another complementary copy was presented to Ulugh Khan Azam (later Sultan Ghiyas uddin Balban), who too gave him twenty thousand *jitals* in reward.[4] The payment of *tanka* (silver coin) is rarely mentioned in the *Tabaqat-i-Nasiri.* The only reference to the *tanka* is found contained in the account of the military expedition led by Ulugh Khan Azam against the Mewati plunderers in 1259. Minhaj states that every soldier who presented the heads of the slain Mewatis was paid one *tanka* (silver coin) per head. Those who brought Mewati prisoners were paid two *tankas* for each one.[5]

Like Minhaj, the other early emigrant poet, Siraji Khurasani also refers to *jital* as the medium of exchange in his panegyric, composed in praise of the crown prince during the reign of Sultan Iltutmish. Once he was rewarded by prince Nasir uddin Mahmud with a horse. The *Amir-i-Akhur* (officer-in-charge of the stable) gave him a defective horse. The poet being grieved complained against the officer and requested for a better one. He says that he sold the horse for three hundred and seventy *jitals* through *a dalal* (broker).[6]

The references to *jital* available in the *Fawaid-ul-Fuad* shows that it remained the medium of exchange through out the thirteenth century and that it was also called *diram.*[7] On another occasion Shaikh Nizam uddin Auliya, mentioning the year AD 1254 refers to the use of silver *tanka* in connection with the payment of a loan and the purchase of a beautiful young slave girl.[8] We also come across the coin, called *nim tanka* (half a *tanka*) in the *Fawaid ul-Fuad* which was in circulation during the thirteenth century.[9] In his account of Sultan Ghiyas uddin Balban and Sultan Jalal uddin Khalji (reigned: AD 1290-6) Zia'uddin Barani furnishes corroborative evidence about *jital.* He incidentally states that the salaries and allowances were paid to the nobles in *jitals.*[10] In describing the payment of *mawajib* (salary and allowances) to the nobles and generosity of certain nobles, Barani rarely mentions the use of silver *tanka.* Highlighting Sultan Jalal uddin Khalji's noble qualities and interest in poetry and literature, he says that when he was elevated by Sultan Kaiqubad (reigned: 1287-90) to the post of *Amir-i-Ariz* (pay master general), he restored Amir Khusrau's deceased father's *mawajib* (pay and allowances) amounting to one thousand and two hundred *tankas* (per annum), to Amir Khusrau.[11] In another context, Barani tells us that when the gold and silver coins were rarely seen, Malik Qutb uddin Alavi, the *naib-i-Mumalikat* under Sultan Jalal uddin Khalji spent two lac *tankas* on the marriage of his eldest son.[12]

It is also worth noting that the *Fawaid ul-Fuad* and the *Khair-ul-Majalis* (the collection of utterances of Shaikh Nasir uddin Chiragh-i-Delhi) not only reflect the increase in the circulation of the silver *tanka* and the introduction of its new fractions since the reign of Sultan 'Ala ud'din Khalji, but also help us in explaining the value of *jital* in relation to the *tanka*. It is a pity that no modern scholar has paid adequate attention to the study of the Delhi Sultanate currency. Simon Digby devotes a section in his essay dealing with the economy of the Sultanate, contributed to the *Cambridge Economic History of India* (vol.1), but he fails to menion the new coins that were introduced during the reign of Sultan 'Ala ud'din Khalji (1296-1315). The new coins were called *ganis* which were a different fraction of the silver *tanka*. Digby simply refers to the views held by different modern scholars about the relative value of the silver *tanka* to the *jital* and accepts that the 'the *jital* changed at 1/48th of a silver *tanka* in northern India and 1/50th in the Deccan after the Muslim conquest of the Deccan'.[13] This is based on conjecture. The evidence contained in the *Fawaid ul-Fuad* helps us in explaining the relative value of the *jital* to the silver *tanka*. While mentioning the *futuh* presented by the thirteenth century Persian poet, Shams Dabir to Shaikh Farid uddin Ganj-i-Shakar (d. AD 1265), Shaikh Nizam uddin Auliya tells us that the poet brought about fifty *jitals*, more or less as offering. The Shaikh had them distributed among the *murids* (disciples) present in the *khanqah*. Further, the Shaikh states that the present *gani* was equal to the *jital* of that time.[14] Moreover, the work, *Fawaid ul-Fuad* contains a reference to *shashgani* (piece or coin worth six *ganis*) along with *jital*. Hasan Sijzi tells us that in Deogiri one of the *murids* of Shaikh Nizamuddin gave him three *jitals* and one *shashgani* to present them to the Shaikh on his behalf.[15] In the *Khair-ul-Majalis* as well, we come across references to the *jital* and the *gani*. Talking about a fellow *murid* (the disciple of Shaikh Nizam uddin Auliya), Shaikh Nasir uddin Chiragh told the visitors that Maulana Fakhr uddin Marwazi adopted the profession of scribe. He made copies of books and sold them. When he brought them to the market for sale, he asked the customer to fix the price of the book. If the latter fixed the price *shashgani* (i.e. six *ganis*), he would sell it for four *jitals* (*Chahargan'i*), i.e. two *ganis* or *jitals* less). 'If some body decided', says the Shaikh, 'to pay twelve *jitals* looking for a blessing, he accepted neither twelve *jitals* nor *Shashganis* (i.e. six *jitals*), only four *jitals* were acceptable'. As he grew old and was not able to carry on his work, Qazi Hamid uddin Multani recommended him to Sultan 'Ala ud'din Khalji for the grant of maintenance allowance. The Sultan fixed one *tanka* as daily allowance. But the Maulana said that he would accept only one *shashgani* that would suffice for his needs. On much persuasion, he agreed to accept two *shashganis*.[16] It should also be added that Barani generally avoids to mention the use of *gani* in his *tarikh*. Even the prices of commodities fixed by Sultan 'Ala ud'din Khalji are mentioned in *tanka* and *jital* . It is only once that he refers to *gani* while describing the withdrawal of copper *tanka* during the reign of Sultan Muhammad bin Tughluq. That when the copper coins were withdrawn and people allowed to change them with silver ones, they brought them to the state treasury and got the *Mohar-i-tanka-i-zar* (gold *tanka*), *tanka-i-nuqra* (silver *tanka*), *Shashgani* and *Dugani* (the coin of two *ganis*) in return.[17] Barani's contemporary, Isami also mentions dugani (piece or coin of two ganis) in his Futuh-us-Salatin.[18]

The corroborative and supplementary evidence available in the contemporary foreign as well as other Indian sources of information may also be referred to. Shihab uddin al-Umari was informed in Damascus by Shaikh Mubarak (an Indian traveller) that the coins in circulation in the Sultanate of Sultan Muhammad bin Tughluq were *yakgani* (one anna of British colonial period), *dugani* (two *ganis*), also called Sultani, *Shashgani* (coin equal to six *ganis* in value), *hashtgani* (equal to eight *ganis*) and *duazdehgani* (the coin worth twelve *ganis*). Thus sixteen ganis made one tanka.[19] Shams Siraj Afif adds that Sultan Firuz Shah (reigned: 1351-88) felt the need to introduce the coin *nimjital* (half of a *jital*) that came to be called *udha*. Likewise, the *dang-i-jital* (one fourth of the *jital* in value and called paisa during the colonial period) was divided into four fractions and known *begha* (later *chhadam*).

What follows from the above discussion is that the expansion of the metropolis of Delhi, socio-economic growth, the progress of trade and commerce and the flow of wealth from the conquest of Malwa, Gujarat and the Deccan under Sultan 'Ala ud'din Khalji not only improved the living conditions of people but also led to the rise of consumerism among the ruling elite and rise in prices. All this necessitated the circulation of silver coins of different denominations in a large number, in order to provide facilities to both the buyers and sellers.

Since the prestige of the Sultan was associated with the coins minted and issued in his name, all efforts were made to maintain their value and standard. Corruption was checked in the royal mint. That is why Amir Khusrau suggests through a specimen *farman* drafted for the guidance of the officers of the state: 'Those who practice fraud by minting spurious coins should be punished, their necks should be struck with the sword, so that the gold concealed by them may be recovered. They should be kept in perpetual fear of imprisonment and punishment'.[20] According to Shams Siraj

Afif, the officials of the royal mint became corrupt during Firuz Shah's reign and used one grain of silver less in minting the *shashgani*. When the matter was brought to the notice of the *wazir*, Khan-i-Jahan Maqbul, the latter instituted enquiry and found out the guilty officials. Kajar Shah, the officer incharge of the mint was given retirement while the corrupt officials were punished and dismissed from the service.[21]

As for the symbolic importance of currency, its circulation signified submission by the people to the King's authority. Therefore, in a newly-conquered territory annexed to the Sultanate, the old currency was replaced by the new coins and the circulation of the coins of the overthrown regions currency was disallowed. Amir Khusrau states in his customary style, 'The royal currency gets circulated in (the newly-conquered) territories, the devilish coins (i.e. the currency of the overthrown regime) called *Achhu* (gold coins), *Padma* (silver coins) and *Qatam* (copper coins) should be superseded through the circulation of royal coins in abundance because the establishment of royal authority and acquiescence by people into it is associated with it (i.e. the sultan's currency)'. Then he concludes his advice with the line, 'The coins act like the compasses under the golden (royal) hand (encircling all)'.[22]

Endnotes

1. Minhaj-i-Siraj Juzjani, *Tabaqat-i-Nasiri,* vol. 1, ed. Abdul Hai Habibi, Kabul, 1963-4, pp. 442-3.
2. Ibid., vol. 2, p. 17.
3. Ibid., vol. 2, p. 8.
4. Ibid., vol. 2, pp. 219-20.
5. Ibid., vol. 2, p. 80.
6. Cf. *Diwan-i-Siraji Khurasani,* ed. Nazir Ahmad, Aligarh: Publication Division, Aligarh Muslim University, 1972, *qasida* No. 47, couplets 25-34, pp. 143-4.
7. Hasan Sijzi, *Fawaid ul-Fuad,* Lahore, 1966, pp. 133-4, 227-8 & 239.
8. Ibid., pp. 112-14, 316-17.
9. Ibid., p. 83.

10. Zia'uddin Barani, *Tarikh-i-Firuz Shahi,* ed. Saiyid Ahmad Khan, Calcutta: Bibliotheca Indica, 1862, pp. 195, 205, 210.
11. Ibid., p. 197.
12. Ibid., p. 202.
13. Cf. Simon Digby, The Currency System, *The Cambridge History of India,* vol., 1, Indian reprint, New Delhi, 1982, ed. Tapan Roy Chaudhary and Irfan Habib, p. 91.
14. Sijzi, *Fawaid-ul-Fuad,* op.cit., pp. 218-19.
15. Ibid., pp. 302-3.
16. Hamid Qalandar, *Khair-ul-Majalis,* ed. K.A. Nizami, Aligarh, 1959, p. 88.
17. Barani, *Tarikh-i-Firuz Shahi,* p. 476.
18. Futuh-us-Salatin, pp. 123-4.
19. Siddiqui, *Perso-Arabic Sources of Information,* p. 133.
20. Cf. Iqtidar Husain Siddiqui, 'The 13th and 14th Century Farmans Concerning the Conduct of Governors under the Sultans of Delhi,' *Islamic Culture,* Hyderabad, (India), April-July, 1991, vol. 65, nos. 2 and 3, pp. 119-46, p. 130.
21. Shams Siraj Afif, *Tarikh-i-Firuz Shahi,* ed. Wilayat Husain, Calcutta: 1891, pp. 348-9.
22. 'The 13th and 14th Century Farmans Concerning the Conduct of Governors under the Sultans of Delhi', Siddiqui, op.cit., pp. 134-5.

Bibliography

Abbas Sarwani, *Tuhfa-i-Akbarshahi,* known as *Tarikh-i-Sher Shahi,* ed., S.M. Imam Uddin, Dhaka: University of Dhaka, 1964.

Abdul Aziz Shams Thanesari, *Kitab-ul-Nujum,* MS, Sir Sulaiman Collection, Maulana Azad Library, Aligarh.

Abdul Haque Muhadis, *Akhbar al-Akhyar,* Matba-i-Mujtabai, Delhi, 1914.

________, *Tarikh-i-Haqqi*, MS, Maulana Azad Library, Aligarh.

Abdul Qadir Badaoni, *Muntakhab-ut-Tawarikh,* Calcutta: Bibliotheca Indica, vol. 1, 1869; tr. G.S.A. Ranking, Calcutta, vol. 1, 1895.

________, *Najat-ur-Rashid*, ed. Syed Moinul Haque, Idara-i-Tahqiqat-i-Pakistan, Danishgah-i-Punjab, Lahore.

Abu Bakr bin Ali Usman al-Kasani, *Farsi Tarjuma-i-Kitab ul-Saidna* of al-Beruni, ed. M. Satudeh and Iraj Afshar, Bunyad-i-Farhang-i-Iran, Tehran, 1325 Shamsi.

Abul Fazl Muhammad al-Baihaqi, *Tarikh-i-Masudi, (*known as *Tarikh-i-Al-i-Subuktigin)* ed. W.H. Morley, Bibliotheca Indica, Calcutta, 1862.

Abu Nasr Muhammad al-Jabbar al-Utbi, *Tarikh al-Yamini,* Arabic text, Lahore, 1300 H.; *Tarikh-i-Yamini,* thirteenth-century Persian translation by Abu-s-Sharaf al-Jurazqani, ed. Jaffar Shiyar, Tehran, 1345 Shamsi.

Afif, Shams Siraj, *Tarikh-i-Firuz Shahi,* ed. Wilayat Husain, Calcutta: Bibliotheca Indica, 1891.

Ahmad bin Umar Ibn Ali an-Nizami al-'Aruzi, *Chahar Maqala,* ed. Mirza Muhammad Qazvini, Leiden: E.J. Brill, 1910.

Ali bin Hamid al-Kufi, *Fathnama-i-Sind,* known as *Chachnama,* ed. Nabi Bakhsh Baloch, Islamabad: Islamic University, 1983.

Ali bin Mahmud al-Kirmani, (also known as Shihab Hakim), *Ma'sir-i-Mahmud Shahi,* ed. Nurul Hasan Ansari, Delhi: Indo-Persian Society, 1968.

'Amid Loeki Sunami, *Diwan-i-Amid Loeki,* ed. Nazir Ahmad, *Majlis-i-Taraqi-i-Adab,* Lahore, 1984.

Anonymous, *Sirat-i-Firuz Shahi,* Facsimile, Khuda Bakhsh Oriental Public Library, Patna, 1999; also MS, Khuda Bakhsh Oriental Public Library, Patna.

________, *Hudud al-Alam,* tr. V. Minorsky, entitled The Regions of the World; 2nd edn. Gibb Memorial Series, London, 1970, no. 11.

________, *Bayaz-i-Tajudin Wazir,* ed. Iraj Afshar and Murtaza Timur, Danishgah, Isfahan, No. 103, 1351 Shamsi.

Arabi, Zain Badr, *Khwan-i-Pur N'imat* (*Malfuzat* of Shaikh Sharafuddin Yahya Maneri), Matba-i-Ahmadi, Patna 1321 H.

________, *M'adan al-M'ani* (*Malfuzat* of Shaikh Sharafuddin Yahya Maneri), 2 vols, Bihar Sharif, 1884.

Ata Malik Juvaini, *Tarikh-i-Jahan Gusha,* ed. Muhammad Qazvini, Leiden: E.J. Brill, 1912, tr. J.A. Bryle, entitled *The History of the World Conqueror,* 2 vols, Manchester, 1958.

'Awfi, 'Sadiduddin Muhammad, *Javami' 'ul Hikayat wa-Livami'ul Rivayat,* vol. 1, Parts I and II, ed. Muhammad Nizamuddin Ahmad, Hyderabad: 1965-6, vols. 2 and 3, ed. Amir Bano Musaffa and Mutahir Musaffa, Tehran: Bunyad-i-Farhang-i-Iran, vol. 4, MS, Patna: Khuda Bakhsh Oriental Public Library.

________, *Tarjuma* (Persian), *Kitab ul-Faraj b'ad ul-Sbidda* MS, India Office Library, London, Ethe, No. 1432.

________, *Lubab ul-Albab,* ed. E.C. Browne and Mirza Muhammad Qazvini, Leiden: E.J. Brill, 1903-6.

Badr Chach, *Qasaid-i-Badr-i-Chach,* Lucknow: Nawal Kishore, AH. 1279,

Zia'uddin, Barani, *Fatawa-i-Jahandari,* ed. Mrs A. Salim Khan, University of the Punjab, Lahore, 1972.

________, *N'at-i-Muhammadi,* MS, No.Tarikh 127, Raza Library, Rampur.

________, *Tarikh-i-Firuz Shahi,* ed. Saiyid Ahmad Khan, Calcutta: Bibliotheca Indica, 1862.

________, *Tarikh-i-Firuz Shahi,* unrevised first version, MS, Bodleian Library, Elliot Collection, No. 353, Oxford and MS. Raza Library, Rampur,

Muhammad, Bihamad Khani, *Tarikh-i-Muhamamdi,* MS Or. 137, British Library, London.

Dharma Swamin, *Biography of Dharma Swamin* (Chaglo tsa-ba chosrje-dpal), vol. 2, tr. G. Roerich, Patna: K.P. Jayaswal Research Institute, 1959.

Fakhr-i-Mudabbir, Muhammad bin Mansur, *Adab ul-Harb wa-shuja,* ed. Ahmad Suhaili Khwansari, Tehran, 1346 Shamsi.

________, *Adab ul-Muluk wa-Kifayat ul-Mamluk,* ed. Muhammad Sarwar Maula'i, Tehran: Bunyad-i-Farhang Iran, No. 212.

________, *Muqadima of Shajra-i-Ansab,* ed. Denison Ross, and published under the title *Tarikh-i-Fakhruddin Mubarakshah Marvar-rudi,* London, 1927. (It has been cited by me as *Tarikh-i-Fakhr-i-Mudabbir).*

Fakhruddin Mubarak Shah (known as Qawwas Ghaznavi) *Farhang-i-Qawwas,* ed. Nazir Ahmad, Rampur, Raza Library, 1999.

Faiz Ullah Binbani, *Tarikh-i-Sadr-i-Jahan,* ed. Iqtidar Husain Siddiqui, Aligarh: Academic Books, 1988.

Fazl Ullah, Rashiduddin, *Jami 'ul-Tawarikh's* part on India, ed. Karl Jahn under the title *Rashiduddin's History of India,* The Hague, 1965.

Firishta, Muhammad Qasim Hindu Shah, *Gulshan Ibrahimi,* known as *Tarikh-i-Firishta,* Nawal Kishore Press, Lucknow, 1281 H.

Firuz Shah, *Futuhat-i-Firuz Shahi,* ed. S. Abdur Rashid, Aligarh: The Aligarh Muslim University, 1954.

Gardezi, Abu Said, *Zain al-Akhbar,* ed. Abdul Ha'i Habibi, Tehran: Bunyad-i-Farhang-i-Iran, 1347 Shamsi.

Hajib Khairat Dehlavi, *Dastur ul-Afazil,* ed. Nazir Ahmad, Tehran: Bunyad-i-Farhang-i-Iran, 1352 Shamsi.

Hamid Qalandar, *Khair ul-Majalis,* ed. K.A. Nizami, Aligarh, Department of History, Aligarh Muslim University, 1959.

Harevi, Saif Jam, *Majmu'a-i-Lataif-o-Safina-i-Zaraif,* MS Or. 4110, British Library, London.

Hasan Nizami, *Taj-ul-Maasir,* MS Add, 1623, British Library, London, Persian Text, ed. Amir Hasan Abidi, (Centre of Persian Research, Iran Culture House, 18 Tilak Marg, New Delhi, 2008), tr. Bhagwat Saroop, published by Saud Ahmed Dehlavi, Delhi: Shaikh Chand Street, Lal Kuan, 1998.

Hasan Sijzi, *Fawaid ul-Fuad,* Lucknow: Nawal Kishore Press, 1302 H., also Lahore: Malik Siraj Uddin & Sons, 1966.

Ibn Battuta, *The Travels of Ibn Battuta,* vol. 3, tr. Sir Hamilton Gibb, Cambridge: Cambridge University Press, 1971; Urdu tr. vol. 1, *Ajaib ul-Asfar,* Maulana Ataur Rahman, Delhi: Rahmani Press, 1348; *Ajaib ul-Asfar,* vol. 2, Urdu tr. Maulvi Muhammad Husaini, rpt, Islamabad: Qaumi Idara Bara-i-Tahqiq Tarikh-o-Saqafat, 1983.

________, *The Rehla,* tr. Mahdi Husain, Baroda, 1953.

Ikhtisan, Muhammad Sadr Ala (bin) Ahmad Hasan Abdusi Dabir, *Basatinul-Urs,* MS No. Add. 7717, British Library, London, tr. with comments; Iqtidar Husain Siddiqui, in *Perso-Arabic Sources of Information on the Life and Conditions in the Sultanate of Delhi,* New Delhi: Munshiram Manoharlal, 1992.

Isami, *Futuh us-Salatin,* ed. A.S. Usha, Madras: Madras University Islamic Series No. 9, 1948.

Jajarmi, Majduddin Abul Maali Muaiyid bin Muhammad, Farsi Tarjuma of *Ihya-ul-Ulum -id-Din* of Imam Ghazzali, MS Or. 8194, British Library, London.

Jalaluddin Ahal Jami, *Faraid-i-Ghiyasi,* ed. Hashmi Moyyid, Tehran: Bunyad-i-Farhang-i-Iran, 1974.

Jamali Kambo, *Qasaid-i-Jamali,* MS, Habib Ganj Collection, Aligarh: Maulana Azad Library.

Juzjani, Minhaj-i-Siraj, *Tabaqat-i-Nasiri,* 2 vols., ed. Abdul Ha'i Habibi, Kabul: Anjuman Tarikh-i-Afghanistan, 1963-4, tr. H.G. Raverty, 2 vols, Calcutta, 1897.

Khusrau, Amir, *I'jaz-i-Khusravi,* 5 vols, Lucknow: Nawal Kishore Press, 1865-7.

________, *Khazain ul-futuh,* ed. Wahid Mirza, Calcutta, 1953; tr. Mohammad Habib under the title *The Campaigns of 'Ala ud'din Khalji,* Bombay: D.B. Taraporewala Sons and Co., 1931.

________, *Masnavi Dewal Rani Wa-Khizr Khan,* ed. Rashid Ahmad Salim, Aligarh: Institute Aligarh College, 1917.

________, *Masnavi Miftah ul-Futuh,* ed. Shaikh Abdus Rashid, Aligarh: Department of History, The Aligarh Muslim University 1954.

________, *Masnavi Qiran us-S'adain,* ed. Muhammad Ismail, Aligarh: Institute Aligarh College, 1918.

________, *Masnavi Nuhsphir,* ed. Wahid Mirza, Calcutta: Oxford University Press, 1950.

________, *Tughluqnama,* ed. S. Hashmi Faridabadi, Aurangabad: Matba-i-Urdu, 1933.

Khwafi, Fasih Ahmad bin Jalaluddin Muhammad, *Majm'ul Fasihi,* vol. 3, ed. Mahmud Farrukh, 1339 Shamsi/1960, 3 vols.

Mahru, Ainul-Mulk, *Insha'-i-Mahru,* ed. Sh. Abdu Rashid, Lahore: Research Society of Pakistan, 1965.

Mir Khurd, Saiyid Muhammad Mubarak Kirmani, *Siyar ul-Auliya,* lith., Delhi, AH 1302, 1885.

Muhammad bin Ali al-Ravandi, *Khulasa-i-Rahat ul-Sudur-o-ayat ul-Surur,* ed. Nazir Ahmad, in *Qand-i-Parsi,* no. 9, New Delhi: Iran Cultural House.

Mushtaqi, Rizq ullah, *Waq'iat-i-Mushtaqi,* ed. Iqtidar Husain Siddiqui and Wiqarul Hasan Siddiqui, Rampur: Raza Library, 2003; tr. Iqtidar Husain Siddiqui, New Delhi: Indian Council of Historical Research, 1993.

Muthar Kara, *Diwan-i-Muthar,* ed. Abdur Razzaq, Patna: Khuda Bakhsh Oriental Public Library, 1998.

Ni'mat ullah Harevi, *Tarikh-i-Khan Jahani*, ed. S.M. Imam al-Din Asiatic Society of Pakistan, Dacca.

Nizamuddin Ahmad Bakshi, *Tabaqat-i-Akbari*, Calcutta: Bibliotheca Indica, 1911.

Nizam ul-Mulk Tusi, *Siyasatnama*, ed. Jaffar Shiyar, Tehran: Shaukat Sihami Kitab ha-i-Habibi, 1960, 1348 Shamsi.

Saiyid Muhammad Husaini, *Javami'ul-Kilem*, ed. Muhammad Hamid Siddiqui, lith., Kanpur, 1356 H.

Shaikh Sharafuddin Yahya Maneri, *Maktubat-i-Sadi*, tr. Paul Jackson under the title *Letters from Maneri*, New Delhi: Horizon India Books, 1992.

Sirhindi, Yahya bin Ahmad, *Tarikh-i-Mubarak Shahi*, ed. M. Hidayat Husain, Calcutta: Bibliotheca Indica, 1931.

Yazdi, Sharafuddin, *Muqadima-i-Zafarnama*, MS, Add, 6538, British Library, London.

________, *Zafarnama*, Calcutta: Bibliotheca Indica, 1888.

MODERN WORKS

Aruni, S. K. Sagar: Provincial Headquarters of the Islamic Deccan, *Bulletin of the Deccan College Research Institute*, Volume 56-57, Pune.

Aziz Ahmad, *Studies in Islamic Culture in the Indian Environment*, Oxford: Clarendon Press, 1964.

Aziz Ahmad, Muhammad, *Political History and Institutions of the Early Turkish Empire*, Lahore, 1949.

Barthold, W., *Turkestan Down to the Mongol Invasions*, tr. V. Minorsky, ed. C.E. Bosworth, London, 1968.

________, *Four Studies in the History of Central Asia*, tr. V. and T. Monorsky, Leiden: E.J. Brill, 1956.

Bosworth, C.E., *The Ghaznavids: Their Empire in Afghanistan and Eastern Iran*, Edinburgh: Edinburgh University Press, 1963.

________, *The Later Ghaznavids Splendour and Decay*, rpt, New Delhi: Munshiram Manoharlal, 1992.

Chaudhuri Tapan Ray and Irfan Habib, eds., *Cambridge Economic History of India*, rpt, Delhi: Orient Longman, 1984.

Digby, Simon, *War-Horse and Elephant in the Sultanate of Delhi,* Karachi: Oxford University Press, 1971.

G.M.Wickens, *Astronomy, Introduction to Islamic Civilization,* ed. R.M. Savoy, Cambridge: Cambridge University Press, 1967.

Habib, Muhammad, *Politics and Society in Early Medieval India,* (Collected Works), 2 vols, Ed., K.A. Nizami, New Delhi: People's Publishing House, 1974 and 1981.

________, ed., *Comprehensive History of India: The Delhi Sultanate,* vol. 5. Delhi: People's Publishing House, 1970.

Habibullah, A.B.M., *The Foundation of Muslim Rule in India,* rpt, New Delhi, 1972.

Hardy, Peter, *Historians of Medieval India,* Westport, Connecticut: Greenwood Press, 1982.

________, 'Didactic Historical Writings in Indian Islam: Zia'uddin Barani's Treatment of the Reign of Sultan Muhammad bin Tughluq', in *Islam in India,* ed., Y. Friedmann, Jerusalem, The Hebrew University, 1984.

________, 'The Duty of the Sultan (in the Sultanate Period): To Further the Material Welfare of his Subjects', *The Concept of Duty in South Asia,* Wendy Doniger O'Flaherty and J.D. Derrent eds., New Delhi: Vikas Publishing House, pp. 147-65.

Harun Khan Sherwani, *The Bahmanis of the Deccan,* Hyderabad, A.P. , 1953.

Hodivala, S.H., *Studies in Indo-Muslim History,* Bombay: The Popular Book Depot, 1939.

Husain, Agha Mehdi, *Tughluq Dynasty,* rpt, Delhi, 1976.

Jackson, Paul, S.J. *The Way of a Sufi: Sharaf Uddin Maneri,* Delhi: Idarah-i-Adabiyat-i-Delhi, 1987.

Jackson, Peter, *The Delhi Sultanate: A Political and Military History,* Cambridge University Press, 1999.

________, 'The Mongol and the Delhi Sultanate in the Reign of Muhammad bin Tughluq', *Central Asiatic Journal,* vol. XIX, nos, 1-2, Wiesbaden, 1975, pp.118-56.

Lal, K.S. *History of the Khaljis,* rpt, New Delhi: Munshiram Manoharlal, 1980.

Majumdar, R.C., ed., *The History and Culture of the Indian People: The Struggle for Empire,* Bombay: Vidya Bhavan, 1975.

Mirza, M. Wahid, *Life and Works of Amir Khusrau,* Idarah-i-Adabiyat-i-Delhi, rpt, 1974.

Moreland, W.H. *The Agrarian System of Moslem India,* Cambridge, 1929, rpt, New Delhi: Munshiram Manoharlal, 1968.

Nazim, Muhammad, *The Life and Times of Sultan Mahmud of Ghazna,* rpt, New Delhi, Oriental Books Reprint Corporation, 1971.

Nigam, S.B.P., *Nobility under the Sultans of Delhi,* New Delhi: Munshiram Manoharlal, 1968.

Nizami, K.A., *Studies in Medieval Indian History and Culture,* Allahabad: Kitab Mahal (W.D.) Pvt. Ltd. 1966.

________, *Some Aspects of Religion and Politics in India during the Thirteenth Century,* 3rd rpt, Delhi: Idarah-i-Adabiyat-i-Delhi, 1978.

Prasad, Ishwari, *History of the Qaraunah Turks,* rpt, Allahabad: Central Book Depot, 1974.

Qureishi, I.H., *The Administration of the Sultanate of Delhi,* Oriental Books Reprint Corporation, 1971.

Shokoohy, Mehrdad and Natalie Shokoohy, "Tughluqabad: The Earliest Surviving Town of the Delhi Sultanate', *Bulletin of the School of Oriental and African Studies* (BSOAS), London, pp. 516-50, vol. LVII, 1994; and part 3, 1999, pp. 421-61.

Siddiqui, Iqtidar Husain, *Perso-Arabic Sources of Information on the Life and Conditions in the Sultanate of Delhi,* New Delhi: Munshiram Manoharlal, 1992.

________, tr., *Waqi'at-i-Mushtaqi* of Shaikh Rizq ullah Mushtaqi, New Delhi: Indian Council of Historical Research, 1993.

________, *Islam and Muslims in South Asia: Historical Perspectives,* Delhi: Adam Publishers, 1987.

________, ed., *Medieval India,: Essays in Intellectual Thought and Culture,* vol.1, New Delhi: Manohar, 2003.

________, *Authority and Kingship Under the Sultans of Delhi,* New Delhi: Manohar, 2006.

Stan Gorn and J.P. Goenka, *The Coins of the Indian Sultanates,* New Delhi: Munshiram Manoharlal, 2001.

Tripathi, R.P., *Some Aspects of Muslim Administration,* Allahabad, 1936.

Zafar ul Islam, *Fatawa Literature of the Sultanate Period*, New Delhi: Kanishka Publishers, 2005.

Index

N

O

P

T